CELLULOID ADVENTURES 3

Great Movies...
Evil Wars

Nicholas Anez

Midnight Marquee Press, Inc.
Baltimore, Maryland, USA

Copyright © 2018
Interior layout and cover design: Susan Svehla
Copy Editor: Janet Atkinson

Midnight Marquee Press, Inc., Gary J. Svehla and A. Susan Svehla do not assume any responsibility for the accuracy, completeness, topicality or quality of the information in this book. All views expressed or material contained within are the sole responsibility of the author.

Without limiting the rights under copyright reserved above, no part of this publication may be reproduced, stored in or introduced into a retrieval system, or transmitted, in any form, or by any means (electronic, mechanical, photocopying, recording or otherwise), without the prior written permission of the copyright owner or the publishers of the book.

ISBN 13: 978-1-936168-82-8
Library of Congress Catalog Card Number 2018952714
Manufactured in the United States of America

First Printing by Midnight Marquee Press, Inc., October 2018

Once more, for Margaret

For Gary and Sue

Whose artistry provides infinite contributions
to the multitude of celluloid adventures.

— For Sgt. Ralph, Terry and Fr. Paul
Anti-war counselors circa 1965 who provided invaluable
information to future draftees on how to evade the draft—
or, if drafted, how to avoid being sent to Vietnam.

"Then Jesus said to him:
Put up again thy sword into its place,
For all they that take the sword shall perish with the sword."
— Matthew: 26:52

"Then I, and you, and all of us fell down
Whilst bloody treason flourished over us."
— Mark Antony (William Shakespeare; *Julius Caesar*)

"The evils of war are great in their endurance
and have a long reckoning for ages to come."
— Thomas Jefferson

"I hate war as only a soldier who has lived it can,
only as one who has seen its brutality, its stupidity."
— Dwight D. Eisenhower

"Mankind must put an end to war
before war puts an end to mankind."
— John F. Kennedy

"Imagine a whole lifetime full of hopes and dreams and ambitions
being wiped out by a two-inch accident like a bullet."
— Chance Wayne (Tennessee Williams; *Sweet Bird of Youth*)

CONTENTS

7	Introduction
14	Jungle Book (1942)
42	They Won't Believe Me (1947)
62	Rocketship X-M (1950)
84	Violent Saturday (1955)
102	Pocketful of Miracles (1961)
123	The Satan Bug (1965)
142	A High Wind in Jamaica (1965)
161	Sol Madrid (1968)
180	The Stalking Moon (1968)
204	The Bridge at Remagen (1969)
230	Lawman (1971)
250	Afterword

INTRODUCTION

The rocketship crashes into the Earth, killing everyone inside.

The father has earned the respect of his son only because he has killed someone.

The woman lies in bed, her life ruined irreparably as the cop walks away from her.

The young girl stares at a toy boat, unaware of the numerous deaths she has caused.

The man with the badge rides away, leaving a trail of lifeless bodies in his wake.

These are all unforgettable endings to great movies that have either been neglected or forgotten. Despite the high merits of these movies, they never received the large audiences they deserved. But it may not be too late for belated recognition.

In this third volume of *Celluloid Adventures*, the spotlight is once again on movies that are unjustifiably underrated or undeservedly unknown. The movies cover a span of three decades, from 1942 to 1971. As in Volume 2, these movies represent a variety of genres. They include a Western that is also a suspense movie, an adventure film that is also a fantasy and a science fiction story that is also a tragedy. There is a movie about children that is not for children, a crime movie that is a social drama and a Western that is both traditional and radical. There is also a film noir that is a morality play, a thriller that is horrifyingly prophetic and a police story about an officer who uses his badge to kill. There is a comedy and a war movie but the comedy has dark overtones and the war movie is anti-military.

Actually, war is a subject of all of these movies. Though this book is primarily about movies, it also evolved into a book about war. As I researched the movies, war in one form or another kept intruding in unexpected ways. The connection of a specific film to war may be direct and concern actual warfare or it may be indirect, due to the experiences of the film's participants, or it may even be allegorical. But, one way or another, the subject of war constantly crept into the narratives.

While this is not a history book, as I gathered information on the following films, it became clear that some historical background of the various wars that the films depict—or reflect in some way—might be conducive to a total appreciation of the movies. In fact, since World War II is so frequently intrusive, a brief summary of that war may be helpful at this point in setting the stage for the discussions of the films. It may also explain how and why the war affected so many Hollywood films and personalities.

Note: I am not a historian. For the historical data within this text, I have whenever appropriate cited the source material. Where no source is cited, I have compiled the data from various encyclopedias. Regarding the information that immediately follows, it would take eminent historians multiple volumes to fully summarize the Second World War. In varying degrees, this rule applies to other wars discussed herein. I provide this admittedly insufficient data only for the purpose of furthering understanding of the specific movies.

In the 1930s, the world was in the midst of the Great Depression. Germany was in particularly severe economic distress due to the 1919 Treaty of Versailles which ended the First World War. Japan was still irate over England's 1923 dissolution of the Anglo-Japanese Alliance. Consequently, Germany and Japan became increasingly nationalistic and attempted to establish domination over their respective regions of Europe and Asia. In 1937, Japan invaded China. In 1939, Germany invaded Poland. England and France declared war against Germany, allegedly to preserve Poland's independence. (At this time, England ruled over the largest colonial empire in history, denying independence to all of her colonies.) The Soviet Union, which had signed a treaty with Germany, also invaded Poland but neither England nor France declared war against the Russians.

British Prime Minister Winston Churchill rejected Germany's offer of peace. After occupying France, Germany launched the Battle of Britain in July, 1940. President Franklin D. Roosevelt, who had promised to keep America out of foreign wars, officially maintained a policy of neutrality. However, in September 1940, he authorized the first peace-time Selective Service Act requiring all eligible males to register for the draft. In March 1941, he passed the Lend-Lease Act to provide war materials and financial aid to England. In June, Germany violated its treaty with Russia and invaded its former ally. Consequently, Roosevelt supplied Lend-Lease aid to the Soviet Union, which under the reign of Premier Joseph Stalin was the most horrific human charnel house in history.

Many political analysts advocated against providing aid to the Soviet Union to support its war with Germany. They believed that if the two totalitarian nations waged a contained war, they might battle for years and cripple one another economically and militarily. Other statesmen were suspicious of Stalin, particularly in view of the emerging facts of his brutal regime. But Roosevelt seemed to believe that he could persuade Stalin, whom he called "Uncle Joe," to convert his nation into a cradle of democracy.

In September 1941, after Japan invaded Indochina, Roosevelt imposed an oil embargo upon Japan and froze all Japanese assets in the United States. Japan's prime minister requested a summit meeting with Roosevelt to discuss peace but was rebuffed. Japan's war faction forced the prime minister out of office. On December 7, Japan attacked the U.S. Pacific Fleet at Pearl Harbor, killing over 2,300 Americans. The next day, the United States joined the Allied Powers which comprised England, the Soviet Union, China and other nations. The Axis Powers were the adversaries and included Nazi Germany and Imperial Japan as well as Fascist Italy and several smaller nations.

During the course of the war, the U.S. drafted more than 10 million men. Though the Axis Powers initially achieved military successes, the Allied Powers steadily gained the advantage. In September 1943, Italy signed an armistice. In May 1945, Germany surrendered. In August 1945, Japan surrendered after the U.S. dropped atomic bombs on Hiroshima and Nagasaki, killing an estimated 220,000 people. World War II officially ended. Official statistics vary but from 405,000 to 418,000 U.S. military personnel died and more than 670,000 were wounded.

World War II was the most catastrophic war in world history and killed more than 60 million people. The majority of these fatalities were civilians who died from disease, starvation, exposure, incineration, strategic bombings by American-British forces and systematic atrocities committed by Japanese, German and Russian troops.

The war empowered the most tyrannical nation in human history. The Soviet Union not only emerged as a global superpower but now controlled a large portion of eastern and central Europe. Conversely, the argument could be made that the Soviet Union won the war in Europe. Over 26 million Soviets died during the war. But Russian military forces decimated the German Wehrmacht. In retrospect, if Germany had not committed the majority of its forces to the Russian front, the course of the war would most likely have been far more extended and cataclysmic. Then again, if the Allies had not capitulated to Stalin after the war, the Soviet Union in subsequent decades would perhaps not have been able to perpetuate far more barbarities upon the world than any nation in the history of the human race.

World War II interrupted the careers of many Hollywood personalities who enlisted in the military to serve their country. The manner in which they served makes for a revealing sub-theme of this book. This journey from the film world to fatigues was also a two-way street. After the war, many former soldiers found their destinies in Hollywood, either by design or a twist of fate. Their stories, too, are equally interesting.

The history of the human race being what it is, it wasn't long before the United States was involved in another war. But this was a cold one and it would be waged against a former ally, the Soviet Union. A synopsis of this war and the events leading to it may once again be helpful to appreciating some of the movies discussed herein.

After the 1917 Russian Revolution, the Bolsheviks defeated the anti-communists and formed the Union of Soviet Socialist Republics under the rule of the Communist Party. Joseph Stalin consolidated absolute power and implemented a repressive political system that enslaved the entire population. Uncle Joe's Great Purge, collectivization, forced labor camps, mass executions and deliberate starvation killed a minimum of 25 million people, with some estimates as high as 50 million.

Following WWII, the United States and the Soviet Union emerged as the world's superpowers. Stalin extended his tyrannical reign to eight European countries that the Allies had ceded to him, including Poland, whose freedom England and France had supposedly declared war to preserve. For communism to survive as a viable economic system, the Soviets had to eradicate capitalism, particularly in America. Thus, in 1947, the two nations became opposing forces in the Cold War which created a continual state of political conflict, espionage and military vigilance. The Cold War (which lasted for 45 years) will make many appearances within the movies highlighted in this book.

To prepare for the insidious possibility of another "hot war" breaking out, Congress passed the Selective Service Act of 1948 to keep military manpower at full strength. Thus, all American males of specific ages had to register for military service and were subsequently eligible to be drafted for a period of two years or longer. The draft will often appear within the discussions of the following movies.

Inevitably, hot wars did break out. Since American and Soviet politicians wanted to prevent nuclear war which would endanger their own lives, both nations engaged in surrogate wars which only killed other people. These wars included the Korean War (1950 to 1953) and the Vietnam War (1964 to 1973). The Korean War, often called "the forgotten war," will be remembered herein at its appropriate time period. As the Vietnam War gradually intrudes into the text, I will offer a brief history of the war to illustrate its pervasive effect upon society as well upon the specific films and their reception.

These hot wars did not alleviate the tensions of the Cold War. Indeed, as the Soviet Union extended its totalitarian control throughout Third World countries, the United States quashed democratic governments in the Third World and supported brutal military regimes as long as they professed to be anti-communist. This global state of affairs was reflected in many Hollywood films, including some discussed in the following pages.

In discussing the causes of war, the subject of colonization of weaker homelands by powerful nations will frequently appear. In addition to forcibly occupying smaller nations and oppressing their inhabitants, the more powerful nations will also inevitably seek to dominate one another. In the study of history, it becomes obvious that humans have developed an infinite capacity to fight wars of one kind or another for reasons that are sometimes necessary, at other times obscure and still at other times pointless. These wars may be hot or cold, national or racial, biological or chemical, cultural or social. And they will all play roles in the films discussed herein.

World War II is the direct subject of only one movie highlighted within the following pages but its impact is felt through many others. The film noir and the crime movie illustrate the repercussions of that war. The thriller warns of the dangers of biological war while the police movie concerns the war against drugs. One Western is about the Indian Wars and the other is a metaphor about American society during the Vietnam War. The movie about children is ostensibly about the war against piracy but suggests a veiled war between children and adults. The comedy wages war against poverty while the fantasy depicts the war that humans wage against animals as well as one another. And the science fiction movie is about the horrors of nuclear war.

There is one inescapable fact that should be mentioned. Within the discussions of the historical backgrounds of the following films, the story of the insidious corruption of the United States of America gradually materializes. Validating the maxim that has been proven so often throughout history, the corruption comes not from external forces but from internal enemies of the constitutional republic and representative democracy that shaped this nation for almost two hundred years. This story emerges stealthily, from beneath the text. But it is there.

However, this book is primarily about movies and the principal purpose of all of the followings films is to entertain. These movies were all made in an era in which the filmmakers on both sides of the camera didn't assume a superior attitude toward audiences; they had respect for the people who bought tickets to see their movies and didn't presume to preach to them. These filmmakers had, in most cases, modest ambitions. While their films may include a message, they primarily wanted to make movies that were entertaining. They achieved that objective, in some cases beyond the scope of their humble intentions. There are a couple of classics here and some great films. Some are just good movies but that is all the filmmakers intended.

The evidence of a good movie is often right up there on the screen, from the direction to the acting, from the script to the music, from the cinematography to the production values. But there are often additional indications that are not instantly apparent. Perhaps it is the fact that the movie remains in your memory long after you have seen it. Maybe it is the characters that remain vividly in your mind. Perhaps the film stirs your emotions in a way that real life does. All of the movies discussed in this book, I believe, have these qualities. Nevertheless, audiences did not patronize them in large numbers.

In Hollywood, a film's status as a success or failure is judged primarily by its box-office performance. In actuality, a film's quality may have nothing to do with its commercial success but grosses are the bottom line in the film capital. Therefore, I have included each movie's domestic theatrical rentals, which were approximately 40% of the total gross, to illustrate its relatively poor performance at the box office in comparison to the money-making hits of the year.

To give an indication of the critical reception each film received, I have quoted many reviews. Most critics reviewed films objectively and astutely. Others allowed their personal agendas to influence their opinions. For instance, see the chapter on a Western (clue: the movie that politically correct watchdogs despised because the villain is an Apache) for a ludicrous review by a critic whose pomposity exceeded her bias. Reference books are equally erroneous; see the chapter on a crime film (clue: the movie that a politician condemned as indecent and disgusting) for an example of arrogance by writers who made a practice of ridiculing not only untalented people but talented ones as well.

When applicable, I have provided a summary of the source material for each movie. Five of the movies are based upon novels. Two others are based upon stories while another is based upon two collections of stories. Three are original screenplays. Interestingly, the exact authorship of one of the original screenplays (clue: the science fiction movie with its controversial message) is still unknown today, due to the political climate of the era in which it was made. The celebrated co-author of another screenplay (clue: the World War II movie with contentious scenes that angered some U.S. veterans) was so upset with the released film that he angrily disowned it.

I have also included a brief production history of each movie, which occasionally can be fascinating. One movie cost only $94,000 and was filmed in 10 days. Another novel was filmed so quickly that the film version was released just as the first edition hardcover was arriving in bookstores. Another film, though based upon a book called one of the best novels of the 20th Century, did not reach the screen for over three decades. During production of one movie, the director developed severe physical and emotional pains because of his anger toward the film's star. While on location for still another production, members of differing religious sects tried to kill one another. And the filming of yet another movie was interrupted by a military invasion!

After filming was completed on these movies, it was then time to present them to the public. The commercial failure of a movie often has a damaging effect upon artists on both sides of the camera and the movies discussed in the following pages illustrate that fact. The film careers of two very popular television stars abruptly ended. One famous Holly-

Robert Vaughn with his Nazi henchmen in *The Bridge at Remagen*

wood director remained bitter for the rest of his life. Another director gave up filmmaking and retreated to academia.

Despite their reception by the critics and the public, all of the movies that I celebrate in this book are the works of talented people who wanted to make something that would interest, excite and please audiences. And they did. They made great motion pictures, with great beginnings, great middles and…

And great endings.

The old beggar smiles mischievously, his words taunting the young woman.

The two simple words of the clerk send shockwaves throughout the courtroom.

The bootlegger and the panhandlers share a joyous celebration.

The virus that could destroy all life on Earth is contained.

The wounded rancher reaches his home after surviving a fight to the death.

The two soldiers embrace warmly, surprised to be alive.

These are memorable endings to superb movies. The creators of these hidden gems deserve to be remembered for their achievements.

JUNGLE BOOK

The setting is India in the early 20th century, during the period known as the British Raj, when India was Great Britain's most prized colony, "the jewel in the crown." In the town square of a large city, an old Beggar offers to tell stories in exchange for a few coins. He survives in this manner from day to day. But there is no bitterness or sadness on his face, just acceptance and wisdom. The daughter of the British magistrate, accompanied by her Indian guide, sights the Beggar and savors his face which seems to contain so many secrets amidst the wrinkles of age. She starts to take his photograph but he objects with some amusement. However, when she gives him a coin, he begins his story. It is a story of the jungle.

This is the beginning of the magnificent 1942 production of *Jungle Book*, also known as *Rudyard Kipling's Jungle Book*. It is both a grand fantasy and an exciting adventure film. It contains scenes of excitement and enchantment that will delight children of all ages. It also contains scenes of poignancy and heartache that will enthrall adults. It is a family film in the traditional sense for it neither patronizes children nor insults adults. Unfortunately, its reputation has suffered over the past several decades for a number of reasons.

In the 1950s, when United Artists initially leased the movie to television, local stations usually relegated it to children's time slots where it was chopped to pieces; one Boston station televised it over the course of a week in five parts during an afternoon children's show. In 1967, when Walt Disney produced his popular animated musical, the 1942 movie was practically forgotten. In subsequent years, while the Disney version maintained its popularity through home video releases, the earlier version suffered the ignominy of falling into

the public domain since United Artists had failed to renew its copyright. Consequently, numerous independent television stations obtained free but shoddy copies of the film which were often unwatchable. With the advent of VHS in 1976, it became available only in cheap, poorly reproduced videocassettes with faded colors and tinny sound. The arrival of DVDs in 1995 continued this custom. This was an unfortunate fate for a wondrous movie that a dedicated artist produced. His name is Alexander Korda.

Alexander Korda was born 1893 in Hungary. In 1911, he entered the film industry by working for Pathé Studios in Paris. He formed his own film company in Budapest and directed his first film in 1914. Over the next several years, he perfected his trade in Hungary, Austria and Germany, where he produced and directed films which eventually led to a Hollywood contract in the late 1920s. But since he lacked control over his Hollywood movies, he returned to Europe and eventually settled in England. At this time, the British film industry was in a dreadful state, releasing only "quota quickie" movies to satisfy the government's mandate that a certain percentage of movies playing in theaters had to be British. Determined to produce prestigious British films, Korda founded London Films in 1932.

Alexander's brothers, Zoltan and Vincent, soon joined him. Zoltan Korda was born in 1895 and, like his older brother, had been a director in his native country. Vincent Korda, born in 1897, was an accomplished artist. In 1933, Alexander directed *The Private Life of Henry VIII*, which became an international hit and made him the savior of the British film industry. He subsequently arranged an American distribution deal with United Artists for his productions, all of which benefited from the talents of his brothers. His productions include such box-office hits as *The Scarlet Pimpernel* (1934) and *Sanders of the River* (1935), which Zoltan directed, as well as such prestigious films as *Things to Come* (1936) and *Rembrandt* (1936), which he also directed. As a result of these films, England became a leading player in the world of motion picture production.

In 1937, Alexander hired famed documentarian Robert Flaherty to direct *Elephant Boy*, based upon Rudyard Kipling's "Toomai of the Elephants," one of the stories in *The Jungle Book*. In his book, *Star of India* (BearManor Media; 2010), Philip Leibfried relates the story of the discovery of an unlikely star. While shooting in India, Flaherty's cinematographer noticed a 13-year-old orphan named Selar Shaik working in the stable of the Maharajah of Mysore and brought him to Flaherty. The boy displayed a natural charm as well as the capability to handle elephants. Flaherty appreciated the boy's instinctive acting talent along with his innate exuberance and immediately cast him as Toomai. But though Alexander approved of young Selar's film presence, he disapproved of Flaherty's documentary-style approach to the story. Once the film crew was back in England, he signed John Collier to write a script that would incorporate Flaherty's footage into a cohesive story. Zoltan directed all of the subsequent dramatic scenes at Denham studios. Meanwhile, Alexander believed that a single name would increase his new star's exotic allure and gave him the name of Sabu. Upon release, the movie was very popular and established Sabu as a major discovery.

Alexander placed Sabu under exclusive contract to London Films and established a home in England for him. In 1938, Alexander produced and Zoltan directed *The Drum* (1938; U.S. title: *Drums*) starring Sabu in the role of an Indian prince who fights his evil uncle with the aid of the British cavalry. The success of this film increased the young star's popularity. In 1939, Zoltan directed the superb adventure film, *The Four Feathers*, which enjoyed worldwide success. Though the setting was the Sudan, there was no suitable role in the story for Sabu. Director George Stevens wanted to cast Sabu in the title role of his film version of Kipling's *Gunga Din* but Alexander would not loan him out. Sam Jaffe, who was 47 years old, played the coveted role and he later stated that he modeled his portrayal on Sabu. (Incidentally, all of these films tend to celebrate British imperialism; Alexander had become a British citizen in 1936 and his brothers would also eventually become citizens of their adopted country.)

Alexander was very eager for another project for his young star. Reportedly, he met Douglas Fairbanks at a screening of *Drum* and acquired

Sabu had a natural ability to develop friendships with the animals.

the rights to loosely remake his 1924 silent fantasy, *The Thief of Bagdad*. Ludwig Berger was the initial director of the sumptuous production which began filming in the spring of 1939 on massive sound stages in Denham Studios. However, Alexander was displeased with Berger's footage and assigned Michael Powell and Tim Whelan to take over the project. Vincent, in his capacities as production designer and art director, built outstanding sets that enhanced the fantasy aspects of the story. Upon the outbreak of World War II in September, Alexander cancelled plans to film on loca-

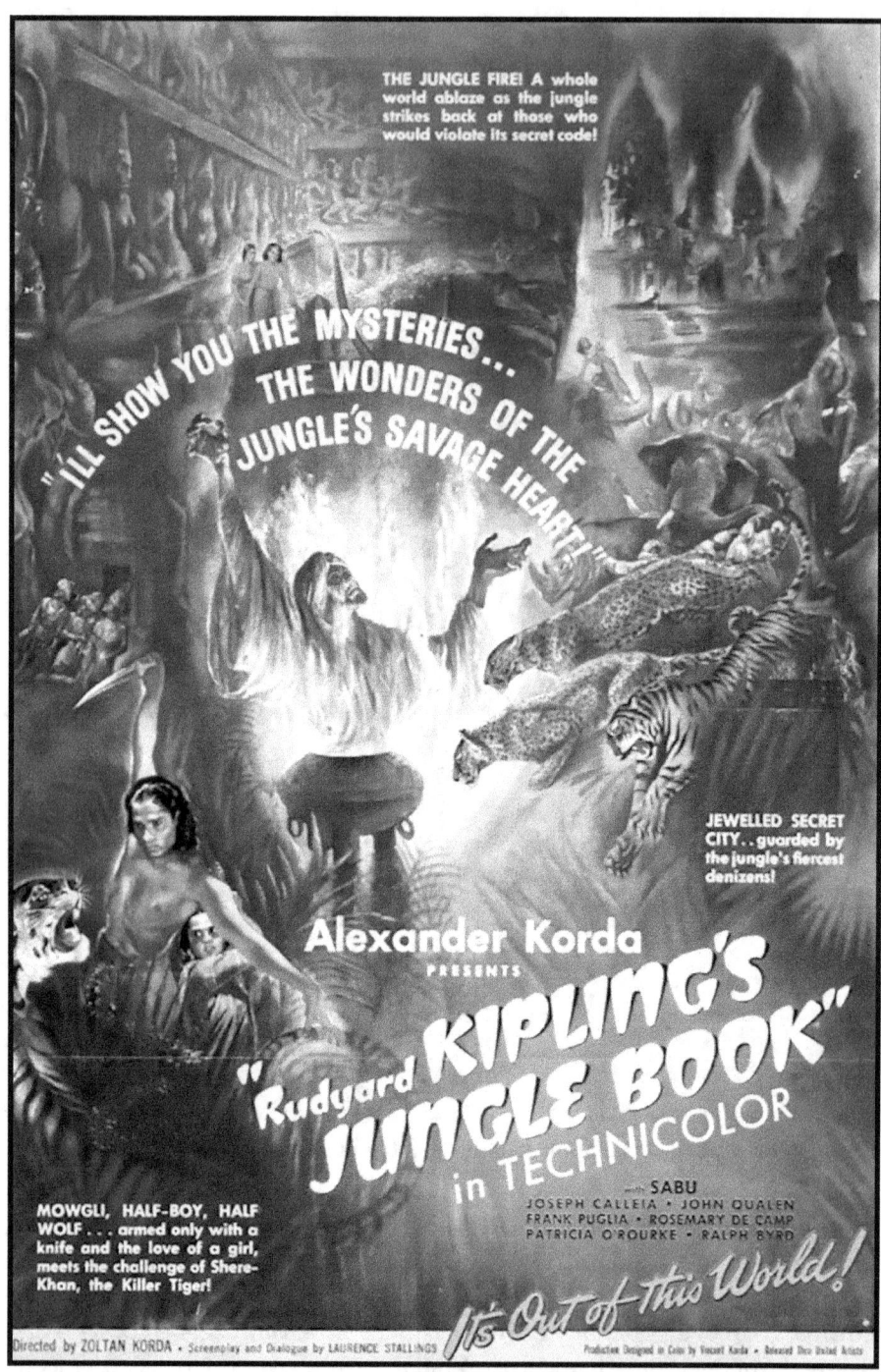

tion in North Africa and eventually moved the production to the United States where Zoltan filmed the remaining scenes; Zoltan did not receive screen credit and neither did Alexander nor William Cameron Menzies, both of whom also directed some scenes. Upon the film's release in 1940, it achieved enormous critical and popular success and certified Sabu as India's first international star. He is totally in his element in the title role of the young Arabian thief and captivated audiences with his natural charm and sincerity. The book, *Alexander Korda's The Thief of Bagdad: An Arabian Fantasy*, by Philip Leibfried and Malcolm Willis (Hypostyle Hall; 2004) provides complete details on the making of this classic film.

In search for another role for Sabu, Alexander found the perfect vehicle: Rudyard Kipling's *The Jungle Book* (which had already provided the source material for *Elephant Boy*) and *The Second Jungle Book*, both of which featured stories about Mowgli, the human child raised by wolves. Rudyard Kipling is known today in some circles for his celebration of British imperialism, which is a limited view of a true literary artist. He was born of British parents in Bombay in 1865. His parents sent him to England at age six for a formal British education, which was not a happy experience, and he was overjoyed to return to India in 1882. He then began his career as a journalist for a local newspaper. Over the next several years, he wrote his distinctively terse and often cynical stories and poems which he eventually published in book form. These works, such as the novella *The Man Who Would Be King*, brought him acclaim in India. When he returned to England in 1889, his celebrity status had preceded him and the press hailed him as a brilliant writer.

Barrack-Room Ballads (which included *Gunga Din*) in 1892, *The Jungle Book* in 1894 and *The Second Jungle Book* in 1895 established Kipling's fame around the world. In 1899, his daughter's death from pneumonia traumatized him and affected his style. His later stories were less romantic and more complex than his earlier works. In 1901, his novel *Kim* became another bestseller but the militaristic tone of *Kim* and other works brought criticism from members of the establishment who opposed British colonialism. His poem *The White Man's Burden* especially incensed anti-colonialists since it suggested that the British had a moral responsibility to bring their superior civilization to the non-English world, or to "new-caught sullen people, half-devil and half-child." However, Kipling also wrote *Recessional*, in which he rebuked imperialists who were "drunk with sight of power" and argued that nationalistic attitudes were irrelevant compared to the eternalness of divinity: "Lord God of Hosts, be with us yet, Lest we forget, lest we forget."

In 1907, Kipling was the recipient of the Nobel Prize in Literature. Over the next several years, he continued to endorse conservative principles, including advocating for increased military spending to prepare for the war that he believed was inevitable because so many countries were promoting nationalism while enlarging their armed forces. His prediction was correct. In 1914, the Great War began; it was also called the World

War and would later be known as the First World War. Kipling encouraged his only son, Jack, to enlist in the military. Jack's death in combat in 1915 devastated Kipling and he suffered feelings of guilt and depression for the rest of his life. Kipling died in 1936. Despite condemnation from detractors who to this day cannot divorce his works from his beliefs, objective literary critics recognize him as a master of prose and poetry, thus assuring his legacy as an exemplary writer.

(The Great War killed approximately 16 million people worldwide, roughly 7 million of which were civilians. It also provided an opportunity for the nations comprising the Triple Entente to expand their colonial powers. Although U.S. President Woodrow Wilson stated that the war was about making the world safe for democracy, subsequent revelations of the Sykes-Picot treaty disclosed that England and France forged a secret agreement to gain control of the Middle Eastern countries, with the third member of the Entente, Czarist Russia, also getting a piece of the pie. This agreement was an egregious betrayal of T.E. Lawrence, better known as Lawrence of Arabia, and of the Arab countries to whom they had promised independence if they sided with the British forces. And it would lead to decades of hatred, strife, war and millions of deaths.)

The two *Jungle Books* have remained immensely popular for decades among readers of all ages. Children can enjoy the stories as fables that use animals to teach moral lessons about such subjects as honesty, respect and fidelity. Adults can enjoy them as allegories with symbolic meanings because, beneath the surface, the stories contain commentaries on politics and society that can range from satirical to solemn. One theme that pervades the books, either directly or allegorically, is that animals may be nobler than human beings. Through his descriptions of the two dissimilar societies, Kipling implies the superiority of animal culture to human culture. The animals have established a set of laws, which they impose upon themselves internally. Humans are incapable of such self-regulation and require an external force to govern their behavior. Though both divergent cultures are able to function separately, trouble is inevitable when they come together. Though Mowgli does not appear in all of the stories, he is the central character of both books and functions as a mediator between the human and animal cultures.

If ever an actor was born to play a role, then Sabu was born to play Mowgli, a fact that Alexander must have immediately recognized. His production of *Jungle Book*, with Zoltan directing, began filming in the summer of 1941. Alexander spared no expense in making the movie, which he filmed entirely in California. In actuality, he had no choice since England was fighting for her survival. The Nazis had taken over much of Western Europe and, though England had thwarted invasion by winning the Battle of Britain, she suffered a crushing defeat at Dunkirk and the

Mowgli (Sabu) and Mahala (Patricia O'Rourke) enjoy the wonders of the lost city.

future looked bleak. However, it is perhaps appropriate that the Kordas would film *Jungle Book* in the U.S. since Kipling had written both books while living in Vermont with his American-born wife.

United Artists released *Jungle Book* in April, 1942. (The reason that the film is known by two titles is apparent from the opening. The first shot of the movie is the cover of a book with two words — *Rudyard Kipling's* — on the cover; the book then opens to the title — *Jungle Book*.) As the credits unfold, it is obvious from Miklos Rozsa's grandly majestic score that this

Sabu earned the trust of the animals by feeding, petting and gently talking to them.

will be a splendid adventure. The music promises action, excitement and wonder. The beginning of the movie is somewhat deceptive as the harmless-looking Beggar seems to mischievously tease the British girl with hints of wild stories of fantasy. Though she is intrigued by his suggestion of exotic adventures and fascinating experiences, she has no way of knowing the price he has paid for his wisdom.

Once the Beggar begins his tale, the setting changes from the village square to a rich, spectacular Indian jungle in which the colors are brighter than they perhaps should be. But that is deliberate. This is not a real jungle but a fantasy jungle in which all of the animals, except one, live in harmony with each other and with nature. There is Bagheera the panther and black prince of the jungle, Baloo the bear who is the teacher of jungle law, Haithi the friendly elephant and Kaa the wise snake. And there is Akela and Raksha, the mother and father wolf, who peacefully raise their cubs in their small cave dwelling. These animals never kill for the sake of killing, the Beggar explains. That is something only man does. And this, he explains, is the story of man versus nature.

Such a battle is taking place in a part of the jungle where humans are building a village. Rao, husband of Messua, places their infant son away from the builders to protect him from harm. But the boy, whose name is Nathoo, wanders away and stumbles into the lair of the wolf pack. He was unaware that he was being stalked by Shere Khan, the killer tiger who does not obey the law of the jungle. Though Nathoo escapes the tiger's wrath, his father Rao is not so fortunate and the tiger kills him. Akela and Raksha protect the human baby from Shere Khan and take him into their home to nurture him along with their cubs. Because he resembles a baby frog, they call him Mowgli, which means "little frog." As he sleeps, he cannot hear the voice of his mother Messua crying out for him.

Many years pass and Mowgli has grown into an adolescent who is friends with most of the animals, especially Baloo and Bagheera as well as Grey Brother, the wolf cub with whom he was raised. He has learned their languages and is able to converse with them in their own tongues. But his one enemy, Shere Khan, still hunts him. Running from the tiger, Mowgli comes upon the village from which he wandered away years before. Never having seen a human being, he sneaks into the village at night to get a closer look. But when he touches fire and screams, the villagers are alerted and instantly see that he is a feral child. Buldeo, the merchant who claims to be a mighty hunter, tries to overpower the boy but Mowgli throws him into a pool of water. Shamed in front of his neighbors, Buldeo wants to cast the boy back into the jungle but Messua offers to raise him in her home with the help of her loyal servant, Durga. Although she doesn't believe that he is her son, she is still filled with sadness for the son and husband she lost. Buldeo warns the villagers that they will all be cursed for letting evil into their village. But Mowgli responds to Messua's warmth and learns his first word in human speech: "Mother."

After several months, Mowgli has learned the customs and language of man. However, he never forgets how Shere Khan drove him out of the jungle, believing that the animal kingdom cast him out of their community because of his fear. When Messua explains the meaning of money to him, he buys a knife from Buldeo who still looks for any opportunity to harm the boy, especially since his daughter, Mahala, is fascinated with him. One evening, Mahala sneaks away with Mowgli to learn the secrets of the jungle. These secrets include a lost city that a great Maharajah once ruled. The city is now deserted and inhabited by the monkey-folk. Hidden beneath the ruins is the monarch's treasure, which an old white cobra guards. Mowgli is tempted to take a jeweled ankus but when the cobra warns him in the language of the snake that the treasure contains death, he heeds the warning and leaves all of the treasure behind. Mahala, however, does take one gold coin with her.

The next morning Buldeo finds the gold coin. When Mahala tells him of the lost city and the treasure, he becomes determined to learn the location of the city and claim the fortune for himself. After accidentally dropping the coin, Buldeo is forced to take two fellow villagers, the Barber and the Pundit, into his confidence. At the same time, Mowgli's animal friends alert him that Shere Khan is nearby. After devising a plan with Kaa to ensnare the tiger, Mowgli finds Shere Khan and taunts the animal. Shere Khan becomes so enraged that he chases Mowgli and, forgetting his fear of water, jumps into the lake to kill the boy. Kaa is waiting and Mowgli, with the help of the python, plunges his knife into the heart of his deadly enemy.

As Mowgli rejoices in his triumph, Buldeo comes upon him and threatens to shoot him if he doesn't reveal the location of the lost city. But Bagheera jumps on Buldeo who thinks that Mowgli has changed into the panther. Now certain that Mowgli is a demon, Buldeo and his cohorts fearfully kneel in front of him. The men hasten back to the village and tell everyone that Mowgli is a sorcerer. When Mowgli returns, he is puzzled by the hostility of the villagers who pounce upon him. Buldeo ties him to a post and whips him while secretly trying to force the location of the lost city from him. But Mowgli refuses to talk, knowing that humans will bring destruction to the jungle. When Messua pleads with him to help himself, he refuses. Mowgli can only feel sadness in his heart. "I was a wolf and the jungle cast me out; I am a man and the man-pack cast me out."

However, Messua cuts him loose, not realizing that Buldeo plans to follow Mowgli to the lost city. After ordering Messua and Durga to be chained, Buldeo and his two henchmen follow the boy. Mowgli deliberately leads them to the city to find out if the cobra spoke the truth about death ensnaring anyone who takes the treasure. The wise cobra's words are soon proven true. Once they find the treasure, the three men begin fighting among themselves. On the way back to the village, the Pundit kills the Barber for the ankus. The next day, he tries to kill Buldeo who throws him into the river and into the jaws of a crocodile. Believing that Mowgli is changing into various animals, Buldeo frantically tries to carry as much treasure as he can back to the village. He reaches the village but without any treasure and tells the villagers that Mowgli has killed the Barber and the Pundit. Almost out of his mind, he takes a torch and starts to set fire to the jungle, hoping to kill Mowgli and all of his animal friends.

Mowgli is now determined to cleanse the jungle of a killer once again, this time not of a tiger but of man. "Men are senseless and cruel," he tells Haithi. "It is not right that man should live here anymore." With these words, he sends Haithi and his herd to destroy the village. But Buldeo's fire is rapidly consuming the village as well as the jungle. As the villagers flee, Mowgli finds Mahala who tells him that Messua and Durga are tied in a hut. After freeing Messua and Durga, Mowgli tells Mahala to lead the villagers to an island in the middle of the lake where they will be safe from the fire. Messua, now knowing that Mowgli is indeed the son she

This lobby card combines various scenes from the film.

lost so many years before, pleads with him to stay with her. However, Mowgli tells her that he belongs to the jungle. As he rides away on Haithi to help his animal friends, Messua watches sadly, knowing that she has lost her son once again.

But has she? The Beggar finishes his tale and tells the English girl that he never got his revenge and that he never became rich. The Beggar is Buldeo who must repeat the tale over and over again to survive. The English girl is not satisfied and anxiously wants to know more. Did Mowgli ever see his mother again? What happened to Mahala? However, Buldeo simply smiles at her. As the camera closes in on him and his face fills the screen, he says to her and to all of us, "That, Memsahib, is another story."

These words were not intended to hint at a possible sequel but to deliberately leave the questions unanswered. This is only one of the many rewards within the screenplay by Lawrence Stallings. In addition to being a screenwriter, Stallings was also a playwright, journalist and literary critic. He achieved fame in 1924 when he co-wrote with Maxwell Anderson the play, *What Price Glory*; the World War I drama would be filmed twice, in 1926 and 1952. Also in 1924, his autobiographical novel, *Plumes*, served as the basis for the renowned 1925 movie *The Big Parade*. The anti-war theme of his play and novel was the result of his own experiences; in WWI, he suffered serious wounds which resulted in the later amputation of his leg.

In adapting Kipling's two books, Stallings invents some characters and rearranges some incidents but faithfully captures the spirit of the stories as well as the characterization of Mowgli. Like the books, the movie is about a boy who is torn between two worlds. It is also about the perennial war between man and nature. He uses events from four of the Mowgli stories to create his script. Unlike the episodic storyline of the original works, incidents and themes from the individual stories merge in order to conform to a conventional narrative structure.

From the first book, Stallings takes events from two stories. In "Mowgli's Brothers," the wolf pack adopts Mowgli. Despite opposition by many of the animals who resent the intrusion of a human into their jungle, Akela and Raksha protect the boy from Shere Khan. They receive support from Baloo the bear and Bagheera the panther, both of whom will become Mowgli's lifelong friends. But, though he grows to be a lad of 17, many of the animals never accept him and he has always been fearful of Shere Khan. As a result, Mowgli leaves the wolf pack to search for his roots in the village of man.

Mowgli has killed his deadly enemy Shere Khan.

Another *Jungle Book* lobby card showing a scene that never appeared in the film.

In "Tiger Tiger," Messua and her husband adopt Mowgli. But the village hunter Buldeo, whose fanciful stories of his exploits Mowgli knows to be untrue, becomes his enemy. When his animal friends tell Mowgli that Shere Khan is hunting him, he devises a plan to trick the tiger into the path of the buffalo herd. The plan works and the herd tramples the tiger to death. As Mowgli stands over the carcass of his enemy, Buldeo comes upon them and tries to take credit for the tiger's death. But a wolf jumps on Buldeo who thinks that Mowgli has transformed himself into the animal. Racing back to the village, Buldeo tells everyone that Mowgli is a demon. When Mowgli returns, the villagers stone him and chase him out of the village. Mowgli now has nowhere to go. "The man-pack and the wolf-pack have both cast me out," he says. "Now I will hunt alone in the jungle."

From *The Second Jungle Book*, Stallings used material from two additional stories to add to his script. "Letting in the Jungle" relates how Mowgli has become accustomed to hunting alone. However, Buldeo has nurtured his hatred of Mowgli and hunts him constantly. On one occasion, Mowgli spies on Buldeo and hears him telling other villagers how he killed Shere Khan and how Mowgli then turned into a wolf. Mowgli also learns that

Buldeo punished Messua and her husband for taking Mowgli into their home by having them beaten and sentenced to death. Upon hearing this, Mowgli returns to the village and frees Messua and her husband, giving them safe passage to another village. Incensed over the way they were beaten, Mowgli decides to drive the cruel humans out of the jungle. With his animal friends, he devises a plan to ruin the villagers' crops and then have the elephants destroy the village.

In "The King's Ankus," Kaa the python takes Mowgli to the deserted lost city in the jungle and they meet the white cobra, guardian of the king's treasure. Mowgli has no need of the treasure but is fascinated by the bejeweled ankus, which he intends to use as a weapon. Though the cobra warns him that it will bring death, he takes the ankus and leaves the city. However, when Bagheera tells him that the ankus is used by man to goad the elephants by sticking it into their heads, Mowgli throws it away. Later, he decides to retrieve it and return it to the cobra. But several men from the village have found it. Tracking the men, Mowgli learns the truth of the cobra's words as the men fight and eventually kill one another over the ankus.

The Second Jungle Book concludes with "Spring Running." Though no direct incidents from this story are in the film, the spirit of the story must have inspired Stallings. Mowgli has sadness in his heart but he does not know why, though Baloo and Bagheera understand the cause of his sorrow. Mowgli has repaid the kindness of his foster-parents by destroying the pack of wild dogs (recounted in the story "Red Dog") that would have killed all of the wolves. He has also purged the jungle of Shere Khan and humans. But Akela and Raksha are now dead. Baloo and Bagheera know that they are old and will soon also die. They tell Mowgli that he has paid all of his debts to the animals but now it is time for him to leave and return to human society. As they tell him they love him, Mowgli sheds tears but realizes that he belongs with Messua, regardless of how destructive humans may be. He leaves the jungle behind him and travels to the far-away village where Messua now lives. But the jungle will always be in his heart.

It is interesting that Kipling ended his book with Mowgli returning to human society but Stallings ends the movie with Mowgli returning to the jungle. The movie ends earlier in Mowgli's life than the book does and we will never hear another story told by Buldeo. So, like the English girl, we will always wonder what happened to Mowgli. We will never know if he remained a "godling of the woods" or if he ever found true happiness with humans. And this is one of the reasons, besides the adventure and the fantasy, that *Jungle Book* is such a memorable motion picture.

Stallings fully captures the essence of Mowgli as a boy who is an outsider in both of his societies. At one point, he tells Messua, "I have a wolf mother, too; these two things fight together in me." This inner battle is so fierce and disheartening to Mowgli that he eventually loses the will to live and is prepared to be burned alive to end his loneliness and his agony. Stallings also totally conveys Kipling's message of the idyllic jungle society and its relatively peaceful existence (except for Shere Khan) as opposed to the hostile and destructive society created by humans. The village that humans erected stands as an intrusive symbol of their arrogance because they constructed it without regard to the animals that inhabit the jungle. Humans then further disrupt the animal society by bringing the sport of killing into the jungle. Along with death comes hatred and greed, emotions which are alien to Mowgli and his animal friends.

In both book and film, Mowgli cleanses the jungle by killing Shere Khan and by destroying the village, thus repaying his debt to the animals that saved his life and raised him. In the movie, however, the cleansing is more complete since Buldeo's fire purges the jungle of all traces of humans. The destruction is also more devastating since it destroys a good part of the jungle. Thus, in the movie the fury of humans will leave an indelible imprint upon the animal community. Therefore, it is not surprising that Mowgli in the movie chooses to stay in the jungle. "I am of the jungle," he tells Messua. "Their lair is my lair, their trail is my trail, their fight is my fight."

However, it is an indication of the movie's complexity and maturity that Mowgli recites these words with a mournful resignation. He knows that he is human but he rejects human society. He chooses to return to the animal

Sabu and Patricia O'Rourke pose for a publicity photo.

world, not because he is one of them but because he has nowhere else to go. He is aware of this and his expression and tone indicate that he will never belong anywhere.

Stallings also makes other changes. In the movie, Shere Khan kills Mowgli's father. In the book, the father survives but he remains a peripheral figure, not as important to Mowgli as his mother. This is perhaps why Stallings eliminates him and replaces him with Messua's servant, Durga. Stallings also creates the character of Mahala as a friend and possible romantic interest for Mowgli. Adding Mahala may appear to be a typical Hollywood cliché but the fact that she is Buldeo's daughter increases the hunter's hatred of Mowgli. Incidentally, Kipling mentions in one of the early stories that Mowgli eventually adapted to human society and married. Thus, even the introduction in the film of a possible mate for Mowgli has its origin in Kipling. Considering the difficulty in shaping the stories into one cohesive whole, Stallings created a remarkably perceptive and intelligent script that holds as much pleasure for adults as well as for children.

Zoltan Korda's direction of the Stallings script is quite exemplary, especially since he must deal with a variety of wild animals, in addition to mechanical snakes. Although trainers were on hand for all of the scenes involving the potentially dangerous beasts, tigers and panthers are not as easily directed as actors. Zoltan also deserves credit for maintaining a fine balance between fantasy and realism, seamlessly blending the two into a cohesive whole. This is particularly commendable in view of the fact that Zoltan wanted to make an adventure movie while Alexander wanted to make a fantasy, which led to an eventual compromise that effectively blended the two elements. Zoltan's expertise with action scenes is certainly evident here, since he splendidly stages them. Mowgli's battle with Shere Khan is particularly exciting and the climactic fire is a visual treat that is as suspenseful as it is harrowing.

Korda also obtains fine performances from his human actors, especially the two antagonists. Throughout his career, Sabu consistently displayed an underrated ability to completely become the character that he played. Although some critics unfairly accused him of repeatedly playing himself, this charge may apply to his debut film *Elephant Boy*, but it is not applicable to his two subsequent Korda classics. As the title character in *The Thief of Bagdad*, his Arabian youth is a mischievous and charming rascal. But his Indian Mowgli is a contemplative, anguished adolescent. It is not easy to make an audience believe in the concept of a feral child raised by wolves but Sabu does this expertly with his skill and his natural ability with animals. Actually, this ability required lengthy preparation since Sabu gradually earned the trust of the various animals over a period of several weeks by staying in their presence, soothing

Messua (Rosemary DeCamp) pleads with Buldeo (Joseph Calleia) to spare Mowgli's life as he Barber (John Qualen) and the Pundit (Frank Puglia) watch.

them with his quiet voice, gently petting them and even feeding them by hand when possible.

Sabu's ability in more intimate scenes also invites believability in his character. When he approaches the village for the first time and sniffs the sleeping humans as an animal would, this could easily have looked ridiculous on screen but he makes it real and convincing. And when he calls for help by howling like a wolf, it is not only credible but emotional as well. His scenes with Messua are especially poignant, particularly as he develops genuine feeling for her. Sabu doesn't just *play* Mowgli; he *is* Mowgli. It is an extremely memorable and definitive portrayal by the 17-year-old actor. As Tony Thomas writes in his book, *The Great Adventure Films* (Citadel; 1976), Sabu's performance in this movie is "the artistic high point in his career and as Mowgli he surely would have pleased even Kipling." Karol Kulik in his biography, *Alexander Korda* (Arlington House; 1975), agrees, writing that Sabu "played his best screen role as Mowgli." Of all of the major actors in the movie, incidentally, Sabu was the only one of natural Indian descent, though this is really irrelevant, since the movie is as much fantasy as adventure. And political correctness, fortunately, was not an issue at the time.

Also outstanding is former Broadway actor and concert singer Joseph Calleia as Buldeo. An exceptional character actor, the Maltese-born Calleia with his sinister features exudes evil into the role of the superstitious, greedy hunter. When Mowgli tosses him like a baby, his expression of shame and fury is palpable. In ensuing scenes, his voice practically drips venom and it is easy to believe that his character is looking for the slightest pretext to kill the boy. His scenes in the lost city and afterward are especially convincing as he manipulates his two cohorts into violence. When Mowgli chases him through the jungle, he projects both terror and fury to such a degree that it is almost pitiable to see a formerly self-possessed man crumble into helplessness. And yet, after creating a truly despicable villain, he is also believable — and initially unrecognizable — as the wizened old Beggar, his mischievous twinkle and wrinkled countenance fully suggesting that the pain and disappointment of his life have indeed made him a poorer but better man. Calleia is such a valuable asset to the movie that it is very fortunate that, shortly after the production began filming, he replaced the actor who had originally been cast in the role.

Rosemary DeCamp, of French and Irish descent, creates a sympathetic Messua. Her grief upon losing her baby at the beginning of the movie is heartrending and sets the tone for her poignant portrayal. Since Messua's relationship with Mowgli is such an integral part of the story, particularly for adult viewers, DeCamp's earnest performance vastly adds to the film's accomplishment. In her autobiography, *Tigers in My Lap* (Midnight Marquee Press; 2000), DeCamp writes about difficulty of filming during the production which stretched to five months due not only to the director's insistence on perfection but to "the extravagant sets, the enormous cast (of humans and animals) and erratic changes in the shooting schedule." In such a volatile environment, it was inevitable that unforeseen problems developed. Some of the incidents, such as several elephants falling into the man-made lagoon, were humorous while others were dangerous. For the crowd scenes, Central Casting sent anyone of Indian lineage, including people of various sects and religions which had been fighting for ages. Hostilities soon broke out among Hindus and Muslims and Sikhs, which led to assorted acts of violence and the destruction by fire of the restaurant tent. But DeCamp and all of the crew kept working like troopers.

Also notable are Norwegian John Qualen as the Barber and Italian Frank Puglia as the Pundit. Ralph Byrd, of British ancestry, as Durga and former Olympic swimmer Patricia O'Rourke (not quite an Indian name) as Mahala also bring the necessary commitment to their roles to make the fantasy believable. By the way, this was O'Rourke's only film role. And also providing invaluable support is Roger, the Bengal tiger, as Shere Khan. Roger injects such believable nastiness into his role as the man-killer that he should have been given a Screen Actors' Guild card.

Vincent Korda's superb art direction is also an extremely integral part of the film's achievement. Most of the filming took place in Sherwood Forest, about 40 miles north of Los Angeles, with Hollywood's General

Sabu and Rosemary DeCamp enjoy the company of tiger cubs.

Service Studios hosting some scenes. As previously noted, the colors are vibrant and striking but it wasn't all natural. Artificial foliage was added to the naturally picturesque area, parts of which were spray-painted to stand out in vivid Technicolor. Vines, bamboo, grass and plants were also imported to give the forest a uniquely distinctive appearance. The brilliant photography by Lee Garmes and W. Howard Greene fully captures the wonder of Vincent's stunningly beautiful sets and the film should be seen on a large motion picture screen to be truly appreciated in all of its glory.

Jungle Book earned four Academy Award nominations, though it did not win in any of the categories. Vincent Korda certainly deserved his nomination for Art Direction, which he shared with Julia Heron for Interior Decoration. What is surprising is that they lost to *My Gal Sal*, a musical comedy. Other nominations include W. Howard Greene for Color Cinematography (*The Black Swan* won), Lawrence Butler and William Wilmarth for Special Effects, Photography and Sound (*Reap the Wild Wind* won) and Miklos Rozsa for Original Score (Max Steiner won for *Now, Voyager*.)

Rozsa's score contains several distinct themes, not only for each of the major characters but for each animal as well. The score includes a rousing central theme for the jungle, a beautiful lullaby for Messua and particularly evocative themes for the dramatic incidents, especially the killing of Shere Khan and the climactic inferno. Different instruments and themes expressively convey the distinctive appearance and qualities of the dissimilar animals. Boisterous tubas accompany Haithi the elephant and string instruments attend to the sleek Bagheera. Piccolos symbolize the chattering monkeys while horns practically duplicate the sound of the hunting call of the wolves. The ominous theme of the killer Shere Khan fittingly utilizes low instruments, including a trombone. The score is a tremendous asset to the film.

Prior to the film's release, the review in *Variety* by "Flin" was unfavorable: "It is something of a shock and a complete destroyer of illusion when Sabu carries on a whispered conversation with his cobras, pythons and wild beasts; sign language might have conveyed all of the necessary dramatic values of their intimacy." Flin missed the point that, preceding the scenes in which Kaa and the cobra talk, the film has already established Mowgli's ability to speak in the tongues of the various animals by showing him talk to Mahala's monkey. Thus, it is understood that when he communicates with other animals, he is speaking in their languages. Flin adds: "Depending almost entirely on the pictorial grandeur, Korda has neglected any but a slight development of the human condition." This is a perplexing criticism since the movie makes cogent points about the relationships of humans to one another, to animals and to nature.

Following the movie's release, other reviews were even harsher. *Newsweek*'s reviewer wrote that the Kordas "have turned out an impressively successful screen novelty [but] when Stallings works in extraneous melodramatics the story turns dull." *Time*'s reviewer didn't like the movie: "This is the Kordas' bold attempt to turn Kipling's tales into a movie; it can't be done; the myth-destroying movie camera produces a laborious tale, saved from disgrace by some of the best Technicolor animal photography extant." Bosley Crowther in *The New York Times* wrote: "Despite commentary on jungle laws and human deceit, there seems little difference between the viciousness of one kind of animal or another; everything seems to be pointed toward the exhibition of violence whether by the animals, the tribesmen or Mowgli himself." Crowther concluded that the director "doesn't put together a solid picture; it is mainly spectacle [and] the film as a whole is ostentatious." These critics sound like a bunch of curmudgeons.

Jungle Book earned $1.3 million in domestic theatrical rentals, far less than *The Thief of Bagdad* earned. Though this was good enough in 1942 for *Variety* to call it a winner for United Artists in an article listing each studio's successes, it was less than anticipated in view of the film's cost. The box office probably would have been higher if not for the time of its release. The Japanese attack on Pearl Harbor had occurred while the movie was in production and UA released the movie four months after the United States entered World War II. So it was a difficult time for a fantasy film to find a large audience, not only in the U.S. but throughout the world since the war vastly limited foreign distribution. The American people were in a mood that fluctuated between trepidation and patriotism. Thus, the top-grossing pictures of the year were the salute to the British civilians at the home front, *Mrs. Miniver*, with $5.3 million and the salute to American patriotism, *Yankee Doodle Dandy*, with $4.7 million. In the adventure genre, *Reap the Wild Wind* earned $4 million and the war movie, *Wake Island*, which was in theaters seven months after the actual battle of Wake Island, earned $3.5 million. In 1948, United Artists re-released *Jungle Book* to profitable returns; in 1953, UA re-released it again, paired with *The Thief of Bagdad* for an unforgettable double feature.

(Miklos Rozsa's score is so opulent that it took on a life of its own. Upon release of the movie, Rozsa adapted the score into a symphonic composition. The symphony, with narration by Sabu, was the first film score from a Hollywood dramatic feature to be released on record. RCA Victor issued the 28-minute composition, called *Kipling's Jungle Book Suite*, in a package of three 78 rpm discs. Although the record label stated that Rozsa conduct-

The film crew prepares to film a scene at the lost city.

ed the Victor Symphony Orchestra for this recording, film historian Rudy Behlmer reports that Rozsa actually conducted Arturo Toscanini's NBC Symphony Orchestra. In 1957, Rozsa recorded another version of the suite in Europe with the Frankenland State Symphony Orchestra, this time with narration by Leo Genn. RCA Victor released this version on one side of a 33⅓ rpm Long-Playing record [LP] as a "New Orthophonic High Fidelity" recording on their specialty Red Seal label which was reserved for classical compositions; Rozsa's *Thief of Bagdad Suite* was on the reverse side. United Artists Records reissued this version in England in 1975. In 1979, Entr'acte Records reissued the original Rozsa-Sabu recording on an LP. And then, in 1997, an historic discovery occurred. The Film Music Society, which at that time was called The Society for the Preservation of Film Music, acquired seven 12-inch acetate discs of Rozsa's original 1942 recordings of the score. In 2004, after a painstaking and extensive restoration process, the organization issued a compact disc of the original recordings.)

The superiority of the Korda movie is evident when compared to later versions of the story. Of course, Disney's 1967 animated movie is not intended to be the subject of serious analysis since it is an amiable children's movie that uses Kipling's stories as a basis for a musical comedy; significantly, Walt Disney told his animators to discard the Kipling books because they were "too dark and dramatic." (Walt died prior to the film's release.) However, the Disney Studio's dreadful 1994 live-action feature has even less relation to Kipling's books, except for the name of the main character. The movie features a 28-year-old actor playing a beefy Mowgli accompanied by animals that appear to be heavily medicated; it includes some fashionable criticism of British imperialism, graphic violence and an inane romance.

In 2016, Disney produced another version which is, in part, a live-action remake of the 1967 movie. Actually, except for the 12-year-old boy who plays Mowgli (and, to put it kindly, is no Sabu), this movie is not really live-action since the animals and the jungle are computer-generated animation. Similarly, the drama as well as the tension and sentiment are equally synthetic. The inappropriate inclusion of two musical numbers from the 1967 version is supposed to generate nostalgia for adults. The comedy is geared toward children while the action scenes are aimed at teenagers. This version is characteristic of movies of its era which typify mechanical and formulaic filmmaking by committee. Moreover, the film politically corrects Kipling's message and creates a fashionable one-world jungle into which Mowgli perfectly adapts, unlike Sabu's lonely outcast who will always be an outsider whether in the human or animal worlds. But its commercial success guarantees that the 1942 movie will further descend into obscurity.

Warner Bros. has produced still another version entitled *Mowgli,* directed by Andy Serkis, scheduled for release in 2019. The filmmakers of this version have announced that their version will be faithful to Kipling. Computer-generated animation will also figure prominently. That is the problem. Computers can create very realistic special effects but they have no heart. Most of today's films are similarly products of factories that are made according to computerized formulas designed to generate as much revenue as possible.

And that is one of the many reasons why the 1942 Korda production of *Jungle Book*, though it was made almost 75 years ago, remains the definitive version. It has a heart. It has a soul. And it has Sabu, the definitive Mowgli. Furthermore, it is one of many testaments to the artistry of the Korda brothers. It was also the last movie on which they all worked together. Following *Jungle Book*, Alexander Korda returned to England where he continued to produce and occasionally direct films. The British government expressed its gratitude for his invaluable contributions to the arts by making him the first person from the film industry to receive a knighthood. Despite occasional setbacks, he remained a vibrant force in the British film industry until his death in 1956. In his honor, the British Academy of Film and Television Arts has established the annual Alexander Korda Award for Best British Film of the Year. Zoltan Korda died in 1961 and Vincent Korda died in 1979.

Jungle Book was Sabu's last movie for the Kordas. After completing this movie, he remained in America and became a United States citizen.

Mowgli and Haithi the elephant lead the animals to safety.

He signed a contact with Universal-International for a series of popular movies, though his roles supporting Jon Hall and Maria Montez in pseudo-exotic adventures such as *Arabian Nights* (1942) and *White Savage* (1943) wasted his proven charisma. In 1943, he joined the U.S. Army and volunteered for hazardous duty with the Army Air Force. He served as a tail gunner and flew 42 missions in the Pacific Theater; on one mission over Borneo, his plane attacked a five-ship Japanese convoy, sinking two ships and a freighter while inflicting damage upon two cargo ships. After a well-deserved furlough, he was preparing for another series of missions when Japan surrendered. Upon his discharge from the military, he resumed his film career. The commercial failure of *Tangier* (1946) was a bad omen. The shocking wreckage of the war had destroyed the market for the kind of mediocre adventure films he made for Universal.

One of the effects of the war upon Sabu's homeland was the Bengal Famine of 1943. In the book, *Churchill's Secret War: The British Empire and the Ravaging of India During World War II* (Basic Books; 2010), author Madhusree Mukerjee blames Winston Churchill for the tragedy. Though the Battle of the Atlantic prevented commerce from other countries, Churchill's decision to use India's resources to wage war reduced vital provisions even further. Following the Japanese occupation of nearby Burma, Churchill feared that India would be the next target for invasion. Thus, his War Cabinet confiscated provisions and barges that were used for transportation of food. This was supposed to deprive the Japanese of supplies but it was the poverty-stricken people of Bengal who suffered deprivation. Hyperinflation drove the price of food, especially rice, to exorbitant levels. In some provinces, corrupt Indian bureaucrats aligned with the upper classes hoarded food for themselves. Subsequently, Churchill refused to send emergency food supplies and diverted food from famished Indians to stockpiles in Britain. Exact statistics are difficult to obtain but estimates of deaths due to the famine begin at one million. (Satyajit Ray's 1973 film, *Ashani Sanket*, aka *Distant Thunder*, depicts the effects of the famine on one rural village.)

Incidentally, as a possession of Britain, India declared war upon Germany in September 1939 and the Indian Army eventually contributed over two and one-half million soldiers to the Allied Forces along with financial and industrial assistance. Nevertheless, Churchill continued to try to suppress the freedom movement in India. During World War II, India suffered approximately 87,000 military deaths. (More than 40,000 members of the India's revolutionary faction, believing that colonialism was more evil than Nazism or Fascism, joined the Axis Powers.)

After the war, India emerged as one of the world's largest industrial powers and was in a position to demand independence from England which was practically bankrupt. In 1947, India achieved sovereignty and an increasing number of Indians felt free to openly express their antagonism toward England. In some quarters, this animosity extended to Indians who had aligned themselves with the British. Consequently, some Indians resented Sabu because he had left his native country to live in Britain. Their resentment increased when he became an American citizen.

In the late 1940s, Sabu appeared in two British movies for Michael Powell and Emeric Pressburger. The 21-year-old actor impressively played his first adult role in *Black Narcissus* (1947), which the team directed. In this renowned film about Anglican nuns facing temptation, his portrayal of an Indian prince is a supporting role but an important one since his character's cologne gives the film its title. In *The End of the River* (1948), which the team produced, he is equally fine as a Brazilian native on trial for murder, though the film is disappointing. He then appeared in two more Universal programmers but their commercial failure ended his contract with the studio.

Throughout the 1950s, Sabu's film career reached a low point as he appeared in cheap B movies that played the bottom half of double bills. He also had supporting roles in two Italian films and one German film. He auditioned for a role in an Indian film but the producer rejected him, probably due to the resentment noted above. His non-film career was more successful. He toured Europe with two circuses and was a very popular attraction to audiences that had only been able to see the Korda classics after the war. He eventually returned to the U.S. and invested in real estate, a contracting business and a furniture store which he owned with his older brother. In the 1960s, his film career appeared to be on the upswing again. He played supporting roles in two major movies, *Rampage* (1963) and *A Tiger Walks* (1964), but he tragically died of a heart attack at the young age of 39 before the latter film was released.

(During this period, India was in turmoil. Although the world now vividly remembers the Cuban Missile Crisis of October 1962, another equally severe crisis simultaneously occurred. While President John F. Kennedy and Premier Nikita Khrushchev were engaged in resolving the crisis in Cuba, the India-China War erupted. *JFK's Forgotten Crisis: Tibet, the CIA and the Sino-Indian War* by Bruce Riedel [Brookings Institute Press; 2015] describes the diplomatic negotiations that JFK utilized to prevent all-out war between the two nations. The Cuban and Asian crises con-

vinced JFK of the necessity ending the Cold War and also of ending his country's colonialism. But these attempts ended with his death. His successors continued the policies of imperialism and ensured that the Cold War would endure. As the United States and the Soviet Union battled to expand global control, India wanted a peaceful relationship with both superpowers. However, the Indo-Soviet Treaty of Peace, Friendship and Cooperation of 1971 infuriated President Richard Nixon and his Secretary of State Henry Kissinger. India was a democracy while Pakistan was a military dictatorship. But since Pakistan was an enemy of the Soviet Union, Nixon provided military and financial aid to Pakistan. *The Blood Telegram: Nixon, Kissinger, and the Forgotten Genocide* by Gary J. Bass [Knopf; 2013] chronicles the subsequent slaughter of hundreds of thousands of civilians in East Pakistan and the mass exodus of millions of people into India.)

As previously mentioned, for many years, *Jungle Book* was available only in cheap videos which greatly diminished the film's reputation. However, in 2011, Criterion released a DVD version on its Eclipse label, which is the company's low-budget subsidiary. Presented as part of a three-movie set entitled *Sabu!* (the others are *Elephant Boy* and *The Drum*), this disc, with its vastly improved visual clarity containing brighter images and more solid detail, is a huge improvement over the past shoddy releases. Though it still falls short of Criterion's high-quality presentation of *The Thief of Bagdad*, it is nevertheless a huge step in the right direction. Turner Classic Movies also deserves credit for presenting the improved version, thereby attracting a whole new generation of fans for the movie and for Sabu's memorable performance.

But there is even more hope. Rudy Behlmer reports that the UCLA Film and Television Archive has preserved a 35mm nitrate Technicolor dye-transfer print of the movie. And Britain's National Film and Television Archive has restored the movie from its original three-strip Technicolor materials to generate a new Eastmancolor negative. So the movie still exists in all of its pristine natural glory. Hopefully, someday the restored movie will be shown in revival theaters on giant theater screens and released on a special edition DVD with suitable commentary by film historians.

But that, Memsahib, is another story.

CREDITS: Producer: Alexander Korda; Director: Zoltan Korda; Screenplay: Laurence Stallings, Based Upon the Books by Rudyard Kipling; Production Design: Vincent Korda; Cinematography: Lee Garmes, W. Howard Greene; Editor: William Hornbeck; Music: Miklos Rozsa; Special Effects: Lawrence Butler

CAST: Sabu (Mowgli); Joseph Calleia (Buldeo); Rosemary DeCamp (Messua); John Qualen (The Barber); Frank Puglia (The Pundit); Patricia O'Rourke (Mahala); Ralph Byrd (Durga); John Mather (Rao); Faith Brook (English Girl); Noble Johnson (Indian Guide)

THEY WON'T BELIEVE ME

Laurence Ballentine is a heel, a liar, an adulterer and a thief. He casually discards his mistress who loves him and quickly starts an affair with another woman. He married his wife for her money and is content to live off her wealth while being unfaithful to her. He also appears to be more than willing to kill her. He is the central character of the 1947 movie, *They Won't Believe Me*, a memorable film noir from RKO Radio Pictures.

Film noir flourished in the years following World War II. During the war, the deaths of American servicemen mounted steadily in both the Pacific and European theaters. To give indications of the scope of the butchery, the Battle of Okinawa killed over 12,000 Americans and the Battle of the Bulge killed over 19,000 Americans. In order to justify the sacrifices made by these Americans and their families, the government produced propaganda films which depicted the viciousness of the enemy that was responsible for the enormous carnage in Allied nations. These shocking films showed brutalized victims, mass graves and corpses in an unprecedented way. Such films desensitized many people to violence and death. By the end of the war, society had coarsened and would never be the same. Veterans were similarly forever changed. The fortunate ones were able to readjust to society and resume their lives. But many others were plagued by memories of horror and destruction, death and dismemberment. They were afflicted with physical and psychological wounds that never healed. Some encountered, at the very least, alienation and discontent. Others displayed bitterness, anger and resentment. And still others saw no need to conform to the laws of society and became criminals.

War veterans who returned to Hollywood and European émigrés who settled in the film capital understood this change and produced movies with a specific mood, style and tone that reflected the jaded sensibility and amorality that permeated an American sub-culture. Within this sub-culture, immorality was invigorating and criminality was conventional. French film critic Nino Frank and other film critics noticed this trend in Hollywood films. In 1946, Frank gave a name to this new type of movie: he called it Film Noir, or Black Film. Hollywood filmmakers did not consciously create a new genre and American critics would not adapt this designation for almost three decades. But Frank's label would eventually become part of the cinematic landscape.

Incidentally, in the book, *Blackout: World War II and the Origins of Film Noir* by Sheri Chinen Biesen (Johns Hopkins University Press; 2005), the author declares that the emergence of film noir in Hollywood actually began in the early 1940s during the period in which the government's propaganda films were impacting the population. She correlates the development of the noir style and themes with the social conditions in Los Angeles and production circumstances in Hollywood. Wartime restrictions and anxieties, including fears of Japanese submarine attacks, created an atmosphere in the film capital that was reflected in such films as *This Gun for Hire* (1942) and *Double Indemnity* (1944). This trend fully emerged as a distinctive genre after the war.

Film noir perfectly symbolized the pessimism of post-war society. With its murky lighting and expressionistic cinematography, film noir reflected a world of uncertainty, menace and moral corruption. Random danger lurked behind every shadow and around every corner. Unpredictable violence and unbridled sexuality became normative behavior in an underworld that existed just off the fringes of alleged civilized society. Assaults upon traditional values existed down each dark alley, just off the clean city streets and not too far from spotless suburban avenues. These attacks came not only from external forces but from within the hearts and souls of disillusioned men who had learned how fragile life was. They now felt free to live by their own rules. For these men, temptations that seemed depraved prior to the war now appeared too alluring to resist in an erratic world in which traditional morality just didn't fit in anymore. *They Won't Believe Me* is the story of such a man.

This poster showing Robert Young with a gun is misleading.

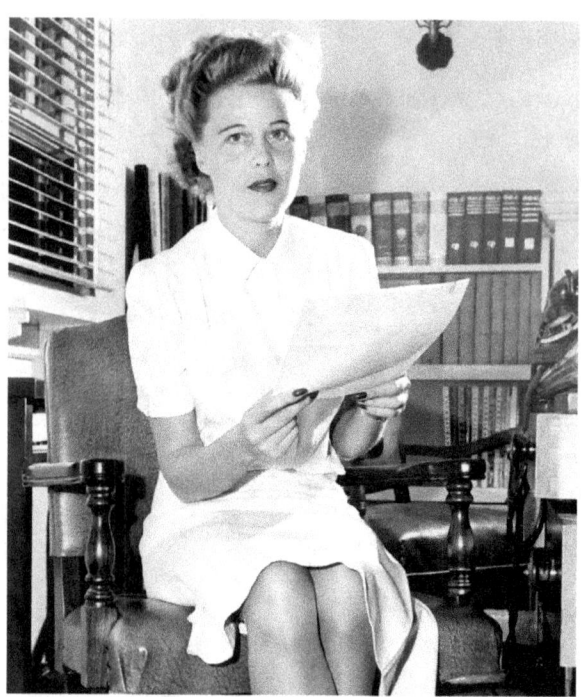

Joan Harrison

Joan Harrison, whose name is forever linked with that of Alfred Hitchcock, is the producer of *They Won't Believe Me*. Born in England, she became Hitchcock's secretary in 1933. In a short time, she started reading scripts and displayed a talent for writing which Hitchcock utilized initially on *Jamaica Inn* (1939), his last British film. She accompanied Hitchcock to Hollywood and subsequently co-wrote four more movies for him: *Rebecca* (1940), *Foreign Correspondent* (1940), *Suspicion* (1941) and *Saboteur* (1942.) In 1943, she left Hitchcock and became a producer at Universal. Robert Siodmak directed her first two productions, *Phantom Lady* (1944) and *The Strange Affair of Uncle Harry* (1945), both of which fit within the category of film noir. However, when Universal substituted an "it was all a dream" ending instead of the original downbeat ending for *Uncle Harry*, Harrison angrily left the studio. She then set up shop at RKO and produced another noir, *Nocturne* (1946), directed by Edwin L. Marin. All three movies proved that Harrison was well-suited to be a producer. At this time, she was one of only three women producers in Hollywood.

RKO gave Harrison the green light for another production and her search for a suitable property led her to British author Gordon McDonell. Several years earlier, during Hitchcock's tenure with David O. Selznick, McDonell's wife had been a story editor at Selznick International. Consequently, Hitchcock and Harrison became friendly with the McDonells. In 1942, when Hitchcock informed the writer that he was looking for a new project, McDonell remembered a plot that he had previously considered developing. He expanded the idea into a story for Hitchcock that the director used as the basis for *Shadow of a Doubt* (1943). Four years later, Harrison may have remembered the success of that film because it was McDonell who provided her with another intriguing story, also unpublished, that would be the basis for *They Won't Believe Me*.

To adapt the story into a screenplay, Harrison signed Jonathan Latimer, who had written *Nocturne* for her. Latimer was the author of several mystery novels written in the 1930s featuring Bill Crane, an alcoholic private detective. In 1937, Latimer started to write screenplays, initially providing the scripts for several B movies. In 1941, he wrote his most notorious novel, a hard-boiled mystery called *Solomon's Vineyards* about a private eye who calls himself Karl Craven; (the book was so sexually graphic—for its time—that an uncensored version was not published in the U.S. until 1982). As a script writer, he eventually graduated to A movies and wrote the acclaimed noir, *The Glass Key* (1942). During World War II, he interrupted his film career to serve in the Navy for three years. Upon his return to Hollywood, he resumed his screenwriting career with *Nocturne* and followed it with *They Won't Believe Me*. The script is quite incisive with sharp dialogue and plausible characterizations.

Irving Pichel signed on to direct the film. After graduating from Harvard University, Pichel worked at various jobs before arriving in Hollywood in 1931 and becoming an actor. He soon also started directing and eventually gave up acting completely. In 1932, he co-directed *The Most Dangerous Game* for producer Merian C. Cooper. This film and *She*, which he also co-directed for Cooper in 1935, would be his only prominent films of the 1930s. Most of his other films, for which he received sole director credit, were low-budget B movies. By the end of the decade, however, he had developed a reputation for being a proficient director who brought craftsmanship to a variety of genres. As a result, he earned assignments on A films and he received plaudits for such movies as *Hudson's Bay* (1941), *The Moon is Down* (1943) and *O.S.S.* (1946).

Though Pichel infrequently ventured into noir territory, he clearly demonstrated an aptitude for the genre with *They Won't Believe Me*. He takes full advantage of the film's intricate narrative development which utilizes flashbacks by a man on trial for murder. The director creates a feeling of escalating despair for the protagonist by periodically returning to the courtroom and focusing on his increasingly haggard appearance that suggests the futility of his fight for his life. By placing typically noir scenes involving adultery and duplicity in outdoor settings, he succeeds in creating an unusually cynical visualization of the main character's moral decadence. With the assistance of cinematographer Harry Wild, Pichel generates a feeling of escalating gloom.

Harry Wild was quite familiar with film noir, having bought his talents to such films as *Murder My Sweet* (1944) and *Cornered* (1945). He also had previously worked with Joan Harrison on *Nocturne*. Wild was one of RKO's chief proponents of the studio's expressionistic technique that distinguished their noirs. For *They Won't Believe Me*, he brings this stylistic low-key photography particularly to the scenes that take place at night.

His delicate control of light and shadow, for instance, is evident as Larry stalks through the ranch, gun in hand and murder on his mind. But Wild also adds a different coating to settings which are not usually associated with noir. Through his camera, even wide open spaces seem to reflect human corruption and convey a frightening ambiance.

The credits of *They Won't Believe Me* occur over a tranquil outdoor scene, not the kind of setting usually associated with film noir. But the menacing tone of Roy Webb's score already indicates that all is not as it outwardly seems. It is obvious that the ensuing story is not going to reflect the serenity of the setting. The beautiful canyon, graced by a waterfall and stream, will symbolize a woman's broken dreams and be the site of her death. It will also be the locale of Larry's ultimate affront to her memory. This hidden valley will figure prominently in the film and will represent the contrast of natural splendor with human decadence.

The movie starts in a courtroom where Larry Ballentine is standing trial for the murder of Verna Carlson. The prosecution has concluded its case and now it is time for the defense. Only one witness will testify for Larry and it is Larry himself. As he takes the stand in his immaculate white suit, he appears to be a distinguished gentleman, the kind that should never be accused of such a horrible crime. However, the hostile manner in which the jurors stare at Larry indicate that the prosecution has presented a formidable argument to convict him. Even the expression on Larry's face is already pessimistic. His only defense is to tell the truth which will be sordid and shameful but hopefully will exonerate him. Thus, the flashback commences.

Larry's story begins at Nick's, a small restaurant in New York City where the Wall Street broker is enjoying a luncheon with his lover, writer Janice Bell. After they part, he walks by a jewelry store and sights a gold cigarette case which he impulsively buys for her. The fact that his wife, Greta, greets him warmly upon his return home doesn't seem to be a problem for him. Also present is Greta's Aunt Martha along with other guests. It is quite clear that Martha has contempt for Larry and castigates him for not remembering his fifth wedding anniversary. Larry cannot resist wiping the malicious smirk off her face and presents Greta with the case that he bought for Janice.

When Larry meets Janice for another rendezvous, Janice tells him that she can never see him again, even though she loves him. Being a friend of Greta, she feels guilty over her relationship with Larry and has asked her company for a transfer to Montreal. But Larry tells her that he is leaving Greta and will meet her at the station. Back at his apartment, Larry is packing when Greta informs him that she is aware of his intention to leave her for Janice. She also tells him she has rented a home in Beverly Hills and that she has bought for him an interest in a brokerage firm in Los

Larry Ballentine (Robert Young) and Verna Carlson (Susan Hayward) share a tense moment.

Angeles. He must choose between Janice, which means losing his wife's wealth, or continued security and an important position. His period of indecision is very brief. Janice travels to Montreal alone.

Larry knows that he has been bought but he enjoys his new position in the Los Angeles brokerage firm. He also enjoys the presence of Verna Carlson, a brazen secretary who is the mistress of Larry's partner, Mr. Trenton. Larry is soon also having an affair with Verna who frankly tells him that she only likes men who have money. Since Larry also enjoys wealth, they make a perfect pair. One evening at a restaurant, Larry sees Janice who has been transferred to Los Angeles. She is quite bitter and doesn't want anything to do with him, particularly after seeing him with Verna. If Larry is bothered by her emotional pain, he doesn't show it. Eventually, Greta learns of the affair with Verna and again proceeds to take him away from the object of his affection. She sells Larry's interest in the brokerage firm and purchases an isolated ranch in the country. Once again, she gives him a choice. He can have Verna and unemployment or come with her to the ranch. Larry travels with Greta to his new home, leaving behind another wronged woman.

At the ranch, Larry feels trapped. The closest neighbor is Mr. Thomason who runs a general store a few miles away. To Larry, the mountains seem like the walls of a prison. But Greta is happy, especially since she

Larry and Verna have an awkward meeting with with a bitter Janice Bell (Jane Greer).

has a new friend, her palomino stallion. She particularly enjoys riding to a valley at the base of a waterfall. Down a steep path is a ravine with a stream and she enjoys staying there, her faithful palomino watching over her. But Larry is restless and searches for an excuse to go to Los Angeles. Ironically, Greta gives him that excuse when she tells him that she wants to build a guest house for Aunt Martha and suggests that he contact an architect.

In Los Angeles, Larry tells Verna that he is definitely leaving Greta and going to Reno for a divorce. But he cannot part with Greta's wealth and commits a clever act of thievery. He leaves a note for Greta telling her of his plans and then meets Verna who surprises him by displaying her lack of concern for the money. He surprises even himself by tearing up the check for funds that he has embezzled. As evidence of his genuine feeling for Verna, he places a wedding ring on her finger. However, as they drive to Reno, an accident leaves their car a fiery wreck. When he awakens in a hospital ward, Larry learns that the police assume that the body burned beyond recognition is that of Greta. He realizes that, since everyone believes that Greta is dead, he can return to the ranch and kill her, thereby inheriting her wealth. However, upon returning home, he finds the palomino standing at the top of the canyon. Nearby is the note that Larry left for Greta. Down in the ravine lies the body of Greta who has either fallen while in a state of despair or committed suicide. As the palomino watches, Larry drops her body in the stream.

Larry is now a wealthy man and travels extensively but he doesn't seem very happy. He finds some comfort in Jamaica, primarily because he finds solace by a pool of dark water. The pool is similar to the one in which Greta's body lies hidden and his despondent expression indicates that he seems to find it inviting. One day he is surprised to see Janice who is apparently part of a tourist group. They quickly re-unite and he appears to find happiness again. After she persuades him to return to Los Angeles, however, he learns that their reunion was not an accident but was arranged by Trenton who is searching for Verna. Trenton then learns that Verna met Larry at Thomason's store before she disappeared. He concludes that Verna was blackmailing Larry who then killed her and disposed of her body at the ranch. He brings his evidence to Lieutenant Carr of the police who obtains a search warrant for Larry's property. The search includes the hidden valley where the police find the palomino lying near the pool, apparently suffering from a fall. In the pool is Greta's decomposed body, believed to be that of Verna. Larry is arrested for murder.

[Spoiler Alert] As the flashback ends, Larry looks like a beaten man, a mere shadow of the debonair man that he used to be. Telling the complete story has perhaps allowed him to see himself as he really is. After the jury withdraws to decide his fate, Janice visits him in his cell. She tells him that she believes in his innocence but he has little hope that the jury will agree. Returning to the courtroom, Larry doesn't see any hope or encouragement in the expressions of the jurors. The verdict is passed from the jury foreman to the bailiff to the judge and then to the court clerk to read aloud. But Larry doesn't want to hear the verdict that he is certain is coming. Sighting an open window, he races toward it and is about to jump when an officer shoots him, his lifeless body falling back to the floor. After the uproar in the courtroom subsides, the judge asks the clerk to finish reading the verdict to officially conclude the case. The clerk reads the decision of the jury and states in a loud, clear voice: Not Guilty.

The last scene of *They Won't Believe Me* is a shocker. Even after repeated viewings, it still sends chills through the spine. The manner in which director Pichel fills the screen with the clerk's face as he states the verdict packs an emotional wallop. If Larry had only waited a few moments, he would have heard his vindication. But it was not to be. After Larry's sins had caught up with him, there was no way that he could ever live happily, not with Janice and not with himself.

This ending is perfectly in accord with all that has preceded it. This is a typical noir world, one that is unpredictable and dangerous, especially for those who believe in love. Both Janice and Greta suffer emotionally

Larry and Verna plan a future together.

for loving the wrong man. Verna remains in control of her relationship with Larry only until she falls in love and then suffers the same emotional pain. Similarly, it is when Larry chooses love over money that fate takes Verna away from him. He bitterly responds to his loss by reverting to his former self and planning the murder of his wife to replace his lost love with wealth.

After Larry inherits Greta's wealth, the malaise he experiences indicates that something has changed within him. The happiness that he thought riches would bring him has eluded him. There are clues concerning the factors that led to his change. His expression when he finds Greta's body reveals no pleasure and even some regret, indicating that it is doubtful that he would have killed her as he had planned. Although he had told Verna that Greta would probably find another man, he could not have been more wrong. When he finds her body, he realizes just how much she loved him. It is thus unsurprising that he contemplates suicide. It is an indication of his guilt regarding Greta that he spends hours and days considering a similar watery grave for himself.

However, when Janice comes back into his life, he experiences happiness, which indicates that he now realizes that love is more important than wealth. It is ironical that fate again intervenes and leads to his arrest for a crime that he did not commit. This sequence is accompanied by other indications of Larry's guilt. As he walks through his property with Carr and the other officers, he only mildly objects to their search. When the officers sight the wounded palomino, he only slightly resists going down to the ravine even though he must know that the horse is there because of

Greta's body. It is as though something within him wants to be punished. And there is almost an expression of relief on his face when Carr, looking down solemnly, asks him to come to the stream.

The ultimate irony of Larry's life is that falling genuinely in love has awakened his conscience and it is his conscience that will deny him happiness. In Larry's mind, he deserves to be condemned because remorse has accompanied his transformation. He knows that he is indirectly responsible for the deaths of both Verna and Greta. Consequently, after telling the truth in the courtroom, he has no faith that such truth will vindicate him because, even though the truth absolves him of actual murder, it does not absolve him of culpability. He believes that he must be punished and he feels certain that the jurors will come to the same conclusion. Thus, Larry receives the punishment that he desires and Janice will have the comfort of knowing that the man she loved was not a murderer, either in fact or by a jury's verdict.

There is another aspect to *They Won't Believe Me* that makes the movie intriguing. The three women in Larry's life are nice people who will all fall in love with a scoundrel. Janice is consumed with so much guilt that she is willing to uproot her entire life to get away from the man she loves. Verna initially has a cynical opinion of herself as a mercenary but, when she falls in love, she becomes unselfish and caring. Greta admits that she lost her self-respect when she married Larry but she obviously is in love with him. Her expression of hopeful enthusiasm when she brings Larry into the ranch is especially sad because viewers already know that he regards the ranch as a cage. All three women are believably realistic which predisposes viewers to realize that Larry must have some inner qualities that are not immediately visible. This heightens the impact of the ending because Larry dies when there is hope for him.

Minor characterizations are equally adroit, indicating the extra care injected into the film. Lieutenant Carr has a casual attitude toward his job and toward this particular assignment. When he discovers Greta's body, it is by chance and when he asks Larry if he can identify the body, it is as though he is asking him the time of the day. Trenton is also not the usual spurned lover. His expressions and tone reveal his contempt for Larry even before he loses Verna, thus adding to the complexity of their professional as well as personal relationship. Mr. Thomason initially seems like a stereotypical jovial storekeeper but his expression of disapproval upon seeing Larry meeting Verna suggests his eventual willingness to testify against him. And Aunt Martha may appear to be a meddling relative but it is very quickly apparent that her distrust of Larry is justified.

Robert Young, who portrays Larry Ballentine, is famous today primarily for his starring roles in two television series. After playing the title role in *Father Knows Best* on radio for five years, Young and his production partner revised the concept to soften his character and brought the series to the small screen. He then starred in 203 half-hour episodes from 1954 to 1960. (He again played the wise father in two television movies in 1977.) A second series with Young in 1962 called *Window on Main Street* was unsuccessful but his third endeavor hit the jackpot again. He portrayed the title character in *Marcus Welby, M.D.* from 1969 to 1976 in 169 hour-long episodes. (He again played the good doctor in two television movies in 1984 and 1988.) He achieved immense popularity by personifying two distinct but equally admirable figures—the ideal father and the ideal doctor—that millions of families welcomed into their homes every week. But, prior to his small screen fame, his career included over 90 movies. It had been a long and arduous journey to television eminence.

In 1931, after a period of training at the Pasadena Playhouse, Young signed a contract with MGM. He subsequently worked steadily in mostly routine roles, one exception being a loan-out for Alfred Hitchcock's *The Secret Agent* (1936), in which he played an enemy spy. He was usually cast as an amiable young man in programmers and projected an affable screen personality. Throughout the decade, he appeared in several movies each year without making much of an impact. Director King Vidor came to the rescue and gave him two plum roles, first as a rugged frontiersman in *Northwest Passage* (1940) and then as a proper Bostonian in *H.M. Pulham, Esq.* (1941). Both portrayals illustrated his versatility but MGM still tended to typecast him in lightweight roles.

Following the United States entry into the war in 1941, Young did his part for the war effort by appearing in such patriotic dramas as *Joe Smith, American* (1942) and *Journey for Margaret* (1942). But he remained frustrated with the course of his career and left the studio in search of better parts. Though two successful movies at Fox—the romantic comedy *Claudia* (1943), and the musical *Sweet Rosie O'Grady* (1943)—increased his reputation, challenging dramatic roles still eluded him. He got a big break at RKO when he played the scarred war veteran in *The Enchanted Cottage* (1945), but his character was still a benevolent one and he was anxious to show that he could play other kinds of characters. The role of Larry Ballentine in *They Won't Believe Me* represented a total departure for him—which is why he very much desired it.

Regardless of how surprised his fans may have been upon seeing him as Larry Ballentine, Young delivers a thoroughly persuasive portrayal of an amoral heel. But yet he also projects an emotional richness that creates a character that is more complex than he initially appears. As the story progresses, it becomes clear that Larry is not a total scoundrel and has some positive features. Undoubtedly, Young's amiable screen image perhaps helped to suggest to audiences that Larry possesses some degree of decency beneath the callous surface. As a result, he manages to elicit

Jane Greer, Robert Young and Susan Hayward pose for a dramatic publicity photo.

some sympathy for his character due in part to the essential warmth that comes through in the final scenes. In essence, he was an excellent choice for the role because of his ability to convey both Larry's amorality as well as his belated moral awakening.

Three first-rate actresses provide distinctive portraits of different types of women that are attracted to Larry Ballentine. Jane Greer is Janice Bell, a nice person who is naïve enough to be seduced by a cad and then discarded by him. This was Greer's first starring role in a film, having previously only had supporting parts. Susan Hayward is Verna Carlson whose mercenary desires also give way to Larry's charm. Hayward had appeared in two previous noirs, *Among the Living* (1941) and *Deadline at Dawn* (1946), in which she played generally nice characters; in this film, she initially projects some of the qualities of a typically noir female but she also conveys an inner softness which makes her transformation believable. Rita Johnson is Greta Ballentine who can only display her love for Larry by possessiveness; her syrupy understanding of her husband's errant ways is

underlined with genuine sadness, thus creating a truly poignant character.

In support, Tom Powers exudes hatred as Trenton. Powers began his Hollywood career in 1911 and appeared in numerous short subjects until 1917. He then had a more successful career on Broadway, singing and dancing in many musical comedies (which belies his later identification with stern authority figures). He returned to Hollywood in 1944 to play the doomed husband in the classic noir, *Double Indemnity*, and was equally effective as a detective in *The Blue Dahlia* (1946). George Tyne gives an understated performance as Lieutenant Carr; his friendly yet solid resolve in his scenes with Young add immeasurably to the tension. Familiar character actor Frank Ferguson, who had previously been a director and acting coach (to such future stars as Robert Young) at the Pasadena Playhouse, is persuasive as the defense attorney. And, though uncredited, Milton Parsons registers as the court clerk, despite the brevity of his role. Pale and gaunt, Parsons possessed an ominous voice that complemented his morose appearance. His stunned reaction to Larry's unexpected fate and his rapid composure leads to his memorable close-up and an unforgettable finale.

The music score by Roy Webb is a definite asset to the film. Webb was the musical director at RKO from 1935 until the studio dissolved in 1955. During that period, over 200 films featured his contributions, whether as arranger, conductor or composer. Initially, many of his scores were perhaps trivial and repetitious since they accompanied similarly forgettable films. In the 1940s, however, he displayed a particular skill for psychological thrillers and horror films. For these movies, he composed moody themes that lurk unobtrusively in the background and are discreetly integrated into the film. He tended to avoid flamboyance, preferring a restrained style with softly melodic, minimalist themes. He was particularly adept at scoring dialogue scenes with the result that the music was often not perceptible, though it added immensely to the scene's effectiveness on an unconscious level.

For *They Won't Believe Me*, Webb composed an atmospheric score that is deeply foreboding, beginning with the main title theme which will subsequently intensify all of the suspenseful scenes. The overall tone is ominous and perfectly complements the noir sensibilities that pervade the story. But yet underneath the impression of fatalism is a hint of sadness, which is especially evident in the canyon scenes. It is also during one of the key canyon sequences that the music, in the midst of quieter themes, will erupt angrily to great effect, which was unusual for Webb who used bombast sparingly. It is an extremely effective score that adds considerably to the film's impact. Other notable Webb scores for noir films include *Murder My Sweet*, *Cornered* and, most memorably, *Out of the Past*.

They Won't Believe Me received some very good reviews. "Whit" wrote in *Variety* that "solid scripting and acting give this character study solid potentialities." *Motion Picture Herald* called it "tense and exciting [with] many dramatic moments well-presented by the performers." A.H. Weiler in *The New York Times* called it "a minor but impressive nugget [and] an adult yarn, adroitly spun." He concluded that the film is "wholly edifying and exciting fare [and] engrossing entertainment" and also made note of the "distinctly surprising and explosive climax." The reviewer for *Newsweek* wrote of too many contrived occurrences but concluded that "the lack of realism is offset by the many good things, not the least of which are some clever characterizations, good writing and a startling windup." He also wrote that Robert Young "gives one of his best performances as the weak, distraught charmer." *Time*'s reviewer had some reservations, writing that the film's "semi-maturity is mixed with trashiness" but still called it "a skillful telling of a pretty nasty story." He also praised the performances of Young and Rita Johnson.

RKO released *They Won't Believe Me* on July 16 in one of the peak years of film noir. During 1947, Hollywood released approximately 30 noirs. They included such films as *Kiss of Death*, *Born to Kill*, *Nightmare Alley*, *Dead Reckoning*, *The High Wall*, *The Unsuspected*, *Fallen Angel*, *Lady in the Lake* and *Ride the Pink Horse* (which Joan Harrison also produced). *Crossfire*, in which Robert Young plays a homicide detective, opened one week later on July 22; *Out of the Past*, in which Jane Greer plays the

archetypal femme fatale, opened five months later. Both stars play roles that are exact opposite of, respectively, Larry Ballentine and Janice Bell and they do it with equal proficiency.

They Won't Believe Me did not earn the minimum domestic theatrical rentals to earn a place on *Variety*'s list of Top-Grossing Films of 1947. Comedies were very popular in 1947; within the top-10 grossers are several, including *The Egg and I, The Bachelor and the Bobby-Soxer, The Road to Rio, Life with Father* and *Mother Wore Tights*, all earning approximately $5 million. The adventure film, *The Unconquered*, was also a success with $5.2 million. The highest-grossing noir films are *Body and Soul* with $3.2 million and *Dark Passage* with $3 million. Other noirs on the list include *Crossfire* with $2.5 million, *Nora Prentiss* with $2.4 million, *Brute Force* with $2.2 million and *Boomerang* with $2.2 million. *Out Of the Past*, surprisingly since it is now considered the ultimate noir, is neither on the 1947 list nor, since it was released late in the year, the 1948 list.

The surplus of noir films may have had an impact upon the film's box office but RKO deserves some of the blame because promotion for the movie was practically non-existent. A.H. Weiler writes in his review that the film "slipped into the Palace yesterday with a minimum of fanfare." Betty Young (Mrs. Robert Young) shed some light on the reason for this studio neglect when she told Leonard Maltin in 1986: "(The movie) was very good. It was at a time when RKO changed hands and it just lacked advertising. The picture got lost." Possibly, the new studio chiefs considered *Crossfire* to be more worthy of the considerable publicity that they bestowed upon it, particularly compared to a movie with a serial adulterer as the protagonist. Similarly, the highest grossing film of the year—though it premiered in late 1946—was *The Best Years of Our Lives* with $11.5 million. RKO distributed this renowned Academy Award winner about three ex-soldiers adjusting to post-war life; it was the type of prestigious film with which the studio wanted to be identified, unlike "a pretty nasty story."

After *They Won't Believe Me*, Joan Harrison produced four more movies, including her last noir, *Ride the Pink Horse*, directed by and starring Robert Montgomery. She worked again with Montgomery on two movies: *Once More, My Darling* (1949), a comedy which was atypical for her, and *Eye Witness* (1950), a mystery. In 1951, she produced her last film, *Circle of Danger*, a mystery directed by Jacques Tourneur. For the rest of her career, she worked only in television. In 1955, her former mentor asked her to join him for his television series, *Alfred Hitchcock Presents*. She remained with Hitchcock—initially as associate producer and then as producer—for the entire 10 seasons of the show which eventually became *The Alfred Hitchcock Hour*.

Irving Pichel's ensuing career included one B noir, *Quicksand* (1950), following which he directed the pioneering science fiction movie, *Destination Moon* (1950). Pichel was one of the so-called "Hollywood Nineteen" or "Unfriendly Nineteen." These were members of the film community who were subpoenaed by HUAC and subsequently informed the committee that they would refuse to provide any knowledge about suspected communist agents. Though Pichel was never called to testify, he was blacklisted in 1951 and directed only two more movies, both church sponsored independent productions, before his death in 1954.

Jonathan Latimer's subsequent noir credits include the script for *The Big Clock* (1948) and as co-writer of *The Night Has a Thousand Eyes* (1948); he also contributed, though uncredited, to the script of *The Accused* (1949). The courtroom scenes in *They Won't Believe Me* may have prepared him for some of his future credits, specifically as the writer of 31 episodes of the *Perry Mason* television series from 1958 to 1965.

Robert Young subsequently appeared in two other film noirs: *Crossfire* and *The Second Woman* (1951), playing laudable characters in both films. After two decades in films, his career started to decline but television superstardom was only a few years away. Jane Greer starred in only one other noir, *Out of the Past*, and would be forever associated with the genre due to that quintessential movie; she also worked with Joan Harrison again when she appeared in two episodes of *Alfred Hitchcock Presents* in 1958 and 1959. Susan Hayward appeared in one other noir, *House of Strangers* (1949). Rita Johnson had important roles in two more noirs, *The Big Clock* and *Sleep My Love*, both in 1948, the same year that a head injury destroyed her career. Tom Powers appeared in such noirs as *Chicago Deadline* (1949) and *Scene of the Crime* (1949). George Tyne appeared in the noirs, *Call Northside 777* (1948) and *Thieves' Highway* (1949) before being blacklisted in 1951 for refusing to answer questions about alleged communist affiliations; he resumed his film career in 1964 and thereafter worked steadily as an actor and as a director, mostly in television.

Following its release, *They Won't Believe Me* disappeared into relative obscurity. Some film noir reference books don't even mention it. The more authoritative books do recognize its merits. In *Dark City: The Film Noir* (McFarland; 1984), Spencer Selby calls it a "notable, lesser-known noir with a strong sense of sexual malaise." In *Film Noir: An Encyclopedic Reference to the American Style*, edited by Alain Silver and Elizabeth Ward (Overlook Press; 1979), Robert Porfirio writes that, "The expressionistic photography of Harry Wild and the cunning reverse casting of Robert Young in the role of the cad make this a very unusual and underrated film noir." Porfirio apparently had second thoughts about Young. In the 4th edition of the book entitled *Film Noir: The Encyclopedia* (Overlook; 2010), he writes that, "What is questionable is the reverse casting of Robert Young in the role of the philanderer. We, the film audience, can only believe (Larry) because of the moral authority Young possesses as an icon."

Leonard Maltin concurs with Porfirio's initial assessment of Young. In his *Classic Movie Guide* (Plume; 2010), he gives the film three and one-half stars and calls it a fine James M. Cain-type melodrama, writing that "Young excels in his unsympathetic role (and) Rita Johnson does wonders with her role as his wife." Richard Jewell in *The RKO Story* (Arlington House; 1982) agrees, writing that, "The film is directed in tough but shrewd fashion (and) the top-line actors all give outstanding performances." Jay Robert Nash and Stanley Ralph Ross, in addition to praising Pichel's direction, write in *The Motion Picture Guide* (Cinebooks; 1987): "Young's fans were perturbed that the normally wholesome actor would play such a loathsome character but his performance here is excellent; he delivers an honest portrait that helps the unusual plot twists work well." In actuality, Young is so good that he completely transcends his usual image. Indeed, the stark contrast between his morally disreputable Larry Ballentine and his benevolent television personality reveals the exceptional skill for which he was never given credit. But belated acclaim is better than no acclaim.

For more than half a century, it was not possible to see the original version of *They Won't Believe Me*. In the 1950s, when RKO was struggling to maintain solvency, the studio re-released many of its old films to generate much-needed revenue. Two major movies were usually edited to create a double feature that would not have a lengthy running time. This editing was frequently done at the expense of character development and explanatory dialogue. *They Won't Believe Me* originally was 95 minutes in length but it was edited down to only 80 minutes; 15 minutes can encompass a considerable amount of essential material in a motion picture. It is a testament to the quality of the film that the edited version is still so notable.

However, in 2010, The Film Noir Foundation located the missing 15 minutes, which add substantially to the film's power. The first restored scene occurs in Larry's office and depicts Verna's anger when he breaks a date with her, indicating that she is falling in love with him. The second missing sequence is even more revealing. Accompanying Greta to a concert, Larry sees Verna with Trenton and is quite annoyed while Greta's reaction to his displeasure implies that she may be getting suspicious of him again. Also, Trenton's relationship with Verna is given more depth and shows why he later goes to such lengths to find her and then to bring justice to the man he believes has killed her. The scene in the lobby after the concert shows Greta meeting Verna, Larry's latest mistress. This scene is filled with tension because of the undercurrent of repressed emotions implied in the expressions of the three characters. Upon getting Verna alone, Larry doesn't attempt to conceal his annoyance because of her talk of possible marriage to Trenton which indicates some jealousy on his part. All of these new scenes reveal that Larry's relationship with Verna has progressed from a purely physical one to an emotional one and add to the believability of the subsequent events.

Following this discovery, The Film Noir Foundation presented the complete version of the movie throughout 2011 as one of the highlights of its Noir City Festival. In January, the Foundation premiered the restored movie at the Castro Theater in San Francisco. Foundation president Eddie Muller wrote in the festival's brochure that it is "one of the most unjustly obscure titles of the original noir era." In February, the Foundation brought Noir City to Seattle where the movie played the SIFF Cinema. In April, the Foundation in collaboration with American Cinematheque presented Noir City at the Egyptian Theater in Hollywood. And then

in October, the Foundation brought Noir City to the AFI Silver Theater in Washington D.C. In recent years, it has been steadily attracting new admirers and becoming less obscure, most recently at the 2015 Arthur Lyons Film Noir Festival at the Camelot Theater in Palm Springs. Most certainly, its status will continue to increase. Hopefully, a special edition DVD with commentary by Eddie Muller and other film noir connoisseurs will also someday appear.

They Won't Believe Me is a superb movie that lingers in the mind long after viewing it. It succeeds on every level, as a film noir, as a mystery, as a thriller and even as a romantic tragedy. Primarily, however, it is a morality tale. For in the end, Larry pays the ultimate price because he finally understands the enormity of his sins. His remorse comes too late to save him, not from society, but from himself.

CREDITS: Producer: Joan Harrison; Director: Irving Pichel; Screenplay: Jonathan Latimer, From a Story by Gordon McDonell; Cinematographer: Harry J. Wild; Editor: Elmo Williams; Music: Roy Webb

CAST: Robert Young (Larry Ballentine); Susan Hayward (Verna Carlson); Jane Greer (Janice Bell); Rita Johnson (Greta Ballentine); Tom Powers (Trenton); George Tyne (Lt. Carr); Don Beddoe (Thomason); Frank Ferguson (Defense Attorney); Harry Harvey (Judge); Milton Parsons (Court Clerk); Janet Shaw (Susan Haines); Lillian Bronson (Aunt Martha); Anthony Caruso (Patient); Lee Phelps (Bailiff); Hector Sarno (Nick); Charles Flynn (Gus); Wilton Graff (Prosecuting Attorney); Jean Andren (Maid)

ROCKETSHIP X-M

The year 1950 witnessed the birth of the Science Fiction Movie as a distinctive genre with the release of two movies: *Rocketship X-M* and *Destination Moon*. Prior to that year, many movies contained science fiction elements but they were secondary to the film's primary genre, which could be a crime thriller or a horror movie, a sub-genre of which was the "mad scientist" movie. Futuristic films, such as *Metropolis* (1926) and *Things to Come* (1936), used science fiction to propagate social messages. Prime science fiction subjects — particularly space travel and extraterrestrial life — only appeared in juvenile serials with comic strip heroes like Flash Gordon and Buck Rogers. The genesis in 1950 was related to various social and political factors as well as to some inexplicable events occurring in the skies. It was also related to wars, hot and cold.

The American people had embraced the end of World War II five years earlier with gratitude and relief. But the dust had hardly settled when the United States and the Soviet Union embarked upon the Cold War. After WWII, the U.S. had enjoyed its status as the only nation on Earth to possess nuclear weapons. However, in 1949, the Russians developed their own atomic bomb. Consequently, the frightening prospect of a nuclear war created a pervasive feeling of fear and anxiety within the American people. These feelings, in turn, created suppressed resentment toward the government for not fulfilling its promise to create a safer, more peaceable nation after WWII.

During this period, the House Un-American Activities Committee (HUAC) conducted hearings into the clandestine activities of Soviet sympathizers within America. Although these hearings have been disparaged as witch-hunts, recent revelations have validated their purpose; *Stalin's Secret Agents: The Subversion of Roosevelt's Government* by M. Stanton Evans and Herbert Romerstein (Threshold Editions; 2013) details the extent of Soviet infiltration into FDR's administration and its influence upon American policies during and after WWII. Regrettably, HUAC investigators abused their authority by unjustly persecuting innocent people along with guilty ones. Simultaneously, ambitious politicians like Richard Nixon used the "Red Scare" to advance their own agenda and to increase the power and scope of Federal agencies, particularly the FBI and the CIA. These politicians branded anyone who opposed them as a communist and used such tactics to advance their careers while destroying the lives of their opponents. Embellished reports of secreted insurgents by such politicians had an impact upon the American people. Concurrently, verified accounts of communist espionage rings in the U.S. and the thefts of atomic secrets by Soviet agents heightened concern that the neighbor across the street could be a Russian spy. As a result, fears of infiltration by communists into all facets of American society generated suspicious feelings for anything of a foreign nature.

During this same period, sightings of unidentified flying objects (UFOs) — called flying saucers due to their elliptical shape — occurred regularly. United States military and civilian authorities dismissed such sightings by calling the objects weather balloons, meteors or hallucinations. However, as sightings of UFOs by responsible people proliferated all over the globe, the government's explanations appeared increasingly feeble. Many people began to believe that the government was either lying or was ignorant about the origin of the

saucers. Accordingly, the subject of visitors from other planets, previously found only in science fiction pulp magazines, now became topics of serious discussion in scientific magazines. In 1950, Major Donald E. Keyhoe, a graduate of Annapolis and retired USMC officer, wrote *Flying Saucers Are Real* (Gold Medal; 1950), a groundbreaking work on the subject. Recently, Leslie Kean's *UFOs: Generals, Pilots and Government Officials Go On the Record* (Three Rivers Press; 2011) provides persuasive evidence of continuing encounters compiled by an investigative journalist with impeccable credentials.

Thus, at the mid-point of the 20th century, American citizens had reason to be fearful of threats not only from human enemies but from interplanetary ones. Hollywood wasted no time in exploiting these widespread fears of dangers, both internal and external. From the beginning of the

Cold War, movies began to tap into the new societal fears as "Commies" and "Reds" became the villains in many movies. Some examples include *Conspirator, The Red Danube, The Red Menace, The Woman on Pier 13* and *Walk a Crooked Mile*, all released in 1949. In January 1950, a cheap exploitation film entitled *The Flying Saucer* appeared in theaters; despite the title, it is not a science fiction movie but another anti-communist movie about an American-made aircraft which Russian villains attempt to hijack.

However, though major Hollywood studios considered human aliens to be a lucrative subject for motion pictures, extraterrestrial aliens were something else entirely. While the major studios were reluctant to enter such a commercially untested field, minor studios, were more willing to explore unproven territory. As a result, producers such as George Pal and Kurt Neumann were able to develop risky film projects at smaller studios, specifically Eagle-Lion Films and Lippert Pictures. These two minor studios were relative newcomers and were not in the same league as the majors. But they were willing to take risks.

In 1947, two New York entertainment lawyers, Arthur Krim and Robert Benjamin, acquired Producers Releasing Corporation, a poverty row Hollywood studio. England's J. Arthur Rank invested in the new company to facilitate American distribution for his British productions. Krim and Benjamin changed the name of the studio to Eagle-Lion Films and began producing B movies while also distributing Rank's films in the United

States. The quality of the new studio's productions increased noticeably from the PRC quickies and included such fine film noirs as Anthony Mann's *Raw Deal* (1948) and Alfred Werker's *He Walked by Night* (1949).

Robert L. Lippert was the owner of a chain of theaters in California. Unhappy with the expenses of renting films from the major studios, he formed Screen Guild Productions in 1945 to produce inexpensive B movies. In 1948, he changed the name of the company to Lippert Pictures. Though most of the company's product remained low-budget programmers, Lippert occasionally produced more impressive features, such as Samuel Fuller's *I Shot Jesse James* (1949) and Fuller's *The Baron of Arizona* (1950).

Eagle-Lion Films and Lippert Pictures figured prominently in the development of the science fiction film genre with their respective productions of *Destination Moon* and *Rocketship X-M*. Before specifically discussing the movies, it is important to recognize their impact upon the future of the science fiction genre. Because of the commercial success of these two films, the major Hollywood studios subsequently recognized space travel and extraterrestrial life as serious subjects for films. As a result, major studios produced several classic science fiction movies in the 1950s. They include *The Thing from Another World* (1951) from RKO, *The Day the Earth Stood Still* (1951) from 20th Century Fox, *The War of the Worlds* (1953) from Paramount, *This Island Earth* (1955) from Universal-International, *Forbidden Planet* (1956) from MGM and *Invasion of the Body Snatchers* (1956) from Allied Artists. Since the special effects of these films were primitive, the filmmakers attempted to attract adult audiences by developing intelligent stories to accompany the fantastic trappings. Equally important, the personnel in front of and behind the camera were skillful artists who approached the subject quite seriously and without any trace of condescension.

Unfortunately, while the major studios were producing quality science fiction films, hacks entered the market and exploited the gullible teenage audience with cheap trash containing wretched effects, infantile scripts and slapdash direction. Some examples of the twaddle that flooded the market are *Flight to Mars* (1951), *Cat-Women of the Moon* (1953), *Killers from Space* (1954), *Devil Girl from Mars* (1955), *Fire Maidens from Outer Space* (1956), *Invasion of the Saucer Men* (1957), *Queen of Outer Space* (1958) and, inevitably, *Teenagers from Outer Space* (1959). Heavily advertised and falsely promising sensational scenes, these shoddy movies gradually eroded the market for mature films. Uninformed patrons were unable to discern between such waste and the classics as well as other movies of merit, such as *Invaders from Mars* (1953) and *It Came from Outer Space* (1953) or the two Quatermass films from Britain, released in the U.S. as *The Creeping Unknown* (1956) and *Enemy from Space* (1957). As a result, the genre acquired a stigma associated with worthless rubbish.

By the 1960s, Hollywood had essentially abandoned alien invasion and outer space themes. England produced the only worthy movies about these subjects, such as *Village of the Damned* (1960), *First Men in the Moon* (1964) and *Quatermass and the Pit* (1967; U.S. title: *Five Million Years to Earth*) but they all played to meager audiences. The genre was in danger of being permanently relegated to low-budget exploitation pictures. And then, in 1968, two Hollywood studios — 20th Century Fox and MGM — gambled and lavished huge budgets on space travel movies directed toward adults, the first produced because of the clout of its star and the second because of the clout of its director. Both *Planet of the Apes* and *2001: A Space Odyssey* were commercial as well as critical successes and precipitated the ascendancy of the science fiction genre.

Adult content within the genre declined appreciably with the 1977 release of *Star Wars*, which is basically a Flash Gordon–type action movie. Though entertaining for adolescents, its phenomenal box-office success convinced Hollywood moguls to aim future movies toward the same youthful audience. Thus, science fiction movies that followed contained themes that audiences of that age *think* are adult but are actually adolescent perspectives on such themes. Pseudo-sophistication replaced sophistication. Sexuality replaced mature relationships. Graphic bloodshed replaced implied violence. Most notably, special effects assumed priority. In essence, the teenagers that in the 1950s were the target age group of the cheap B movies became the target age group of the big-budget A movies. Space soldiers with ray guns, comic strip characters and other subjects formerly seen in serials and cheapies now appeared in exorbitantly expensive movies. The marketplace had been turned upside down.

There were a few exceptions. Nevertheless, Phil Hardy nailed it in his seminal book, *Science Fiction* (William Morrow; 1984) when, in comparing movies of the 1950s to those of the 1970s, he wrote of the "radical shift in tone of the science fiction films from a questioning of tendencies within modern society to an unabashed celebration of escapism, gee-whiz heroics and innocence." He also wrote that where films of the 1950s represented "a probing of the fears of the days," films of the 1980s "in their calculated mix of slickness and escapism reflected an avoidance of the issues of the times." By 2018, comic book heroes ruled, representing an unmitigated surrender to mindless diversions and an incapacity to explore the infinite possibilities of the genre. Indeed, most of the mega-hits of today exemplify nothing more than the crass commercialism of the new Hollywood.

However, though science fiction has become the dominant genre at the box office, none of the commercial blockbusters with their gargantuan budgets can surpass the artistry of the 1950s classics. Undeniably, the marked inferiority of the various remakes of several of the '50s classics compared to the original films proves that costly computerized effects have replaced imagination and ingenuity. Today's filmmakers are trying to disguise their dearth of creativity by calling these remakes "reimaginings" or "revisions" but this is gibberish. In actuality, they lack the creativity and imagination of the pioneering filmmakers who blazed a new trail in 1950.

It was back in that year of 1950 — actually late 1949 — that science fiction fans began to read publicity about a film in production from Eagle-Lion Films called *Destination Moon*. Enthusiasts of serious science fiction found the reports very exciting. This was going to be the first major movie to realistically depict space travel. It was being filmed in Technicolor. George Pal, who had achieved fame for his animated "Puppetoon" shorts, was producing. Irving Pichel (who had directed six films since *They Won't Believe Me*) was directing. Esteemed science fiction writer Robert Heinlein was the technical advisor and co-author of the script. Notable artist Chesley Bonestell, upon consultation with the scientific establishment, was creating the special effects, including background paintings for the space scenes and the lunar surface. Due to the stigma associated with the subject matter, second-string actors were playing the major roles but they were performers with talent. Projected cost was approximately $550,000. Following extensive preparation for the special effects, filming began in November 1949 and was scheduled to continue for four months. As the production progressed in Hollywood and in the Mojave Desert, science fiction periodicals and some mainstream magazines provided ongoing details and created an awareness of the movie months before its release.

Naturally, whenever a movie is the recipient of extensive publicity, there are spoilers willing to reap the benefits. While

The astronauts prepare to explore the Martian terrain.

Destination Moon was nearing completion, Lippert Pictures rushed into production a movie that appeared to take advantage of the hype given to the Eagle-Lion film. Trade papers announced the title as *Rocketship Expedition Moon* or *Rocketship to the Moon*. Kurt Neumann was writing, producing and directing the black and white movie. It appeared to lack any bona fide credentials of scientific research. And, like its rival, the leading actors were all familiar to followers of B movies. The movie had a budget of $94,000. Filming began in February 1950 and was scheduled to last a paltry 10 days.

However, there were indications that the movie possibly was not a rip-off. While it is probably true that Robert Lippert approved the production to take advantage of the publicity given to the Pal film, Kurt Neumann may be innocent of the charge of jumping on Pal's bandwagon. According to Bill Warren in his book, *Keep Watching the Skies* (McFarland; 1988), Neumann had been trying to finance a script about an expedition into space for quite a while. Though Pal's movie probably served as the impetus for Lippert's acceptance of the project, Neumann's story may have evolved independently. Moreover, Warren writes that Jack Rabin, who would do the special effects for Neumann's movie, had also previously submitted a moon expedition story to Lippert.

Though aware of the rival production, George Pal continued to painstakingly ascertain that everything about *Destination Moon* was scientifically accurate and state-of-the-art. Pal knew that he was pioneering a new film genre and wanted everything about his project to be perfect. Moreover, he was aware of the tremendous eagerness of science fiction fans that looked forward to seeing his movie and he did not want to disappoint them. However, Lippert Pictures had rushed its movie to completion. Much to Pal's displeasure, the rival movie premiered on May 27, 1950 at the Criterion Theater in New York City. The final title, after threats of a lawsuit from Eagle-Lion, was *Rocketship X-M*. To avoid confusing theater exhibitors, the promotional booklet for the movie stated that, "This movie is not *Destination Moon*."

One month later, on June 28, 1950, three days after the start of the Korean War, *Destination Moon* premiered at the Mayfair Theater in New York City. As promised, the special effects were remarkable. The rocketship's trip through space and the depiction of the moon surface were spectacular, especially in Technicolor. Alas, aside from the effects, the movie is disappointing, due primarily to a script that is fixated on scientific details. Basically, astronauts travel to the moon, explore the surface and return to Earth. Director Pichel is able to display his skill only in the climactic crisis, in which one of the men is willing to sacrifice himself for the crew. Seen today, the movie often resembles a tedious educational film, particularly when Woody Woodpecker makes a guest appearance as an instructor during an animated sequence. It appears dated not only due to its emphasis on what at the time was innovative science but also because of its political message. Since the movie was produced during the Cold War, the primary incentive for going to the moon is to get there ahead of the Russians. The possibility of sabotage is a constant threat. And it is explicitly stated that the first country that can use the moon for the launching of missiles will "control the Earth." Ultimately, the movie — which never fully recovers from Mr. Woodpecker's lengthy cameo — fails due to the script.

Rocketship X-M **artwork by Richard Groh.**

Nevertheless, it should not be forgotten that *Destination Moon* was exploring unknown cinematic territory. For the first time, audiences had an idea of the sense of wonder conveyed by space travel. The suitably eerie score by Leith Stevens efficiently sustains this sense of the fantastic. And the actors convincingly bring a sense of gravity to the project. John Archer, Warner Anderson, Tom Powers and Dick Wesson approach the story with all due sincerity. But the movie fails dramatically, just as Pal's *Conquest of Space* with its similar emphasis on scientific accuracy would do five years later. However, Pal will always deserve praise and gratitude for *The War of the Worlds* (1953), along with *The Time Machine* (1960) and *The Power* (1968), among later films.

(Incidentally, the following year, *The Thing from Another World* also had a far cheaper movie hitching a ride on its coattails. The RKO movie was filmed over a period of three months at a final cost that exceeded $1,000,000. Prior to its release, two producers formed Mid-Century Films and made *The Man from Planet X* in six days at a cost of $41,000; it opened one month earlier than *The Thing* and, due to large audiences in its initial engagements, United Artists acquired it for national release.)

In comparison to *Destination Moon*, *Rocketship X-M* surprisingly emerged as the superior film. The science contained in the film may be intermittently illogical and the special effects are rudimentary; the ship does occasionally appear transparent and the meteor shower is primitively depicted. However, special effects creator Jack Rabin and matte painter Irving Block did the best they could with their limited budget and even more limited production schedule. In any case, the effects are secondary to the story and this is why the movie succeeds. And the subject of war is ever-present. If the Cold War is a supporting player in *Destination Moon*, then World War II and the weapons that ended the war with Japan are the specters that haunt *Rocketship X-M*.

Rocketship X-M begins at the government base at White Sands, New Mexico. After completing medical examinations, four men and one woman attend a press conference hosted by Dr. Robert Fleming who announces the imminent launching of the first manned spacecraft to the moon. He then introduces the crew who will make the journey: Dr. Karl Eckstrom, physicist and designer of the spaceship; Dr. Lisa Van Horne, chemist; Colonel Floyd Graham, pilot; Harry Chamberlin, astronomer and navigator; and Major William Corrigan, engineer. The ship, called RXM, will launch within the hour and is scheduled to reach the moon in 48 hours.

Blast-off occurs as scheduled and the journey through space initially proceeds without incident. Trouble begins when the ship loses power and the cause is traced to a malfunction in the mixture of the fuel. Lisa and Karl disagree on how to solve the problem but Karl makes the final decision. However, the alterations in the fuel mixture cause the ship to rapidly accelerate, rendering the crew unconscious. Upon awakening several days later, they astonishingly discover that the ship has been hurled off its trajectory and is approaching Mars. Realizing that they now have the opportunity to gain knowledge that would far exceed their expectations on the moon, Dr. Eckstrom makes the decision to land on the red planet.

Using oxygen masks (in 1950, some scientists theorized that the planet might have a thin atmosphere), the crew disembarks and begins to explore Mars. Initially, the planet with its barren surface and stark rock formations seems to be totally devoid of life. But then they discover a metal statue half-buried in the sand which is evidence that life once existed on the planet. In the distance, they sight the ruins of what appears to have been an advanced civilization but they also detect a high level of radioactivity which prevents exploration of the ruins. Dr. Eckstrom concludes that the Martians must have destroyed themselves and devastated the planet through atomic warfare.

That evening, Harry notices movements among the distant rocks and, upon investigation, the explorers find footprints. Anxious to discover what kind of life still exists on Mars, Eckstrom and Corrigan try to find the elusive creatures. They eventually glimpse beings on the cliffs above and one who resembles a human female falls. As they try to help her, they see that she is blind. She screams and others who resemble cave men from earth's Stone Age come to her rescue. They are the surviving Martians who have reverted to savagery after becoming mutants due to radiation. The Martians shower boulders upon the two men, killing Corrigan. Though fatally injured, Eckstrom is able to make it back to his crewmates. His dying words are pity for his killers and a desperate plea for the others to return to earth to save the human race from a similar fate.

However, the Martians have followed Eckstrom and attack the remaining crew members. Though Harry suffers a serious wound, Floyd and Lisa carry him back to the ship and blast off for earth. They are determined to inform humankind of what they have learned. En route, Lisa discovers that they do not have enough fuel to land on Earth. As they near their home planet, they are able to contact Dr. Fleming by short-wave radio and give him the details of their discoveries. The message is obvious: the escalation of catastrophic nuclear weapons on earth will destroy the human race just as the Martians destroyed themselves. As they approach their home planet, Floyd and Lisa realize that they love one another just before the ship enters the earth's atmosphere. Fire rapidly consumes the rocketship before it crashes into the Earth.

Back at White Sands, Dr. Fleming confirms the destruction of the ship and the deaths of the entire crew. When the reporters conclude that the expedition was a disaster, Dr. Fleming admonishes them. The knowledge gained by the crew of RXM is invaluable not only regarding further attempts to travel through space but also concerning the salvation of the human race. Secure in this knowledge, Dr. Fleming announces his decision to plan a second expedition which will be called RXM-2.

Despite the hurried conditions under which *Rocketship X-M* was made, it is a notable achievement. Kurt Neumann receives credit for the screenplay with additional dialogue credited to Orville Hampton. However, reports have circulated that blacklisted scenarist Dalton Trumbo wrote part or all of the script. Trumbo was a member of the Communist Party USA. In 1939, when the Soviet Union was an ally of Germany, he wrote the anti-war novel, *Johnny Get Your Gun* as a warning against the United States becoming involved in a European war. After the Soviet Union became an American ally, he advocated for U.S. intervention in the war. During World War II, as one of Hollywood's highest-paid screenwriters, he wrote the screenplays for two patriotic war movies, *A Guy Named Joe* (1943) and *Thirty Seconds Over Tokyo* (1944). During the Cold War, he achieved infamy as one of the "Hollywood Ten" who, when subpoenaed to testify before HUAC, refused to answer any questions; he was convicted of contempt of Congress and served 11 months in a federal prison. Following his release, he wrote screenplays under pseudonyms and by using other writers as fronts.

Trumbo pseudonymously wrote the scripts for two movies subsequently directed by Kurt Neumann: *Carnival Story* (1954) and *They Were*

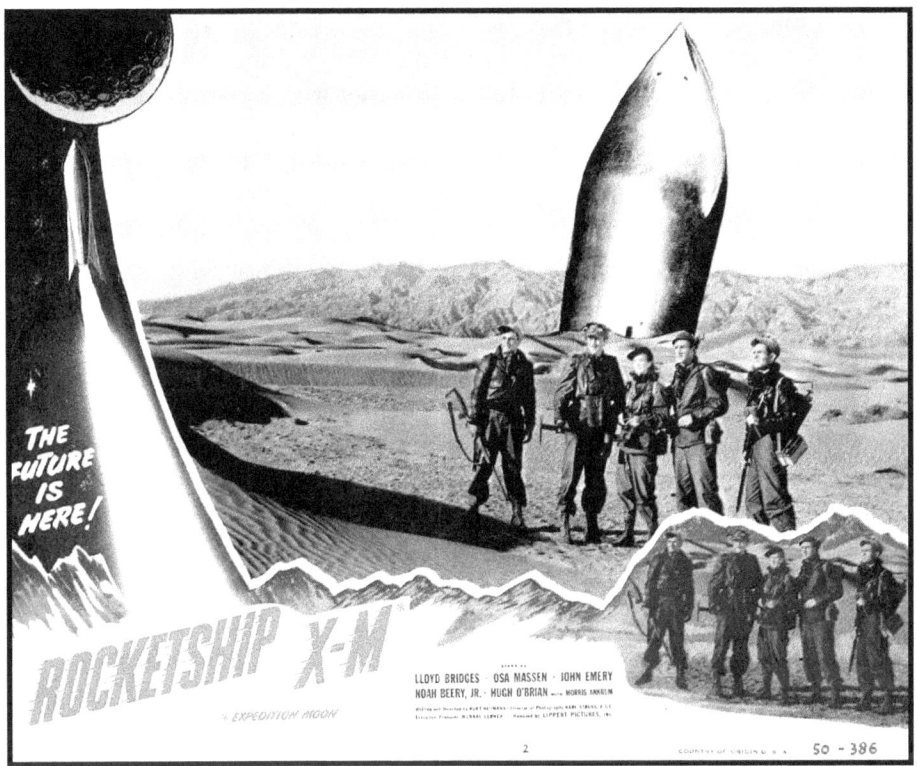

So Young (1955). This suggests that he may have previously worked with the director. In view of Trumbo's pacifist sentiments which were sporadic, depending upon which country was waging war, the message of *Rocketship X-M* appears to be in accord with his beliefs. The objective of the expedition represents the opposite end of the political spectrum as the one expressed in *Destination Moon*: in his presentation to the press, Dr. Fleming suggests the possibility of establishing a base on the moon to "control world peace." (Then again, there may be little distinction between "controlling the Earth" and "controlling world peace.") Similarly, he probably would have advocated the message of the devastation caused by atomic war.

However, there is no documentation of Trumbo's involvement in the script in Bruce Cook's biography, *Dalton Trumbo* (Scribner's; 1977), or in Peter Hanson's *Dalton Trumbo, Hollywood Rebel* (McFarland; 2001), though both books list virtually all of the uncredited scripts he wrote. *Dalton Trumbo: Blacklisted Hollywood Radical* by Larry Ceplar and Christopher Trumbo (University Press of Kentucky; 2015) states the following: "In the fall of 1999, a committee established by the Writers Guild of America was charged with restoring credits to writers who had written under pseudonyms or behind fronts." The committee restored the credits of seven films to Trumbo but "did not recommend correcting the credits of other films," one of which is *Rocketship X-M*. This decision indicates that Trumbo's contributions were either unproven or minor. It should also be noted that the book's index contains a category of Trumbo's "Unlisted Film Scripts" which lists 47 titles; *Rocketship X-M* is not one of those titles. Furthermore, an Appendix contains a category of "Black Market Work" that lists 50 films and his payment, not one of which is *Rocketship X-M*; the movie is also not listed under the category of "Consultations."

Though Kurt Neumann's authorship of the complete script has been questioned, his direction is commendable. Unfairly never considered more than adequate, Neumann was as versatile as he was competent. He came to the U.S. from Germany in 1930 and spent the next three decades directing programmers in virtually every field, including Westerns, mysteries and comedies. He directed Johnny Weissmuller's two best RKO Tarzan movies, *Tarzan and the Amazons* (1945) and *Tarzan and the Leopard Woman* (1946), as well as Lex Barker's worst, *Tarzan and the She-Devil* (1953). Cinematographer Karl Struss, who won the first Academy Award for cinematography in 1927 for *Sunrise* and was nominated three more times, had worked with Neumann on numerous previous films. He again collaborates with him on *Rocketship X-M* and his contribution to the impact of the film cannot be overestimated. The locations of Death Valley and Red Rock Canyon have never seemed so bizarre, thanks to the shadowy photography as well as the inventive placement of the cameras.

Neumann and Struss made a good team and this is apparent throughout the movie. The opening sequence at the press conference creates a dramatic atmosphere that steadily increases as the story progresses. When the fuel crisis occurs, the film assumes a dark, pessimistic mood. The first sighting of Mars is quite thrilling due to the way the camera pans through the spacecraft and then stops as the red planet is viewed through the aperture. Once the crew lands on Mars and starts to explore the planet, the feeling of anxiety gradually escalates as it becomes apparent that the crew is not alone. Struss' decision to use a reddish tint for these scenes effectively accentuates the unnatural aspects of the Martian surroundings. As the humans trek across the bizarre landscape, the environment itself assumes a hostile outlook. The first detection of the Martians is especially well staged while the subsequent action scenes are filled with tension and excitement. And the sudden close-up of the blind Martian woman is shocking in its impact because of the evidence of what has happened to the once-intelligent race.

The perceptive script also allows Neumann to derive a sense of uneasiness from the relationships. The increasing strain among the crew believably develops and reveals some unexpected character flaws as each unexpected predicament takes the crew further away from their planned mission and places them at the mercy of events over which they have

no control. The professional relationship between Karl and Lisa is not as congenial as it initially appeared. Karl's stubbornness in insisting on his formula for fuel alteration appears overly obstinate. Lisa's emotional reaction to her mistake in the calculation of fuel elicits sympathy, particularly since it penetrates her self-confidence. Harry on occasion seems overly sullen and appears to display something less than the right stuff. And the deep friendship between Fleming and Eckstrom adds immeasurably to the impact of the tragic denouement.

    A couple of brief early scenes suggesting a potential romance between Floyd and Lisa are unnecessary. On the flight to the moon, Floyd's flirtatiousness is particularly awkward. Similarly, on the return flight, the development of romantic feelings is inappropriate in view of the recent deaths of Eckstrom and Corrigan. It isn't logical that they would have even a hint of romance on their minds at this time, considering the horror they have been through. However, the film's ending compensates for these deficiencies and justifies such a development. In the climactic scene, when they both know that they are about to die, the warmth they display to one another is logical as well as emotionally moving. At this point, it is psychologically believable that they would be drawn to one another and the change in the relationship is credible.

This last sequence is extremely powerful. After participating in the most important scientific discovery in the history of human civilization, these courageous explorers all die and it seems unjust. In future genre movies, the climactic deaths of leading characters would become a gimmick. But in this film it derives from the progress of the story and the unforeseen events that occur. The epilogue with Dr. Fleming ends the movie on a note of optimism. But the optimism is tainted by the warning that the same human intelligence that has the potential to conquer space also has the potential to destroy the Earth. Five years after Hiroshima and Nagasaki, this was an alarming message.

The ensemble acting is quite convincing by all of the players, which is remarkable considering the circumstances under which the movie was made. For example, in Tom Weaver's book, *They Fought in the Creature Features* (McFarland; 1995), Lloyd Bridges reports that, "When we went out on location to film the scenes on Mars, we went out to Death Valley, and we had to put on our wardrobe and makeup en route, in the plane, so that as soon as the plane landed, we were ready to go to work right away." To some degree, the characters may seem to be conventional, from the stalwart hero to the frosty heroine, from the comic relief to the sturdy commander. But yet all of the players invest their performances with sincerity and are given individual scenes to flesh out their characters, thus taking them out of the narrow range of stereotypes.

Lloyd Bridges is convincing as Floyd Graham, projecting the necessary masculinity for the role but displaying warmth in the climax. Osa Massen is credible as Lisa, conveying both surface efficiency and suppressed sensitivity. John Emery as Eckstrom initially seems to be a typically rigid, by-the-book leader but he provides one the most heartrending scenes of the movie with his last words of compassion for the Martians. Hugh O'Brian successfully creates a portrait of a man whose surface valor slowly succumbs to dread in the face of extraordinary circumstances. Some critics place Noah Beery, Jr.'s Corrigan in the same category as Dick Wesson's comic relief in *Destination Moon*. Though he does provide some humor with his Texas references—admittedly too many, like Wesson's Brooklyn references—Beery was not totally identified with comedy the way that Wesson was, which makes his character more credible.

As Dr. Fleming, Morris Ankrum deserves special mention. An exceptional character actor, Ankrum perfected the role of the stern and dedicated figure of authority, whether it was a military officer or a judge or even an Indian chief. He makes his character's presence felt throughout the film due to the passion he injects into his role. He gives the impression that his heart and soul are invested in the voyage, not for his own glory but for the advancement of humanity. At the end of the movie, his emotional commitment to the crew of the doomed voyage is so compelling that it is apparent that each astronaut's death has killed a part of him. His silent reaction to the fate of his close friend, Karl Eckstrom, is particularly poignant. Consequently, his determination to try again to conquer space is especially stirring.

Another asset to the movie is the score by Ferde Grofe, a classical composer who is chiefly known for his 1931 masterwork, *Grand Canyon Suite*. Classical enthusiasts hail that opus as a very visual work because of the composer's ability to evoke distinct images for the suite's movements. This aptitude led to several film scores in the 1940s. In the liner notes for the 1977 LP soundtrack album for *Rocketship X-M* released by Starlog Records, Kerry O'Quinn reports that Lippert offered Grofe $3,000 to write the score. Due to the meager amount, the composer agreed to write only the basic themes which would afterward be orchestrated and conducted by Albert Glasser. Although Grofe reportedly disparaged film music, his score is one of the most memorable ever composed for a movie from a minor studio. Following a heroic main title theme, the music perfectly complements the action during the countdown and launching of the ship. The jubilant triumph of these early scenes gives way to a sweet melody for the romantic interludes which precede a deliberately uncanny melody, due in part to the use of a Theremin, for the exploration of Mars. Frenetic

The crew of RXM: Harry Chamberlin (Hugh O'Brian), Maj. William Corrigan (Noah Beery, Jr.), Dr. Lisa Van Horne (Osa Massen), Col. Floyd Graham (Lloyd Bridges), Dr. Karl Eckstrom (John Emery).

music that manages to convey both the terror of the explorers and the deformities of their pursuers enhances the chase scenes. Grofe's contribution to the movie is of tremendous value, despite his disdainful attitude.

Trade paper reviews for *Rocketship X-M* must have pleased Lippert. *Variety*'s reviewer, "Brog," liked the film: "The subject of space travel has been excellently presented. [The movie is] a thriller that raises the hackles and is a top-notch small-budgeted exploitation feature;" Brog added that "Neumann gains potent realism by a matter-of-fact approach and the restrained playing of the six principles; he keeps the footage constantly at the shock stage through a sustained feeling of excitement and expectancy." The reviewer for *Film Daily* wrote that the film is "intelligently conceived and admirably executed [and is] a far better treatment of the subject than has ever been given in films." Reviews in the mainstream media were ambivalent. *Newsweek*'s reviewer called the movie "a solaropera" but concluded that Neumann "uses his scientific mumbo-jumbo for melodrama and the result is a workmanlike development of a fascinating theme." Howard Thompson in *The New York Times* wrote that the actors "look silly throughout the picture," adding that "if things are really as dull out there as Neumann would have us believe, science is in for a big surprise." Thompson must have lived a very exciting life if he considered the discovery of extraterrestrial life to be dull; however, he praised the "nice, unpretentious suspense and some clever photography."

Rocketship X-M did not earn the minimum amount of $1 million in domestic theatrical rentals to earn a place on *Variety*'s list of Top-Grossing Movies of 1950. There are 95 movies on the list and *Destination Moon* is Number 88. But an accompanying article states the following: "A vogue which hit during 1950 was the pseudo-science films. The first of these, *Rocketship X-M*, will earn domestically about $650,000, which is great in view of its $94,000 budget. *Destination Moon* is in color and cost more but will earn about $1.3 million." The blockbuster, *Samson and Delilah*, was at the top of the list with $11.5 million. Just below and earning in the $4 million range were such films as *Battleground*, *King Solomon's Mines*, *Cheaper By the Dozen*, *Annie Get Your Gun*, *Sands of Iwo Jima* and *Broken Arrow*. Religious spectacles attracted huge audiences while adventure films, war movies, musicals, family comedies and Westerns were also popular. Science fiction was still a novelty but the profits of the two movies, though small by major studio standards, proved to Hollywood that there was an audience for such films.

However, the profits were not large enough to keep the two minor studios afloat in an industry that the majors dominated. Eagle-Lion dissolved in 1951; Arthur Krim and Robert Benjamin subsequently took over United Artists and had better luck. Lippert Pictures lasted a few years longer, in part due to an arrangement with Britain's Hammer Films to release their productions in the U.S. At that time, Hammer was producing mostly crime films. Lippert went out of business in 1955, the year before Hammer started to concentrate on science fiction and horror.

While Robert Lippert took advantage of Pal's publicity, he could have made an exploitation movie with a hack crew. As has already been noted, such garbage in the science fiction genre would become the norm later in the decade. He could very easily have dumped such a movie on the market to cheat indiscriminate audiences out of a few quick dollars. Instead, he oversaw a project of quality and intelligence.

A Martian mutant shows no mercy toward the astronauts.

Osa Massen and Lloyd Bridges in a publicity photo.

And while he may have had to suffice with low-tier actors, he hired performers who were all very skilled. Afterward, these actors all continued with their careers, possibly forgetting the inexpensive picture that had taken up less than two weeks of their lives.

Lloyd Bridges stated that at the time he viewed *Rocketship X-M* as just another B movie which would do nothing for his career. After playing the heroic Floyd Graham, Bridges gave one of his finest performances as a degenerate killer in *Try and Get Me!* (1950). But he achieved fame on television later in the decade with the series, *Sea Hunt*. Hugh O'Brian also became a star on the small screen a few years later with the series, *The Life and Legend of Wyatt Earp*. Osa Massen deserved better but played mostly supporting roles in her career, doing a great deal of television throughout the 1950s. John Emery also never rose above supporting actor level, being the kind of performer who had nothing distinctive about him but always registered. Noah Beery, Jr. continued his lengthy career as a character actor and achieved some degree of fame in the 1970s with a supporting role on the television series *The Rockford Files*. Morris Ankrum remained a familiar and imposing presence in films and on television. For many viewers, he is perhaps best remembered as the judge in 22 episodes of the *Perry Mason* television series, which is appropriate casting since he was a graduate of the USC School of Law.

After *Rocketship X-M*, Robert Lippert produced other science fiction movies, all mediocre. He dissolved Lippert Pictures in 1955 and formed Regal Films as a subsidiary to 20th Century Fox to produce B movies for the studio. In 1957, he signed Kurt Neumann to direct *Kronos* and *She-Devil* for Regal. *Kronos*, in which Morris Ankrum and John Emery have roles, has some interesting elements but *She-Devil* (which has no relation to Tarzan's nemesis) is awful. Incidentally, *She-Devil* co-starred John Archer, the star of *Destination Moon*. In an interview with Tom Weaver, Archer expresses pride in *Destination Moon* and annoyance toward the rival film. "Ours was in color and it was going to be great," Archer states, "so Lippert jumped the gun with that other movie and got it out a couple of weeks ahead of ours and it did steal our thunder. Our movie was getting a lot of attention during production and they stole a bit of that for themselves. But there was nothing we could do about it." However, Archer must have gotten over his resentment because there are no reports of his punching out either Lippert or Neumann.

Neumann spent most of his career in B movies and programmers—except for his last movie, *The Fly* (1958), which Lippert initially planned as an inexpensive black-and-white programmer. In Tom Weaver's book, *Attack of the Monster Movie Makers* (McFarland; 1994), screenwriter Harry Spaulding states that Lippert brought George Langelaan's story of the same title to Fox but the studio decided to film it as an A movie in color and didn't want Lippert to release it under his B unit. However, Lippert did produce both of the B sequels, neither of which approached the quality of the first film (which

The crew of RXM experience their first view of Mars.

remains superior to the pretentious 1986 remake.) Sadly, Neumann died shortly after the release of *The Fly* and couldn't enjoy the success of his best-known film.

In view of its significance to the development of the science fiction genre, it is unfortunate that *Rocketship X-M* is relatively unknown today. In actuality, even upon its release, it didn't have much of an opportunity to attract audiences. Unlike the major studios, Lippert Pictures didn't own theaters and didn't have the clout to open the film in the best theaters. In most cities, it played second-run theaters and, as it gradually made its way to smaller venues, it was frequently the lower half of a double feature. Only a few years later, it started appearing on local television stations where it was cut to ribbons to accommodate copious commercials.

The current availability of *Rocketship X-M* on home video has made it more accessible. However, some haughty members of the post-*Star Wars* generation tend to condescendingly ridicule its archaic special effects and faulty science. They disdainfully sneer at the fact that the Martians are portrayed by men in loin cloths and skull caps, believing that this humanoid appearance is scientifically implausible; they fail to grasp that this deliberate similarity to human beings makes audiences aware of what the future of humanity might contain, which would not have been possible if the Martians were alien in appearance. These modern critics also snark at the film's alleged sexism due to some lines of dialogue. They ignore the fact that it is Lisa's research that has made the expedition possible and some seem to particularly resent the fact that she is shown to be a woman as well as a scientist, which reveals more about them than about the movie.

For these mocking skeptics, the most egregious plot point is the fact that the ship's new trajectory leads directly to Mars. They claim that the chances of this happening are about one in a billion. However, as Eckstrom stares in astonishment at the red planet ahead of them, he rejects the possibility that mere chance could have carried them precisely to Mars. He can only conclude that, "We must pause while something infinitely greater assumes control." Eckstrom is implying that a divine hand has guided them to Mars for a specific reason, which it will become clear is to prevent the annihilation of humanity. Earlier in the movie, Corrigan has hinted at a similar reason for the loss of power when he states: "Maybe somebody don't want us to get where we aim to get." Of course, cynics tend to scoff at such an explanation due to their anti-theology prejudice, which determines their critical evaluation. They must have an apoplectic fit when they hear Lisa's last words, which imply heavenly comfort just prior to her death.

Rocketship X-M does not display the high quality of the 1950s classics or the costly special effects of modern blockbusters. But yet, though it is very primitive in comparison, it is far more memorable than many of these recent spectacles. It is totally adult in its approach and execution. It features a script that is stimulating and disturbing, not because of computerized effects but because of its ideas. It features credible characters with genuine emotions, unlike the synthetic characters with artificial emotions that populate current movies. It contains images and scenes that were provocative upon release and remain challenging today.

And it is even—quite literally—poetic. On the journey through space and before any hint of tragedy, Floyd recites to Lisa a line from Rudyard Kipling's narrative poem, *Tomlinson*: "The wind that blows between the worlds is cutting like a knife." Kipling's message was biblical in reference, affirming that human beings reap what they sow. This message will propel RXM-2—and hopefully save humanity.

Rocketship X-M was the first adult science fiction movie about space travel and contact with extraterrestrial life. It is also one of the best.

CREDITS: Presentation: Robert Lippert; Producer/director: Kurt Neumann; Screenplay: Kurt Neumann; Additional Dialogue: Orville Hampton; Cinematographer: Karl Struss; Editor: Harry Gerstad; Music: Ferde Grofe; Musical Director: Albert Glasser; Special Effects: Jack Rabin; Visual Effects: Irving Block; Executive Producer: Murray Lerner

CAST: Lloyd Bridges (Colonel Floyd Graham); Osa Massen (Dr. Lisa Van Horne); John Emery (Dr. Karl Eckstrom); Noah Beery, Jr. (Major William Corrigan); Hugh O'Brian (Harry Chamberlin); Morris Ankrum (Dr. Robert Fleming); Patrick Ahern (Reporter); Sherry Moreland (Martian Girl); John Dutra (Doctor); Katherine Marlowe (Reporter); James Conaty (Doctor #2); Judd Holdren, Stuart Holmes, Bert Stevens, Sam Harris, (Reporters)

VIOLENT SATURDAY

20th Century Fox released the 1955 crime film, *Violent Saturday*, after a minor controversy. Because the movie features an Amish farmer as a pivotal character, the studio had planned a gala premiere for the movie in Lancaster, Pennsylvania. However, after watching the movie, the mayor of the city cancelled the premiere because he thought it was too violent and indecent.

It is not a particularly violent movie, certainly not by today's standards. But, in 1955, even implied violence could be contentious. One scene in particular, involving the killing of a criminal by an Amish farmer, elicited harsh condemnation from some critics. But the film depicts this scene and other scenes of violence with restraint. The movie is also not indecent in any sense. There is no nudity and there are no bedroom scenes, both of which were not allowed in the mid-1950s. However, the rendering of such subjects as murder, adultery, alcoholism and voyeurism must have been the source of the mayor's outrage. But once again, the film depicts these themes in a non-exploitational manner.

Violent Saturday is a heist movie in which three criminals arrive in a small town to commit a bank robbery. But other heist movies of the decade, such as *The Asphalt Jungle* (1950), *The Killing* (1956) and *Odds Against Tomorrow* (1959), concentrate on the criminals as well as the preparation, execution and consequences of their crime. Though the criminals of *Violent Saturday* are main characters, the movie's primary focus is upon several citizens of the town and the manner in which the crime will impact their lives. And though the setting of the movie is a small town, that town is clearly a reflection of American society in the 1950s.

Violent Saturday is also, though covertly, a movie about war. World War II had ended 10 years earlier but, though the United States emerged as a militarily and morally superior nation, the optimism of the American people gradually faded. Instead of the peaceful world that was supposed to blossom after the war, the atomic weapons that had hastened the end of the war created the precarious Cold War. Adding to the feeling of anxiety was the onset of another hot war in Korea. American troops had been home for only five years or less — many servicemen were not demobilized until 1946 or 1947 — when the Korean War started. This did not sit well with the American public. At this time, it may be useful to provide an overview of the Korean War and its aftermath.

In 1910, Japan annexed Korea and implemented an oppressive reign. After WWII and the defeat of Japan, the Soviet Union and the United States vied for control of Korea. Consequently, the Allied Powers divided Korea along the 38th Parallel with the Russians occupying the north and

This advertisement for Violent Saturday exploits its lurid elements.

the Americans occupying the south. In 1948, the Russians established a communist government in North Korea with Kim Il-sung as ruler. Kim Il-sung, a disciple of Joseph Stalin, assumed total control over the populace through purges, labor camps and mass executions. Also in 1948, the U.S. promoted the election of anti-communist Syngman Rhee as president of South Korea. Rhee established an autocratic rule and suppressed dissent through similar methods of imprisonment and executions.

Soviet troops withdrew from North Korea in late 1948 and American troops withdrew from South Korea in 1949. In June 1950, North Korea invaded South Korea. President Harry Truman was under pressure to intervene, particularly since he had been criticized for "losing" China the year before when Mao Zedong's Communist Party had taken control of China and, shortly thereafter, signed a treaty with Stalin. Truman committed American forces, under the umbrella of a United Nations military effort, to enter the war in defense of South Korea. China aided North Korea militarily, sending in over one million troops, while the Soviet Union provided economic aid.

The United States drafted over 1,500,000 men during the Korean War. Unlike WWII, the Korean War did not elicit widespread support from the American people. Americans who had so recently suffered the hardships of WWII resented having to again make sacrifices, both human and material. And many people found it difficult to accept their countrymen dying for a foreign nation. Truman, aware of this resentment, did not ask for a declaration of war from Congress. He tried to make the public accept the war by calling it a "police action." Consequently, people who didn't have a relative in the military developed feelings of indifference about a conflict that wasn't even called a war.

Approximately 1,790,000 American troops served in Korea. They all knew that they were not involved in a police action; they were fighting and dying in a war. The armistice in 1953 was a stalemate; it re-established the border between the two Koreas at the 38th Parallel with neither side victorious. U.S. military statistics included over 36,000 deaths and more than 92,000 wounded. The ambiguous conclusion to the war shattered the image of United States primacy.

(In *The Korean War: A History* [Modern Library Reprint; 2011], author Bruce Cumings provides an account of the historical factors that led to the war, emphasizing its origin as a civil war, its relation to colonialism, the atrocities committed by both sides and the similarities to the following decade's war in Vietnam.)

Meanwhile, the American public just wanted to forget the Korean War, in part because of their own anxieties. At this time, Americans were increasingly worried about a possible atomic war. Since the beginning of the decade, the government had been producing films instructing citizens on ways to survive an atomic blast. An animated film taught children how to "duck and cover" at the first sign of an attack. Other films trained adults on how to react if they heard the warning sound of air raid sirens. In 1952, the U.S. tested its first hydrogen bomb which was 50 times more destructive than the atomic bombs dropped on Japan. The following year, the Soviet Union developed its own hydrogen bomb. Americans realized that no amount of training could save them if such powerful bombs struck their country and consequently felt very vulnerable.

By the middle of the decade, as a consequence of the Korean War and the threat of atomic war, the resentment toward the government that many people within American society had suppressed just a few years earlier now began to find expression. A growing sense of apprehension and hostility began to infect the national psyche. People needed an outlet for their frustration, their anxiety and their antagonism. Beneath the surface of the calm and decent culture of the mid-1950s, a steaming cauldron of violence and sexuality was boiling and would fully erupt the following decade. *Violent Saturday* is a depiction of a society on the verge of upheaval, with references to hot and cold wars implicit throughout the storyline.

The basis of *Violent Saturday* is a novel of the same title by W.L. Heath that Harper & Brothers published in 1955. Three men — Harper, Dill and Preacher — arrive in the town of Morgan, Alabama with a plan to rob the town's only bank. Perhaps because they are from Memphis, they share the racism of the town's citizens, including Shelley Martin and his wife,

Helen. Shelley works in the town's primary industry, a fabric company managed by the owner's son, Boyd Fairchild, whose wife, Emily, is cheating on him. Elsie Cotter, the town librarian, is in a financial crisis and steals a purse. Sugarfoot, the hotel bellhop, has the habit of searching guests' rooms and finds a shotgun inside Harper's suitcase. Harry Reeves, the bank manager, is obsessed with Miss Benson, a new nurse in town. The lives of all of these people will converge on the next day, Saturday.

On Saturday morning, the three criminals kidnap Shelley and plan to use his car for the robbery. They take Shelley to a barn and leave a fourth man, Slick, to watch him. Shelley, aware that Helen will be at the bank, knows that he has to escape. Boyd drives Emily to the bank and waits for her in a pool hall while Elsie deposits the stolen money from her purse. After Harry leaves the bank to follow Miss Benson, the robbery commences but Harry's return causes the robbers to shoot him and Emily. Meanwhile, Shelley overpowers Slick but the return of the robbers precipitates a gun battle in which Shelley kills Preacher and Dill. Shelley is a hero, though he feels guilty for the manner in which he killed Dill. And the police continue to scour the area for Harper, his capture inevitable.

Violent Saturday was author Heath's first novel and reflects the amorality that flourished in some segments of society during the Cold War. (Heath received the Distinguished Flying Cross for his service as an aerial radio operator in the Army Air Corps during WWII.) The novel is a candid portrait of a small Southern town in the middle of the 20th Century. He doesn't make any moral judgments about the town's residents but displays them as they are, warts and all. Primarily through dialogue, he paints a vivid portrait of self-absorbed people who are blind to injustice and prejudice. It is a portrait that is harshly

truthful and yet sadly sympathetic. However, readers of crime fiction were disappointed in the novel because the crime itself is not part of the main narrative. Though the author gives every indication that the bank robbery will be the climax of the novel, he instead only relates what happened after the fact as participants describe the events. Similarly, readers of conventional literature considered it to be pulp fiction because of the crime theme.

20th Century Fox acquired film rights to *Violent Saturday* prior to publication and studio chief Darryl F. Zanuck put the production on the fast track. He assigned it to producer Buddy Adler who had recently left Columbia Pictures. This was Adler's first film for Fox and he hired Sidney Boehm to write the screenplay. Richard Fleischer signed on to direct and filming began in December 1954 in Bisbee and Tucson, Arizona.

While the movie was in post-production, the novel made its first appearance in the February 1955 issue of *Cosmopolitan* with the magazine's cover proclaiming it "The Suspense Novel of the Year." (In the 1950s, *Cosmopolitan* was not the pathetic pseudo-porn that it is today; it was a magazine of quality which included articles, stories and an abridged novel in every issue.) Although the Table of Contents promised the "Complete Mystery Novel," it was a condensation. The subsequent publication in April of the full-length novel in book form coincided with the release of the movie version and publicized it. On the dust jacket of the first edition of the hardcover book, it states: "Impressed with its dramatic impact and vividness, Darryl Zanuck purchased the movie rights to *Violent Saturday* and has made a major film of it."

Many reviews of the novel mentioned the upcoming film version. Barbara Klaw in *The New York Herald Tribune* wrote that the novel "reads like a movie thriller and is tense, engrossing and economical." R.J. Kauffman in *The Nation* wrote that, "the book is compact, firmly plotted and, particularly in the last half, exiting. It is at once conventional and fresh enough so that it can be expected to make a good and successful movie." Richard Lister in *The New Statesman* wrote that, "it is remarkably accomplished for a first novel [and] is wonderfully taut and brilliantly planned." It is very rare for people to read a book review of a new novel and then be able to immediately see the movie based upon it but that was the case with *Violent Saturday*. However, there are differences between the novel and film.

The beginning of the film version of *Violent Saturday* is similar to that of the novel, though the setting is different. Harper, the leader of the hoodlums, arrives in the Arizona mining town of Bradenville in the guise of a jewelry salesman. His partners, Chapman and Dill, soon join him and they make a detailed preparation for the bank robbery which will take place the next day, Saturday. They are unaware and unconcerned of the many problems of the town's residents. And the residents are equally unaware of the criminal activity that will soon tear apart their town. Many of the citizens of Bradenville are all self-centered to some degree and have no idea that the outside world is about to make their own troubles seem petty by comparison.

And there certainly are plenty of problems. Shelley Martin, an engineer, served the government during the war by staying home and increasing copper production at the mine that he manages. Shelley's son, Billy, has to fight other children who brag about their fathers' wartime exploits. Boyd Fairchild, son of the mine's owner, is aware that his wife, Emily, has been unfaithful to him and drowns his sorrow in liquor. Emily spends her spare time at the local country club with Gil Clayton, a local gigolo, while Linda Sherman, the new company nurse, has her eye on Boyd. Librarian Elsie Braden, who is in danger of losing her house to the bank, steals a purse. Bank manager Harry Reeves hides in an alley every night and watches Linda undress. And staying apart from everyone is the local Amish farmer Stadt, who detests violence and wants nothing to do with the society that surrounds him.

The night before the robbery, the three hoods have a drink at the local bar. Dill wants to please Harper and tries not to show his anxiety. Chapman, cool and calm, finds Dill amusing. In the same bar, Boyd is slowly getting drunk and flirts with Linda. But Linda takes Boyd home and admonishes Emily. She states that she will accept Boyd's offer to run away with him if Emily doesn't stop publicly shaming him. The advice seems to have its effect on Emily who pleads with Boyd for a chance to save their marriage. He happily agrees and they make a plan to withdraw money from the bank for a second honeymoon. Meanwhile, Elsie also has decided to pay off her loan with the money from the purse. And Shelley is hoping to mend fences with his son.

Harper's plan involves stealing a car which the robbers will use for the getaway. He has chosen the Stadt farm, which doesn't have a telephone, as a rendezvous with a fourth hoodlum, Slick, who will meet them with a truck after the robbery. Shelley is conducting routine business when the hoods hijack his car and take him prisoner. The hoodlums take Shelley to Stadt's farm and tie him up, along with Stadt and his family, leaving Slick in charge. As he struggles to free himself, Shelley quickly discovers that he can expect no help from Stadt because of the farmer's pacifist beliefs.

Harper, Dill and Chapman burst into the bank but Harry's foolish attempt to be a hero unleashes Dill's savagery. There is an explosion of gunfire that makes victims of both Harry and Emily. The three men race from the scene with their loot and return to the farm only to find that Shelley has disposed of Slick. He also now has Slick's gun and the keys to the truck. A gun battle erupts and, although the criminals outnumber Shelley, Stadt still refuses to help him. But when the robbers injure one

Shelley Martin (Victor Mature) unties the hands of farmer Stadt (Ernest Borgnine) and his wife (Ann Morrison).

of Stadt's children, the farmer finally realizes that he cannot stand by and do nothing. After Shelley kills Harper, Dill is about to shoot Shelley when Stadt plunges his pitchfork into Dill's back. In the epilogue, Boyd is grief-stricken over Emily's death, the recovering Harry confesses to Linda about his peeping and Shelley now has his son's respect because of his heroic actions.

Violent Saturday seamlessly blends together a crime drama with a social drama. Each character has qualities that were very familiar to audiences of the 1950s. These are not just stereotyped characters but real human beings whose dialogue and behavior bring them realistically to life. And they are all involved in personal crises with their blistering emotions lurking just beneath their calm exteriors. None of them have any idea that all of their problems are about to converge in bloodshed. The sudden carnage that erupts at the bank almost serves as an overt representation of their pent-up passions.

Shelley Martin just wants to be a good husband and father and he hopes that his son will become more understanding as he grows older. This family dilemma is not in the novel and makes Shelley more deserving of sympathy than his novel's counterpart. The significant factor of Shelley's character is that, despite his son's shame as well as his own guilt for not serving in the military, he has no desire to be a hero. A quirk of fate forces him to assume such a stance and thrusts him into circumstances which provide him with no alternative. He may not have served in the World War but hometown events draft him into a local war and he serves with distinction, thus freeing himself of guilt.

Boyd and Emily Fairchild are both weak and self-centered, due in part to their affluence. Boyd doesn't have the strength to leave his wife and finds solace in liquor, though his relationship with Linda, not in the novel, makes him less of an object of derision. Emily is aware that she is a tramp and doesn't seem to care. It is only when she realizes that she may lose Boyd to another woman that she resolves to start a new life with him. But the moral laxity of both Emily and Boyd has made them vulnerable to outside forces; they have no defenses against unseen enemies who are prepared to brutalize anyone who is weaker than they are. And Boyd learns that neither his wealth nor his social standing can shield him from evildoers.

Elsie Braden is trying desperately to hang on to her home. She does not have the responsibility for her elderly father, as her novel's counterpart, and this increases sympathy for her since she is so alone. She would never have considered stealing money if not for the fact that she sighted the mislaid purse on the same day that pitiless Harry Reeves informs her of the consequences of her late mortgage payment. Harry, who enjoys the power of his position at the bank, probably never would have deviated from his priggish life if not for the presence of Linda Sherman under whose spell he becomes powerless. He is a young single man, not the novel's older man with grown children, and this tends to make his character less shameful than the novel's Harry who should know better at his age. His brush with death awakens his conscience regarding Linda and will also make him more sympathetic to Elsie. He learns that the capitalism symbolized by the bank must be tempered with mercy.

The farmer Stadt is a new character, along with his wife and children, and his presence is responsible for the film's most controversial question. Is violence the only way to confront evil when it intrudes upon your peaceful existence? Stadt is only interested in raising his family to live by his principles of love and pacifism. But three men who don't believe in ei-

Banker Harry Reeves (Tommy Noonan) and teacher Elsie Braden (Sylvia Sidney) learn each other's secret in a dark alley.

ther love or pacifism force him to decide if his beliefs are appropriate to the modern world. It is fate once again that brings Harper to the Stadt farm and compels the farmer to commit an act that shatters his religion's most holy directive. He learns that he cannot isolate himself and his family from the rest of the world. He learns that violence unimpeded will proliferate.

The hoodlums, as in the novel, are also not stereotypes. Harper is a cold and calculating professional on the surface but yet he displays an almost paternal concern for Dill. He meticulously plans the robbery and leaves nothing to chance, not wanting to hurt anyone only because he knows that killing innocent people will increase the chance of their capture. Dill, in contrast, is only interested in building his career as a criminal and doesn't care who he hurts as long as he impresses Harper. His anxiety combined with his psychopathic tendencies makes him the most dangerous member of the trio. Chapman is an expert at cracking safes and is proud of his skill. Due to his bookish appearance, he appears to be a harmless businessman.

On Saturday, the hoodlums will forcibly and viciously intrude upon the lives of the townspeople with an explosion of violence that will tear the town apart. Though the story takes place within a time span of two days, the film provides a microscopic view of the main characters whose flaws are exposed to the audience but not to their neighbors. They continue to pursue their daily lives while being totally unaware of the presence of an evil force that can extinguish them in a heartbeat. The film faithfully transports this theme from the source novel. Unlike the novel, the movie can be interpreted as a Cold War allegory. To the townspeople, the three men are strangers—or foreigners—and it will soon become clear that they embody an anarchic disrespect for freedom and life. Only the same kind of violence that they exhibit can stop them.

Sidney Boehm started his screenwriting career in 1947 and scripted many hard-boiled crime dramas. He received an Academy Award nomination for *Atomic City* (1952), a Cold War thriller in which communist spies kidnap a nuclear physicist's son. He also won an Edgar Award from the Mystery Writers of America for his screenplay for the film noir, *The Big Heat* (1953). His script for *Violent Saturday* adds some characters from the novel and eliminates others. He changes the setting from a small town in Alabama to a small town in Arizona and eliminates the racism of the main characters. Though the locale is the antithesis of the usual noir setting, the characterizations of the three criminals contains archetypal noir sensibilities. Unlike the novel, the bank robbery is the culmination of the movie and the subsequent gun battle is also dissimilar. But the behavior of most of the characters remains unchanged. Despite the differences, the film achieves the novel's objective of illustrating the horrifying effects of violent crime upon ordinary people.

Dill (Lee Marvin), Chapman (J. Carrol Naish) and Harper (Stephen McNally) hold Shelley captive.

Richard Fleischer originally intended to become a doctor but somewhere along the way the theater bug bit him. He left Brown University and cancelled plans to go to medical school, choosing instead to study at the Yale School of Drama. After he formed a theater group, a talent scout from RKO spotted him and brought him to Hollywood in 1942. He started directing shorts which led to his assignment to the studio's B-picture unit and his first full-length movie in 1946. Though he eventually hoped to graduate to A movies, the revolving production chiefs at RKO never gave him the opportunity. But then he directed the minor film noir gem, *The Narrow Margin* (1952) in only 13 days. His imaginative use of the confined space of a train is particularly impressive but it is only one of the qualities that elicited positive reviews from critics. The movie put him on the map and into the realm of A movies.

In 1954, Fleischer directed *20,000 Leagues Under the Sea* for Walt Disney and its tremendous success paved the way for a career that lasted an additional three decades and more. Many of his movies have stood the test of time, including the adventure movie, *The Vikings* (1958), the courtroom drama, *Compulsion* (1959), the biblical spectacle, *Barabbas* (1962), the science fiction thriller, *Fantastic Voyage* (1966), and the definitive Pearl Harbor movie, *Tora! Tora! Tora!* (1970). These indicate the range of genres

in which he worked but he also made Westerns, fantasies, musicals and a swashbuckler. Because he was adept with so many genres, some critics consider him to be only a reliable craftsman. In reality, he chose not to impose a personal style upon his films but instead allowed the subject matter to determine the type of proficiency he exhibited.

Violent Saturday was Fleisher's first film after the Disney blockbuster. Although in Cinemascope and color, it contains some elements of his black-and-white noir thrillers. He uses the widescreen effectively during the opening pre-credits sequence and particularly during the climactic gun battle at the Stadt farm. He carefully builds suspense by creating an atmosphere of tension beneath the illusory harmony of the town's facade. His staging of many integral scenes conveys a sense of oppressiveness within the small town, primarily because the major characters are all struggling with emotional dilemmas. And though they are unaware of the impending menace, the director never lets viewers forget it because of the manner in which he juxtaposes the townspeople with the criminals.

The bank robbery is especially compelling because he and Boehm have carefully prepared viewers for the convergence of all of the sub-plots with the crime. By the time of the climactic sequence, the tension has increased to such a degree that the violence is almost a catharsis, however brutal and saddening it may be.

Fleischer's sympathetic treatment of these characters elicits emotional commitment from viewers which explains why the film lingers in the mind. This is in contrast to some of his later crime dramas. For instance, in films such as *The Boston Strangler* (1968), *The Last Run* (1971) and *The Don is Dead* (1973), he presents his characters in a cold and detached manner. *The New Centurions* (1972) is an exception and, like *Violent Saturday*, also achieves a degree of uncharacteristic poignancy.

In Fleischer's best films, regardless of the genre, he benefited from the assistance of accomplished actors. Victor Mature has often been described as a "beefcake" actor due to his muscular physical presence. As a result, pompous critics often denigrated him. For instance, Michael and Harry Medved named him as one of "The Worst Actors of All Time" in their contemptuous book, *The Golden Turkey Awards* (Putnam's Sons; 1980). While they probably thought they were being witty, the Medveds only succeeded in displaying their eligibility for "The Most Ignorant Critics of All Time."

After dabbling in various businesses, Victor Mature went to Hollywood in 1936. He studied at the Pasadena Playhouse and made his film debut in 1939. Following his leading role in *One Million B.C.* (1940), he signed a contract with 20th Century Fox and starred in several films. During World War II, he joined the Coast Guard and served a three-year tour of duty, reaching the rank of chief boatswain's mate. Following his return to Hollywood, he displayed his versatility with impressive performances as an ex-convict in *Kiss of Death*, (1946), the Biblical hero in *Samson and Delilah* (1949) and a ruthless warrior in *The Egyptian* (1954). In 1955, in addition to *Violent Saturday*, he played the title role in *Chief Crazy Horse* and an uncivilized trapper in *The Last Frontier*. As Shelley Martin, he conveys a sense of uncertainty when facing a problem, whether it is his son's tears or a loaded gun pointed at him. In contrast to his usual vigorous image, his pained expressions suggest vulnerability and fear. This was Mature's only film with Richard Fleischer.

Richard Egan taught judo and close combat (knife and bayonet) fighting in the Army during World War II. Following his discharge with the rank of Captain, he earned a bachelor's degree from the University of San Francisco and a master's degree in Theater History from Stanford University. After teaching public speaking at Northwestern University, he made his first film appearance in an uncredited role in 1949. 20th Century Fox signed him to a contract and, after several supporting roles (including *The*

Glory Brigade in 1953 and *Demetrius and the Gladiators* in 1954, both starring Mature), he graduated to leading man. In 1955, he had starring roles in four other movies and played such varied characters as a Southern-born lawyer (*The View from Pompey's Head*), a Spanish soldier (*Seven Cities of Gold*) and a South African outlaw (*Untamed*) as well as a standard male lead (*Underwater*). Like Mature, Egan's screen personality usually projected vigor and Boyd Fairchild is an atypical role for him. Nevertheless, he is believable and is particularly poignant in his concluding scenes. Egan reunited with director Fleischer for *These Thousand Hills* (1959).

Stephen McNally's Harper is another of his many villainous roles throughout his career. McNally, a graduate of Fordham Law School, practiced law for several years in the 1930s. He quit his practice to pursue his childhood dream to be an actor. In the early 1940s, he had many small roles on the stage and in films under his real name of Horace McNally. In 1948, he changed his name to Stephen and got his breakthrough role as the rapist in *Johnny Belinda*. Subsequently, he alternated between playing villains and heroes, usually playing the latter in B movies. (Two movies in which he starred—*Wyoming Mail* in 1950 and *Split Second* in 1953—feature Richard Egan in supporting roles.) In 1955, he guest-starred in several television series and appeared in one other feature, a B Western, *The Man from Bitter Ridge*. Whether hero or villain, McNally projected an image of a tough, no-nonsense character and he brings this quality to the role of Harper. He didn't make another movie with Richard Fleischer.

In support, Ernest Borgnine is memorable as Stadt. Borgnine joined the Navy after high school and served four years prior to discharge in 1941. He re-enlisted after Pearl Harbor and reached the rank of Gunner's Mate during the war. After returning to civilian life, he studied drama in Connecticut and then apprenticed at the Barter Theater in Virginia for four years. He began his film career in 1951, usually playing heavies, most notably in *From Here to Eternity* (1953) and *Demetrius and the Gladiators*. His career was in a villainous rut until 1955 when Delbert Mann chose him to star in the film version of a teleplay called "Marty" that he had originally directed in 1953 for the *Philco Television Playhouse* (with Rod Steiger). Then Borgnine returned to supporting role status as the farmer Stadt. Though the character is obstinate at the beginning, he gradually expands Stadt into a troubled person with genuine moral dilemmas. Upon seeing his family threatened, his expressions of confusion and indecision perfectly reflect his agonizing internal conflicts. As he reaches for the pitchfork, his expression combining hesitation, agony and fury is truly haunting. Borgnine worked again with Richard Fleischer in *The Vikings* and *Barabbas*.

Lee Marvin (who was also in *The Glory Brigade*) had a reputation as an incorrigible adolescent. He joined the U.S. Marines and received a medical discharge after being wounded in the Battle of Saipan. Returning to civilian life, the former PFC (Private First Class) displayed symptoms of what would later be called Post Traumatic Stress Disorder and would last for the rest of his life. He was working as a plumber's apprentice in New York when members of a community theater persuaded him to appear in a play. After acting on the stage, there was no turning back. He appeared in his first movie in 1950 and soon made his mark playing villainous roles, most notably in *The Big Heat* and *The Wild One* (1954). He makes Dill a repellant character. Pacing nervously the night before the robbery, he is almost comical as he blames his ex-wife for his sinus problems. But Dill, who makes snorting on an inhaler seem perverted, is a sadist who will kill without hesitation. And yet he wears pajamas to bed and this little touch somehow makes his wanton killing even more horrifying. Two decades after a supporting role in their first collaboration, Marvin headlined *The Spikes Gang* (1974) for Fleischer.

Borgnine and Marvin first appeared together in the 1953 Western, *The Stranger Wore a Gun*. In 1955, they were both quite visible in many supporting roles; Borgnine appeared in six movies while Marvin appeared in seven. They also co-starred in *Bad Day at Black Rock*, which had been released three months prior to *Violent Saturday*. *Marty*, featuring Borgnine's first starring role for which he won the Best Actor Academy

The bank robbery in progress.

Award, opened in the same month as *Violent Saturday*. Almost a decade later, Marvin won his Best Actor Academy Award for *Cat Ballou* (1964), though his performance in that movie really isn't noteworthy compared to his unforgettable portrayal of Liberty Valance in the 1962 Western classic (guess the title). The two actors subsequently appeared together in *The Dirty Dozen* (1967) and *Emperor of the North* (1973) as well as in the television sequel, *The Dirty Dozen: the Next Mission* (1985).

J. Carrol Naish, who started his career in the mid-1920s, was an accomplished character actor who always submerged himself within his role, whether as the amoral safecracker in this film or as chief Sitting Bull in the film of the same title the previous year. Though of Irish ancestry, he had the ability to credibly portray characters of many nationalities and races, appearing variously as a Mexican, an Italian, a Frenchman, a Russian, an Indian, an Arabian and, even — though rarely — an Irishman. Born in 1896, Naish served his country by playing Japanese villains at least three times during the war years. In 1955, he appeared in six movies, playing totally dissimilar roles in each one. By the way, Naish's dialogue with a boy during the robbery in *Violent Saturday* is priceless.

Veteran actress Sylvia Sidney, who began her film career in 1929, is notable as Elsie Braden. She creates a credible portrait of a woman who has been pushed to the brink of desperation. Her glee at catching Harry peeping just after he has cruelly threatened to ruin her life is quite satisfying. Amusingly, an incident which occurred during pre-production obviously impressed Richard Fleischer. Prior to rehearsal, Fleischer met with Sidney and provided a lengthy summary of her character's back-story as well as the necessary motivations for her behavior. After this lengthy speech, Sidney smiled and said, "Just tell me when to cry." Fleischer used this line as the title of his autobiography that Carroll & Graf published in 1993.

Former Navy sailor Tommy Noonan, whom Darryl F. Zanuck personally chose for the role of Harry Reeves, makes his character suitably hypocritical with just the right degree of sliminess. Virginia Leith brings warmth and allure to Linda Sherman; she deserved a more notable film career but didn't get the right breaks. Margaret Hayes initially is persuasively frosty as Emily and makes her transition quite affecting. Hayes also had a significant role in *Blackboard Jungle*, which had been released the previous month; this film, in which a war veteran-teacher confronts juvenile delinquency in a high school, is another depiction of the societal turmoil of the post-war 1950s. Brad Dexter, though his role is brief, makes an impression as Gil Clayton, Emily's country club lover. Dexter, who served in the Army Air Corps during the war, would later achieve some degree of reverse fame for being the forgotten member of *The Magnificent Seven* (1960).

Upon its release, *Violent Saturday* received some excellent reviews. *Variety*'s reviewer wrote that, "Fox has what looks like a sleeper in this taut melodrama," adding that it is "a masterful piece of storytelling." The reviewer for *Time* wrote: "It is a big, rough savvy sort of pell-meller, perhaps the best thing of its type that Hollywood has offered in 1955. The morality of violence is brought vividly into question and has seldom been answered with more pith and natural majesty." *Newsweek*'s reviewer called it "good entertainment," adding that the director "has a story that is sound enough; his cast is pretty good and the personal narratives are tied up in a neat if obvious bundle." Lee Rogow in *The Saturday Review* wrote that "the bank-robbing sequence and the battle between Mature and the criminals in the Amish barn are suspenseful action at their best." But Bosley Crowther in *The New York Times* wrote that it "is vicious and sadistic." Calling the characters a "passel of modern misfits," Crowther concluded that the movie "appears to have no other purpose than to titillate and thrill on the level of guarded pornography." The mayor of Lancaster, Pennsylvania must have loved this review.

Variety's annual list of Top-Grossing Movies for 1955 includes 105 films. Movies about World War II topped the list: *Mister Roberts* earned domestic theatrical rentals of $8.5 million and *Battle Cry* followed with $8.1 million while *The Sea Chase* and *To Hell and Back* also scored with $6 million each.

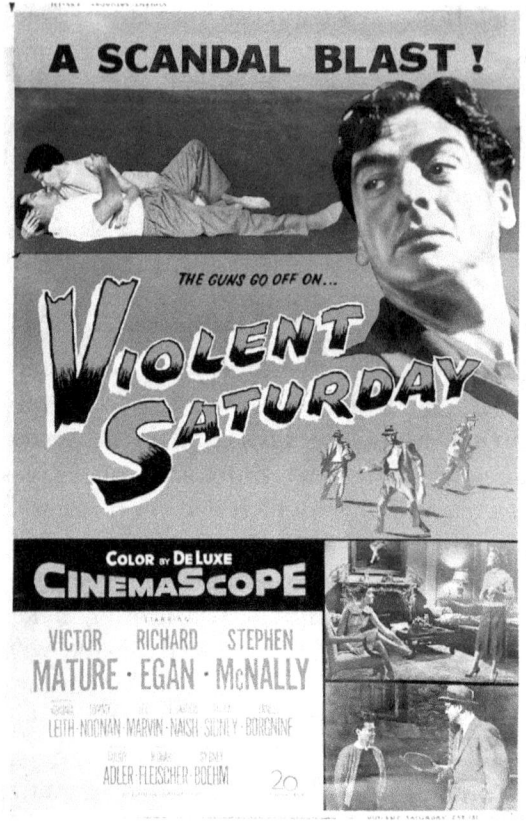

The most successful crime film was *Pete Kelly's Blues*, the Jazz Age gangster drama, which earned $5 million. *The Desperate Hours* followed with $2.6 million. Two crime films reflected aftermaths of the war: *The Phenix City Story*, in which an ex-soldier finds tyranny in his hometown after defeating it abroad, earned $2.2 million while *House of Bamboo*, in which ex-soldiers create a criminal syndicate in occupied Japan, earned $1.7 million. *Violent Saturday* is at the bottom of the list at Number 98 with $1.25 million. Other crime movies of the year include *Kiss Me Deadly* (another vision of the unstable 1950s with its theme of post-nuclear paranoia), *The Big Combo*, *Hell on Frisco Bay*, *I Died a Thousand Times* and *New York Confidential*. Some films reflected the Cold War: *Trial* is a courtroom drama about the Communist Party's exploitation of racial prejudice and *Shack Out on 101* features Lee Marvin as a communist spy called "Slob."

However, *Violent Saturday* is more than a solid crime drama. It is more than a story about war and peace. The setting of the Arizona mining town suggests a modern Western and the climactic gunfight in the barn could easily have taken place in the previous century. The movie also features some elements from the previous year's *The High and the Mighty* and other later imitative disaster movies in which various people from differing backgrounds suffer a shared crisis. More precisely, it recalls the previous decade's *Kings Row* and presages *Peyton Place* of three years later, both of which expose the intimate secrets of small town inhabitants.

In Douglas Brode's book, *The Films of the Fifties* (Citadel; 1976), he writes: "In many respects, *Violent Saturday* presented the definitive study of America during the decade. Every detail, from the clearly representational characters to the very geography of the town, helped make it a perfect representation of Fifties mentality." The fact that it still resonates over half a century later is testament to its power. Perhaps it is even more powerful today than it was back in 1955 because now it has an additional implication; despite all of the problems people had back then, they still experienced guilt and shame and still believed in sin and morality. This was before the modern concept of moral relativism made such terms obsolete.

In view of this, many of today's younger moviegoers consider *Violent Saturday* to be quaint. Guilt and shame are alien concepts to them. They expect that a movie about sexuality and violence should include soft-core pornography and gratuitous bloodletting. In contrast, this movie appeals to intelligent adults, not dolts who have to see everything in graphic detail to understand what is happening. The artistic level of motion pictures has dumbed down to attract simpletons who delude themselves into believing that their acceptance of sleaze indicates maturity, not realizing that it reveals cultural idiocy. This type of moviegoer that Hollywood shunned in the past is now the target audience of major studio movies made with actors that Victor Mature could swat like a fly and by directors who couldn't shine Richard Fleischer's shoes.

Violent Saturday deserves to be better known than it is. However, as with other neglected movies, time often has a tendency to redress past wrongs. In March 2006, The American Cinematheque presented a tribute to Richard Fleischer at the Aero Theater in Santa Monica with presentations of eight of his movies, including *Violent Saturday*. Six days later, Fleischer died. In May 2006, the Egyptian Theater in Hollywood presented a two-film memorial tribute to the director, one of which was *Violent Saturday*. In February 2008, the Film Forum Theater in New York City, presented *Violent Saturday* in a new 35mm Cinemascope print for a week-long engagement; at the conclusion of more than one of its showings, the audience responded with a round of applause. And in 2011, the new specialty DVD label, Twilight Time, chose *Violent Saturday* as one of its inaugural releases.

The makers of *Violent Saturday* did not intend for it to be to be a classic. They only designed it to be an entertaining and gripping thriller. They succeeded admirably.

CREDITS: Producer: Buddy Adler; Director: Richard Fleischer; Screenplay: Sidney Boehm, Based Upon the Novel by W.L. Heath; Cinematographer: Charles Clarke; Editor: Louis Loeffler; Music: Hugo Friedhofer

CAST: Victor Mature (Shelley Martin); Richard Egan (Boyd Fairchild); Stephen McNally (Harper); Virginia Leith (Linda Sherman); Sylvia Sidney (Elsie Braden); Margaret Hayes (Emily Fairchild); Ernest Borgnine (Stadt); Lee Marvin (Dill); J. Carrol Naish (Chapman); Tommy Noonan (Harry Reeves); Dorothy Patrick (Helen Martin); Billy Chapin (Steve Martin); Brad Dexter (Gil Clayton); Ann Morrison (Mrs. Stadt); Kevin Corcoran (David Stadt); Donna Corcoran (Anna Stadt); Noreen Corcoran (Mary Stadt); Boyd Morgan (Slick); Ellene Bowers (Bank Teller)

POCKETFUL OF MIRACLES

The setting is Broadway in the 1930s. The bedraggled old woman in tattered clothes walks down a busy street carrying a basket. She cries out, "Apples for sale!" and has to practically force one into a man's hand. It is the Christmas season and the numerous shoppers carrying gifts don't even seem to notice her or deliberately choose to ignore her. And then the credits of the movie begin. *Pocketful of Miracles* is the title and it is a delightful movie that upon release received unfavorable reviews by most critics and was a commercial failure.

The basis of the movie is a story by Damon Runyon. Runyon was born in 1880 in Kansas and was raised in Colorado, where he began his newspaper career. In 1898, he joined the U.S. Army during the Spanish-American War. (This war lasted three and one-half months. The American defeat of Spain ended the Spanish Empire and expanded America's role as a colonial power; the United States annexed the Spanish colonies of Guam, Puerto Rico and the Philippines and also established a military base in Cuba at Guantanamo Bay. Many Filipinos resented being occupied again and rebelled; the Philippine-American War, or the Philippine War of Independence, began in 1899 and lasted for three years until the American victory. Incidentally, in 1899, Rudyard Kipling altered his poem *The White Man's Burden* and gave it the subtitle: *The United States in the Philippine Islands*.)

Following his discharge, Runyon returned to Colorado and worked for several newspapers. In 1910, he moved to New York City and achieved distinction as a sports writer. He also became friendly with various shady characters who inhabited New York's underworld, some of whom he celebrated and romanticized in his articles. He wrote in a flamboyant style which attracted a multitude of fans. By the 1930s, millions of people read his syndicated column and made him the nation's most popular journalist.

However, Runyon's fame is due primarily to his short stories about Broadway and its inimitable inhabitants during the Prohibition. He wrote these stories in such a distinct style that the term "Runyonesque" would be coined to apply to any fiction about the characters and milieu he described so colorfully. He developed a uniquely vernacular style which features a blend of proper speech and quaint slang. The narrator usually recounts the tale in the present tense and never uses contractions in his speech. The main characters are typically hoods, hustlers, bootleggers, thieves, gamblers and assorted misfits of society, all of whom have amusing nicknames.

In October 1929, *Cosmopolitan* magazine published a story by Runyon entitled "Madame La Gimp." Dave the Dude is a hood whose unnamed henchman narrates the story which begins with a "busted-down old

Spanish doll" known as Madame La Gimp telling her troubles to Dave. Years before, she had sent her daughter Eulalie to Spain to live with her aunt. She has since been pretending in her letters to Eulalie to be married to a wealthy man and living in an upscale hotel. But now Eulalie is bringing her fiancé and his parents to New York. Count Romero, her fiancé's father, has to make certain that Eulalie's parents are socially acceptable before he will approve the marriage. Since Dave is a sucker for anyone in trouble, he hatches a plan to set up Madame in a ritzy hotel with a rich husband. To play the husband,  Dave enlists Judge Henry Blake, a former financier who lost his shirt in the stock market. Dave's wife, Billie, recruits jazz dancer Missouri Martin and a squad of beauticians who turn Madame into a society matron. The meeting with Eulalie and her fiancé's family at the pier works perfectly but Dave can't resist impressing the Count and hatches a plan to stage a grand reception at the hotel with all kinds of dignitaries in attendance. Characters like Big Nig, Rochester Red, the Paleface Kid and Death House Donnegan pretend to be everyone from the Mayor and the Police Commissioner to various celebrities like Al Jolson and Rudy Vallee. After the Count gives his blessing, Eulalie and her fiancé elope while Madame La Gimp and Henry Blake also decide to get married. And Dave the Dude feels very pleased with himself, except that he demands that his hoods immediately return all stolen goods to the hotel.

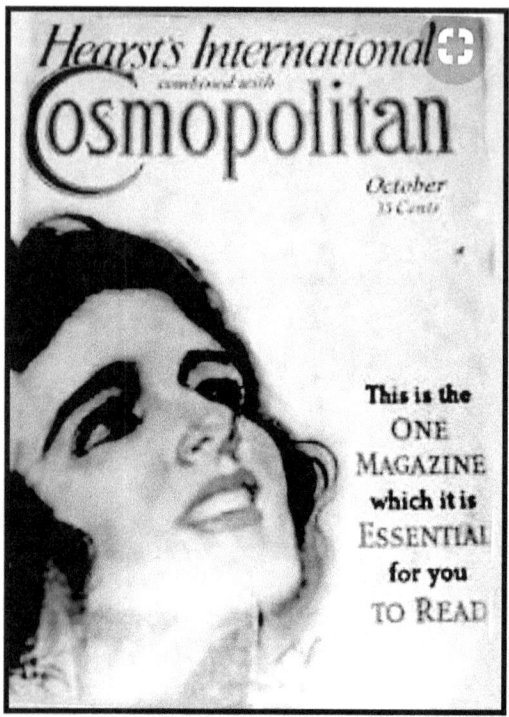

Damon Runyon's multitude of fans enjoyed the story. But the timing of its publication may have prevented many of his followers from being able to appreciate it. The *Cosmopolitan* issue featuring the story appeared just prior to October 29, 1929, a day known as Black Tuesday. This was the day of the stock market crash in which stockholders lost $40 billion. The crash was one of the major causes of the subsequent Great Depression which began in the United States and quickly spread all over the world. The devastating effects included bank failures, loss of income, obliteration of personal savings, countless home foreclosures and extensive unemployment—25% in the United States, higher in some other countries. National and world economy steadily declined and, by 1933, poverty and despair had become a way of life for millions of people. For many of them, the only pleasure they could afford was to see a movie; the average price for a theater ticket in 1933 was 25 cents and, in rural areas, 10 to 15 cents.

The Great Depression was a factor leading to World War II. Harsh economic times tend to lead to the rise of nationalism and militarism. Germany's economy and unemployment were singularly terrible because of the massive reparations that it had to pay after the First World War. In the 1920s, Germany borrowed money from foreign banks to pay this debt. During the Depression, American banks recalled the loans which collapsed Germany's industry, further increasing poverty. In the United States, President Herbert Hoover believed that it was not the government's duty to resolve the economy and urged patience. This antagonized a population that included one-fourth of the workforce being unemployed and millions living in despair. As a result, he was defeated for re-election by Franklin Roosevelt who established a series of programs known as The New Deal to restore prosperity. These programs included the Social Security Act, unemployment insurance and the Work Progress Administration. In general, FDR's domestic policies were invaluable in providing assistance to millions of Americans. In the international arena, his anti-colonialist views were also potentially beneficial to oppressed people worldwide. However, some historians believe that FDR's reaction to the burgeoning war in Europe had adverse consequences. Indeed, just as Roosevelt blamed Hoover for the Depression, Hoover blamed Roosevelt for WWII. *Freedom Betrayed: Herbert Hoover's History of the Second World War and its Aftermath* (Hoover Institute Press; 2011), edited by George Nash, presented Hoover's analysis of how Roosevelt's foreign policy combined with Churchill's machinations pulled the U.S. into WWII and expedited the Soviet Union's rise to global power. A.J.P. Taylor's *The Origins of the Second World War* (Hamish Hamilton; 1961) is an insightful exploration of the human follies and political intrigues that led to the war. Pat Buchanan's *Churchill, Hitler and the Unnecessary War* (Crown; 2008) is a further indictment of Britain's prime minister and attributes his imprudent diplomatic decisions, in tandem with those of other European statesmen, for causing WWII.

It was also in 1933 that Harry Cohn, the chief of Columbia Pictures, deduced that "Madame la Gimp" would be the kind of story that would be a perfect vehicle for his studio's foremost director, Frank Capra. Just as "Runyonesque" became an adjective for literature that emulated the author's style and characters, "Capraesque" would eventually become an adjective for films that emulated the kind of movie associated with the director. In general, such films depict individual acts of courage, usually by a "common man" or an underdog against immense obstacles, that produce beneficial effects for society. Dave the Dude's ultimately successful quest to help Apple Annie certainly had these qualities.

Frank Capra was born in Sicily in 1897 and his family immigrated to the United States in 1903. He attended college to study engineering but became interested in the theater. He served briefly in the U.S. Army during the First World War. (President Woodrow Wilson had been re-elected in 1916 with the slogan, "He Kept Us Out of War!" Not quite. In April 1917, he officially declared war against Germany and the United States entered "the Great War" after the war had been raging in Europe for three years. Approximately 116,000 U.S. military personnel died during the course of the war which lasted another 19 months. And the maliciously punitive Treaty of Versailles made the German people receptive to the appeal of the Adolph Hitler's Nazi Party and practically guaranteed the Second World War.)

Capra was discharged from the Army after he caught the Spanish Flu. (Incidentally, this epidemic killed more than 43,000 American servicemen in 1918 and 1919.) He then obtained work as an extra in movies. Over the next several years, he found jobs in and out of the movie business and eventually worked his way up to gag writer, editor and director of shorts. He directed his first feature in 1926 and, the following year, Harry Cohn brought him to Columbia. Capra developed an innovative directorial style which utilized semi-improvisation and overlapping dialogue; he also eliminated dissolves as well as the exits and entrances of characters. Capra's movies gradually raised the studio from minor to major status.

At Columbia, Capra also formed a working relationship with screenwriter Robert Riskin, which would prove to be very fruitful for his career. Riskin was a skilled playwright whose works contained an intrinsic sense of dramatic structure fused with clever plots and distinctive characterizations. He wrote the screenplay for *American Madness* (1932), which Capra directed, but their official alliance began with their adaptation of "Madame La Gimp." Though Capra was initially reluctant to accept the project, Cohn convinced him of the story's potential appeal to a population depleted by the Depression. And it was Riskin who fully realized that potential. He expanded the story, fleshed out the characters and infused the story with emotion. He injected some degree of sarcasm but still affirmed the natural decency of people of all levels of society while glorifying the triumph of the human spirit.

In Riskin's script, Dave the Dude is the same good-hearted hood but he is also superstitious. Madame La Gimp's name is changed to Apple Annie, reflecting her "profession" as a seller of apples instead of old newspapers. Dave buys an apple every day from Annie and considers this his good luck charm. As in the story, Annie has sent her daughter—her name changed to Louise—to Spain but, instead of being raised by relatives, is in a convent for which Annie has been paying with her money and the money of other beggars, all of whom have agreed to help Annie with her pretense of being a society matron.

The crisis begins when Louise informs Annie that she is coming home with her fiancé, Carlos, and his wealthy parents, Count and Countess Romero. Annie is devastated and proceeds to get drunk. After hunting her down, Dave knows that he has to solve her problem to keep receiving his

Frank Capra in the 1930s.

daily apples so he hatches a plan with his reluctant henchman, Happy McGuire, to trick the Count. Instead of the story's "ever-loving wife," Dave has a "long-suffering girl friend," Missouri Martin, who has the task of transforming Annie into a dowager with the name of Mrs. E. Worthington Manville. Dave also convinces pool hustler Judge Henry Blake to pretend to be Annie's husband. The charade works initially but the Count insists on meeting all of the wealthy friends of the Manvilles. Once again departing from the story, instead of doing it out of the goodness of his heart, circumstances force Dave into arranging a party. He enlists the aid of all of his gang members who then rehearse their roles as aristocratic dignitaries in Missouri's nightclub. However, the police are growing increasingly suspicious of Dave's activities, which seem to be connected to the disappearances of several reporters. They surround the club, prevent Dave and his hoods from going to the hotel and arrest Dave. Just as Annie is about to tell the truth to the Count, the police and politicians whom Dave has told of Annie's predicament all arrive at the hotel to save Annie from disgrace.

After Riskin finished his script, eventually titled *Lady for a Day*, Capra started casting. Columbia was not a major studio at the time so he had difficulty getting the stars he wanted, including James Cagney or William Powell for Dave and Marie Dressler for Annie. He eventually signed Warren William and May Robson for the two leading roles. Filming went smoothly and it was with this movie that Capra perfected the themes with which he would become associated, specifically the nobility of his "little people" in the face of oppression and their triumph over the cruelty of a pitiless social order.

Harry Cohn was so pleased with *Lady for a Day* that he arranged for it to debut at New York City's Radio City Music Hall in October 1933. The film became an instant hit with the public and with critics. It was Columbia's first picture to earn a Best Picture Academy Award nomination, though this was due in part to the desire of the Academy members to display their empathy with the victims of the Depression. It also earned nominations for Capra, Riskin and Robson. Damon Runyon was so delighted with the movie that he publicly praised Riskin for improving his story. The movie did not win any awards but it established Capra's status in Hollywood as a major film director.

According to some film historians, Capra's prominence started with *Lady for a Day*. His next film, the hugely successful *It Happened One Night* (1934), certified Capra's position as Columbia's foremost director; it also won Academy Awards for Best Picture and for Capra as Best Director. In rapid succession, Capra then made *Broadway Bill* (1934), *Mr. Deeds Goes to Town* (1936), *Lost Horizon* (1937), *You Can't Take It With You* (1938) and *Mr. Smith Goes to Washington* (1939). All of these movies were for Columbia and all—except *Mr. Smith*—were written by Riskin. Capra and Riskin then founded Frank Capra Productions and arranged for Warner Bros. to release their first independent movie, *Meet John Doe* (1941) with Gary Cooper. This film turned out to be their last direct collaboration. Riskin had become increasingly unhappy that Capra was seemingly taking full credit for their films and wanted to branch out on his own. It was the end of a fertile relationship that produced many memorable films. It should also be noted that, aside from the innate quality of the films, some critics with liberal political convictions praised the movies because of their harsh portrait of symbols of capitalism, such as politicians, bankers and industrialists.

Capra remained at Warner Bros. to direct the film version of the Broadway play, *Arsenic and Old Lace* which is not a Capraesque story but was a surefire hit in view of the play's immense popularity. In the midst of filming, the Japanese attacked Pearl Harbor and the United States declared war. At age 44, Capra enlisted in the Army Signal Corps and subsequently directed eleven documentaries, including the celebrated *Why We Fight* series; one of these, *Prelude to War* (1942) won an Academy Award for Best Documentary. Meanwhile, Riskin was also producing propaganda films; he had joined the Office of War Information and was in charge of the overseas motion picture division for the duration of the war.

In 1945, upon his discharge from the military, the Army awarded Capra the Distinguished Service Medal. He returned to Hollywood and, due to his desire for independence from studio interference, formed Liberty Films with his production partner, Samuel Briskin. Directors George Stevens and William Wyler subsequently joined Liberty as partners. For his first Liberty feature, Capra directed *It's a Wonderful Life* (1946), for release by RKO. Today, this is his most popular movie and many critics consider it to be his last great movie. After this film, according to some film historians, he started his decline and never rose again. In reality, of the five ensuing movies that he directed, only two are misfires while two others are very good and one is a splendid swan song, though at the time he didn't intend it to be his last movie.

Following *It's a Wonderful Life*, Capra moved to MGM and made his second Liberty film, an adaptation of another Broadway success, *State of the Union* (1948). This insightful political drama contained the director's familiar populist theme and was successful with the public and the critics. However, due to financial problems caused by the commercial failure of *It's a Wonderful Life*, Capra and Briskin sold Liberty Films to Paramount Pictures in return for Paramount stock and a five-film deal for each of Liberty's director/partners. Capra directed his next two movies for Paramount: *Riding High* (1950) was a remake of *Broadway Bill* that used Riskin's original screenplay for the earlier film and *Here Comes the Groom* (1951)

was based upon a script that Riskin had previously sold to Paramount. Possibly, Capra felt insecure without a Riskin script or a hit play. However, a reconciliation with Riskin was not possible; his former colleague had suffered a stroke and was not able to work. Both of the Paramount films are not up to Capra's—or Riskin's—standards and are, at best, mildly amusing musical comedies. Subsequently, Capra retreated to television to direct four documentaries.

In 1956, with the approval of Harry Cohn, Capra decided to remake *Lady for a Day* for Columbia and he wisely knew that Robert Riskin's original script would have to be the bedrock of any new version. But Riskin had died in 1955 and other writers had difficulty preparing a new script that pleased both Capra and Cohn. Meanwhile, a play entitled *A Hole in the Head* opened on Broadway in 1957 and Frank Sinatra, who had bought the rights, asked Capra to direct the film version. Capra placed the *Lady for a Day* remake on the back burner and, after an eight-year hiatus from movies, directed the comedy-drama that was a commercial success. But though the public liked it, many critics may have allowed their politics to determine their negative assessment of the movie. They criticized the film because it lacked the sharp satire and liberal viewpoint that had distinguished the director's renowned films of the past. In their viewpoint, Capra had betrayed them by making an enjoyable movie about family relationships that reflected the surface values of the 1950s.

Count Romero (Arthur O'Connell), Louise (Ann-Margaret) and Dave the Dude (Glenn Ford) await the arrival of the guests.

For his next movie, Capra resurrected his idea to remake *Lady for a Day* and brought the project to United Artists which had released *A Hole in the Head*; it must have seemed like a sure bet to UA executives since Capra wanted to cast Frank Sinatra as Dave the Dude and the Capra-Sinatra combination had been very successful. Capra approved of a new screenplay, entitled *Pocketful of Miracles*, credited to Hal Kanter and Harry Tugend which was based upon Riskin's script for the original film. To add more spice to it, Capra enlisted the aid of Jimmy Cannon, the eminent sports writer who had a special affinity for Runyonesque jargon. In fact, Cannon had been a protégé of Damon Runyon and often emulated his style. However, Sinatra declined the role, as did Capra's second choice, Dean Martin. Then, according to Capra's autobiography, *The Name Above the Title* (MacMillan; 1971), Capra had a chance meeting with Glenn Ford in a restaurant and Ford offered to play the lead role.

Glenn Ford was born in Canada in 1916 and moved to California with his family when he was a youth. He started acting in high school and had his first feature film role in a 20th Century Fox B movie which led to a contract with Columbia Pictures. Shortly after appearing in his first Columbia movie, he became a naturalized citizen. In 1941, though he had received a deferment from the draft because he was his mother's sole support, he enlisted in the Coast Guard Auxiliary and served three nights a week and on weekends. His career began to take off with his appearance in the 1941 Universal film, *So Ends Our Night*, which led to more important roles at Columbia. Nevertheless, in December 1942, he interrupted his film career to join the Marine Corps as a private. After serving for two years at Camp Pendleton at San Diego, he was medically discharged (because of duodenal ulcers) as a sergeant.

Ford returned to Hollywood and had some difficulty resuming his career until Bette Davis persuaded Warner Bros. to borrow him from Columbia to co-star with her in *A Stolen Life* (1946). Columbia subsequently cast him opposite Rita Hayworth in *Gilda* (1946), which began his stardom. During the 1950s, Ford headlined numerous movies and proved to be a versatile actor, starring in various genres. His successful films include *Blackboard Jungle* (1955), *Ransom* (1956), *3:10 to Yuma* (1957) and *Don't Go Near the Water* (1957). It was also in 1957 that he joined the U.S. Naval Reserve and was commissioned as a lieutenant commander with an assignment to serve as a public information officer. In 1958, Quigley's Annual Top-Ten Money Makers Poll named him the Number One Box-Office star of the Year.

In view of Ford's status and popularity, he was an excellent choice to play Dave the Dude. However, it is debatable whether the restaurant meeting happened quite the way Capra reported. In his biography of his father, *Glenn Ford: A Life* (University of Wisconsin; 2011), Peter Ford reports that it was agent Abe Lastfogel who arranged for Glenn Ford to star in the film. After a series of meetings with United Artists executives and various agents, Capra writes in his autobiography that he was forced to accept Ford as associate producer of the movie. This would be the beginning of his resentment of Ford. (Film historian Joseph McBride would later claim that Capra's autobiography is filled with contradictions and untruths.)

Capra's initial choices for the role of Apple Annie were Shirley Booth and Helen Hayes. Booth declined, believing she couldn't top May Robson, but Hayes signed on. Capra signed Shirley Jones for Queenie but shortly thereafter, according to Capra, Ford demanded that Hope Lange be cast in the role. However, Ford later claimed that he was not aware of Capra's preference for Jones and didn't demand but only suggested Lange, his romantic interest, for the part. But Capra states that he was forced to cast Lange whom he believed was too young for the role; actually, she was three years older than Jones. Furthermore, this delayed start of production which resulted in Hayes leaving due to a scheduling conflict. Bette Davis, whose career was in a slump after three decades as a major star, then accepted the role opposite Ford, whom she had chosen to play opposite her 15 years earlier. Meanwhile, Capra's anger toward Ford magnified.

Quite probably, Capra was incensed by the changes in the film capital and needed a scapegoat for his anger. Ford was a convenient target, especially since his salary was higher than the director's. Thus, in his autobiography, Capra seethes with fury as he describes the making of the movie. He writes that the film was "shaped in fires of discord, filmed in an atmosphere of pain, strain and loathing." Capra also relates how he suffered from intense headaches every night of filming and had to be given daily shots of sodium phosphate to be able to work. Regarding his many complaints about the film's star, Peter Ford reports that, following the publication of Capra's autobiography, his father sent Capra a telegram which succinctly stated: "What a shame you did not have the guts to say this to my face—what you said in the book."

Despite all of these problems, the production wrapped and United Artists sneak-previewed *Pocketful of Miracles* in Oakland, California in October 1961. The audience enthusiastically enjoyed the movie. They laughed, cheered and heartily praised it in their review cards. Another sneak preview in Riverside resulted in the same kind of positive reaction with a lengthy round of applause at the end of the screening. As a result of these and other previews, Hollywood insiders predicted an immense commercial success. The movie also seemed to be a good candidate for Academy Award nominations in many categories, which meant that it had to open before the end of the year.

There was one problem. United Artists had four other major releases opening in December, all of which had already been booked into the preeminent first-run theaters in Los Angeles and New York. They were William Wyler's *The Children's Hour*, Billy Wilder's *One, Two, Three*, Stanley Kramer's *Judgment at Nuremburg* and Robert Wise and Jerome Robbins' *West Side Story*. UA planned extensive promotional campaigns for these movies prior to their exclusive first-run engagements which the studio hoped would extend for several weeks before gradually branching out to other parts of the country. Due in part to the shortage of first-run theaters, UA executives decided to premiere the Capra movie for only one week in two New York theaters and then open it in 200 cities and in 600 neighborhood theaters during the Christmas season. (Though normal today, this type of saturation booking was unusual for a major movie in 1961.)

The review in *Variety* by "Tube" prior to the film's release might have influenced this decision: "Once upon a time, a sweet sentimental fairy tale would have been a shoo-in for a happy ending at the wicket windows. But today, the tracks are faster, the stakes are stiffer and the pot of gold more elusive." Since the review concluded by saying that the movie "should be a satisfactory box-office candidate especially as a yuletide attraction," UA executives may have decided to make the movie available to as many people as possible while they were filled with the Christmas spirit. It was a miscalculation. Capra's former production partner, Samuel Briskin, viewed the movie at a Directors Guild screening and cautioned Capra against letting UA release it cold around the country before the public could have the opportunity to hear about it. Because it was old-fashioned,

he advised Capra, the movie needed special handling and would benefit from word of mouth. But UA proceeded with its plan.

On December 19, 1961, *Pocketful of Miracles* opened in all parts of the country. Reviews were mostly negative as many critics accused Capra of being out of touch with the supposedly sophisticated 1960s and for not realizing that old-fashioned sentiment was too corny for modern audiences. More than one critic used the hackneyed "Capracorn" label to describe the movie. Such critics viewed themselves as too urbane for the kind of sweet story that audiences and critics in 1933 had found entertaining. Because they were unable to detect the movie's multi-layered themes, they condescendingly dismissed it. They condemned it because to praise it would have meant, in their snobbish views, that they were as out of date and unfashionable as they believed Capra to be.

Newsweek's reviewer gave the movie a rare favorable review, writing that, "It is happy news that, after 40 years, Capra's ways are as sure as ever [and] he has used Damon Runyon's story with pure guile." The reviewer praised Davis, calling her, "a masterpiece of touching grubbiness and, later, as an image of elegance." The reviewer for *The Hollywood Reporter* also liked it, calling it, "a Christmas sockful of joy, funny, sentimental and romantic." Unfortunately, A.H. Weiler's review in *The New York Times* was far more typical. Weiler wrote that "the bloom is off Mr. Runyon's gilded lily [and] time has dulled the point of the jest." He adds that "a

world faced by grimmer problems seems to have been excessively tough competition for this plot." Arthur Knight in *The Saturday Review* wrote that the movie was "overlong, over-elaborate and makes the fundamental error of taking its people seriously." However, he also writes: "Honesty compels me to add that the audience seemed to be having a grand time."

In actuality, audiences everywhere who had an opportunity to see the movie also had a grand time. But the window of opportunity was too narrow. UA's decision to dump the movie into any available theater doomed its chances. As positive word of mouth was just beginning to spread, the movie had vanished.

The box-office returns were unsatisfactory. For 1961, the big comedy hits on *Variety*'s annual list of Top-Grossing Films of the Year were two Disney films, *The Absent-Minded Professor* and *The Parent Trap*, both with over $9 million in domestic theatrical rentals. Since *Pocketful of Miracles* was released at the end of 1961, it was on the 1962 list with a disappointing $2.4 million. The comedy successes on the 1962 list were *Lover Come Back*, which was released the same week as the Capra film, and *That Touch of Mink*, both with $8.5 million, while Disney's *Bon Voyage* earned $5.5. Comedies at the bottom of the list included *Gigot* with $1.6 million and *The Pigeon That Took Rome* with $1.4 million. Regarding the other UA December 1961 releases, *West Side Story* was at the top of the list with $18 million while *Judgment at Nuremburg* earned $3.9 million; *One, Two, Three* also disappointed with $2.3 million and *The Children's Hour* flopped with $1.5 million.

Crushed by the film's commercial failure, Capra angrily placed the blame on Glenn Ford and studio politics while ignoring UA's dreadful marketing decision. In his book, he suggests some kind of pseudo-mystical explanation. In brief, his audience of "regular people" chose to reject his movie because they sensed that he had sold out his trademark of artistic integrity by compromising with studio executives and with Ford. In Capra's analysis, his "John and Jane Does" sensed somehow that he had betrayed them and, as a result, stayed away from the movie.

This is poppycock. In the early 1960s, Disney comedies and bedroom comedies — especially with Doris Day — attracted huge audiences. *Pocketful of Miracles* did not fit into either category and needed careful promotion. It was undeniably an old-fashioned movie and required distinctive advertising to attract the kinds of large audiences that had loved it at the previews. United Artists executives displayed tremendous ignorance by insisting that the movie had to open during the Christmas season. (In 1947, *Miracle on 34th Street* opened in May and was a huge commercial success.) UA should have postponed opening the movie until suitable theaters in the major markets could be secured; it could then have premiered in exclusive engagements in New York and Los Angeles, followed by a promotional campaign to develop anticipation for it across the country. UA blundered badly and the movie suffered as a result.

Pocketful of Miracles follows the same basic story of the original, with significant changes and some expansion. With a 136-minute running time, it is 40 minutes longer than the original film. Once again, the setting is New York City during the Depression. The movie opens at a bankrupt nightclub formerly owned by Rudy Martin, whom the mob has rubbed out because he owed money to everyone, including Dave the Dude. Rudy's daughter, Elizabeth, offers to pay off her father's debts at $5 a week, which would take a few lifetimes. Dave doesn't think the club is worth much but he gets a brainstorm and decides to turn the club into a classy speakeasy with Elizabeth, called Queenie by her father, as the star. And then the main story begins.

Dave is a prosperous bootlegger who is on the verge of forging an alliance with a big-time Chicago crime boss, Steve Darcy, for control of the Manhattan territory. But Dave's superstition about his lucky apples from street peddler Apple Annie threatens to destroy his confidence when he cannot find her. From this point on, the storyline is similar to the original. Tracking Annie to her room, he finds her on the verge of suicide. Annie's daughter, Louise, is due to arrive with her fiancé's family believing her mother is a Manhattan socialite. For his own benefit, Dave decides that he has to help Annie. With his loyal henchmen, Joy Boy and Junior, he devises a plan to transform Annie into a proper society matron with all the trappings of affluence. As in the original, the scheme gradually becomes increasingly elaborate and almost ends in disaster as the police close in on Dave and prevent his plan from taking place. But Dave's heartrending explanation leads to a spectacular finale in which politicians and dignitaries save the day for Annie.

Many current film reference books compare *Pocketful of Miracles* unfavorably to *Lady for a Day*. Leslie Halliwell in his annual *Film Guide* (HarperCollins) calls the movie, "a boring, overlong remake (with) dated themes." Leonard Maltin in his annual *Movie & Video Guide* (Signet) writes that, "Capra's remake is just as sentimental but doesn't work as well." Phil Hardy in *The Gangster Film* (Overlook Press; 1998) calls it a "wheezy and outmoded vehicle." And Joseph McBride, in his biography of the director, *Frank Capra: The Catastrophe of Success* (Simon & Schuster; 1992), labels it "a bloated, unfunny, maudlin and thoroughly insincere film." He adds that "it is so shockingly inferior to *Lady for a Day* that it effectively ended his career."

In actuality, Capra signed on to direct two more features in the mid-1960s — *Circus World* and *Marooned* — but he backed out of both due to conflicts with other personnel or disagreements about the script. While this may be an indication of his increasingly sour personality in his later years, the fact remains that he could have directed both movies if he had played the Hollywood game of "getting along." The industry had changed since the 1930s and 1940s and he had to adjust like so many other directors from that era. It appears that he was unable or perhaps unwilling to do so.

Some admirers of *Lady for a Day* suggest that its commercial success proves that it is a better movie than the remake which failed at the box office. However, *Lost Horizon*, *Meet John Doe* and *It's a Wonderful Life* were also box-office failures. In assessing the commercial fates of both films, it may be helpful to consider the economic environments in which they were released. In 1933, Depression-weary audiences could identify with Apple Annie, if not directly then because her type was so visible. They also wanted to believe that politicians and wealthy people would help a destitute peddler. Such a message gave them hope, which they desperately needed. In 1961, because the Depression was a distant memory, there was no direct frame of reference for many moviegoers who didn't realize how terrible it was during that period. Thus, the remake had to succeed purely on an entertainment level which it arguably could have done if not subjected to poor marketing decisions.

Pocketful of Miracles succeeds in being amusing and dramatic, hilarious and poignant. It is more than just a comedy, which is perhaps why so many scenes remain memorable. The entire movie, like so many individual sequences, is clearly designed to evoke simultaneous and often opposite emotions. The main plot of Dave the Dude going to incredible lengths to help Annie and the happy ending that results from his actions leaves audiences with pleasant feelings. At the end, it is true that Dave and Queenie may live happily ever after and even the politicians seem to have been softened by the entire affair. However, the street beggars remain on the edge of society, discarded misfits pleading for handouts to survive each day while the upper crust return to their mansions.

Numerous other scenes are simultaneously funny and distressing, amusing and sad. Annie has been able to deceive her daughter because a kindly clerk at a posh hotel has been allowing her to use the hotel's address as her own. When the clerk loses his job because his employer has discovered his deceit, his life is destroyed. And yet Annie is too preoccupied with her own problems to care and he is never seen again. On a different level, when disbarred alcoholic Judge Blake saves the entire plan from ruin by his expertise with billiards, neither Dave nor anyone else has any time to hear of his accomplishment, which will remain unacknowledged.

With all due respect to Robert Riskin, whose splendid script is the solid foundation of the remake, the expansion of his screenplay by Hal Kanter and Harry Tugend adds to the emotional impact of the film. By showing Dave's introduction to Queenie and the circumstances of their initial meeting, the relationship assumes a deeper emotional content. Also, the scenes with Steve Darcy provide a greater sense of urgency for Dave

as he hastens to wrap up the charade with Annie so he can finalize his deal with Darcy. When he decides that Queenie is more important to him than rising to the top of the bootlegging business, this decision increases the degree of his sacrifice. While one miracle of the title may be Annie's transformation into a lady, another miracle is Dave's transformation from an amoral hood into a noble hero. Similarly, Queenie emerges as a three-dimensional character instead of the cipher represented by Missouri Martin.

Furthermore, the dialogue—aided immensely by Jimmy Cannon's contributions—is priceless and contains innumerable memorable lines recited by a gallery of unforgettable characters, from Dave the Dude to Apple Annie, from Queenie Martin to Soho Sal, from Joy Boy to Junior, from Cheesecake to Weasel, from Knuckles to Mallethead. Never have so many of Damon Runyon's characters journeyed from the page to the screen so faithfully and with the assistance of such an impeccable cast. Indeed, Capra was fortunate to obtain not only his stars but a gallery of wonderful character actors.

As Dave the Dude, Glenn Ford gives a terrific performance. As a confident and self-centered hood, he initially projects indifference and cynicism. But as the unfolding events gradually force Dave to shed his hard exterior, Ford successively projects anger, confusion, exasperation and desperation. He is argumentative one moment, frantic the next, and then flustered as one seemingly impossible obstacle after another threatens to upset his plan. He can be boyishly enthusiastic and then helplessly despondent. But when it is all over, Dave will have sacrificed all of his personal desires, first for Annie and then for Queenie. Ford perfectly captures all of these emotions and qualities. His portrayal of Dave the Dude is essential to the film's accomplishment.

Bette Davis is believably squalid as Apple Annie and equally credible as the Mrs. E. Worthington Manville. She minimizes her familiar mannerisms to create an initially pathetic but ultimately sympathetic character who has sacrificed everything for her daughter. She initially projects a hardness for her character but this trait dissolves as she displays a vulnerability that makes audiences understand completely why so many people are willing to come to her aid, from her squad of peddlers to haughty members of high society. It is a marvelous performance.

Hope Lange, previously noted for dramatic roles, displays unexpected comic talent as Queenie Martin. At the outset, she conveys a demure appearance as a waif-like young girl but is equally persuasive as a more sophisticated showgirl. Despite Capra's objections, she makes Queenie's transition believable and gives a fine performance. Thomas Mitchell, who had worked with Capra on three previous films, totally owns the role of Judge Henry Blake and projects sensitivity underneath his hustler's facade of apathy. Arthur O'Connell is equally fine as Count Alfonso Romero; because of the character's stuffiness, he could have come off as an unlikable snob but the actor's innate warmth eventually reveals a man who just wants what is best for his son.

However, it is the wide gallery of character actors that adds so much spice to the film. Sheldon Leonard, Barton MacLane, David Brian, Mike Mazurki, Fritz Feld, Benny Rubin, Willis Bouchey and Jerome Cowan are just a few of the talents that make valuable contributions to the movie. Edward Everett Horton is hysteri-

Apple Annie (Bette Davis) sheds tears as Queenie (Hope Lange) and Dave the Dude read the letter from Louise.

Queenie prepares for a dance number.

cal as Hutchins the butler while Peter Falk as Joy Boy and Mickey Shaughnessy as Junior, Dave's two most trusted sidekicks, are together worth the price of admission. And Jack Elam pretending to be a dignitary is equally uproarious.

No offense to the actors in the original film but they mostly emerge as second best. Warren William achieved popularity in the early 1930s portraying superficially charming but ultimately unscrupulous and amoral cads. But comedies were not his specialty and, though quite fine as Dave the Dude, he lacks Glenn Ford's natural warmth. As Apple Annie, May Robson is very good but her suffering occasionally crosses the line into maudlin overdrive, which Bette Davis avoids. Glenda Farrell is too brassy and lacks Hope Lange's softer qualities. Basically, the supporting actors do not have the endearing screen personalities of their counterparts in the remake. Guy Kibbee and Halliwell Hobbs are good character actors but they are no match for Thomas Mitchell and Edward Everett Horton. Ned Sparks, whose monotone becomes monotonous, pales next to Peter Falk. Nat Pendleton is good as Shakespeare but he cannot measure up to Jack Elam as Cheesecake. Admittedly, Jean Parker is a better Louise than Ann-Margaret, whose mannered performance is distracting. And Walter Connolly's performance as the Count is as effective as that of Arthur O'Connell.

Widescreen and color are also valuable additions to the remake. The Panavision screen is used to great effect in the crowd sequences, including the opening scenes on Broadway as well as the climactic celebration. The preparation for the reception, in which Dave's guys and Queenie's dolls try to learn etiquette, encompasses more details and is far more hilarious. The more intimate scenes also benefit from the widescreen which fully captures the squalor of Annie's room. Capra also uses color efficiently, often using subdued colors to reflect the emotions of various characters. In general, color and widescreen bring the fairytale aspects of the story more fully to life while it also increases emotional involvement with the characters.

Basically, the two movies illustrate Capra's growth from a pacesetter developing his trademark skills to a gifted artist at the top of his form. *Lady for a Day* is an entertaining movie but it is somewhat dated today because it is intrinsically aware of the era in which it was made. In 1933, Capra was hoping for an end to the Depression and allowed his empathy to occasionally take precedence over his craft, which accounts for some saccharine moments in the film. In 1961, Capra knew that the Depression had ended, due to the advent of World War II (during which lucrative government contracts along with the draft vastly reduced employment and spurred economic growth). Consequently, he treats it more dispassionately, allowing his characters to transcend their environment and assume less pathos. In general, his inspired direction expertly balances scenes of merriment with scenes of warmth but without the sporadic mawkishness of the original. To sum up, this is one of those rare instances in which the remake is superior to the original.

(Just for the record, in 1989, Jackie Chan directed and starred in a Hong Kong-produced movie entitled *Ji ji*. English titles include *Mr. Canton and Lady Rose* and *Miracles*. The story concerns a country boy named Cheng Wah Kuo who comes to the big city and is quickly swindled. After reluctantly buying a rose from Madame Kao, who survives by selling flowers in the streets, Cheng helps a dying crime boss who makes him the new leader of his gang. Cheng turns the gang away from crime and buys a nightclub to give a young singer a chance to become a star. Now having money and a girlfriend, he credits his good fortune to Madame Kao from whom he buys a rose every day. A crisis occurs when Madame tells him that her daughter, who believes that her mother is a rich society matron, is coming to the city with her fiancé and his wealthy parents. Cheng then sets Madame up in a ritzy hotel with his hoods posing as high society friends. Meanwhile, conflict with a rival gang leads to action sequences that showcase Chan's expertise as a martial artist. Thankfully, Chan didn't call his character Cheng the Dude.)

Pocketful of Miracles received three Academy Award nominations, including one for Peter Falk for Best Supporting Actor. Other nominations were for Best Costume Design and Best Original Song. It didn't win in any of the categories. At least, Glenn Ford won the Golden Globe for Best Actor in a Musical or Comedy. Bette Davis received a Golden Globe nomination for Best Actress but didn't win. Perhaps proving that Frank Capra was totally incorrect about the quality of his last film, The Director's Guild of America nominated him for Outstanding Directorial Achievement.

Damon Runyon died in 1946, leaving a legacy of immortal characters. Robert Riskin died in 1955; he was nominated five times for Best Screenplay award, all for Capra movies, and won for *It Happened One Night*. Frank Capra died in 1991; he received six Best Director nominations and

GLENN FORD BETTE DAVIS HOPE LANGE ARTHUR O'CONNELL FRANK CAPRA'S Pocketful of Miracles
PETER FALK THOMAS MITCHELL EDWARD EVERETT HORTON MICKEY SHAUGHNESSY

won three times for *It Happened One Night*, *Mr. Deeds Goes to Town* and *You Can't Take It with You*, all graced with Riskin scripts. Maybe Capra and Riskin needed each other. At least, Capra's last film was a collaboration, in a sense, of the two artists.

There are many memorable moments in *Pocketful of Miracles*, not the least of which is the one when Joy Boy exclaims: "She's like a cockroach what turned into a butterfly!"

CREDITS: Producer/Director: Frank Capra; Associate Producers: Glenn Ford, Joseph Sistrom; Screenplay: Hal Kanter, Harry Tugend, Based Upon a Screenplay by Robert Riskin and a Story by Damon Runyon; Cinematographer: Robert J. Bronner; Editor: Frank P. Keller; Music: Walter Scharf; Title Song: James Van Heusen, Sammy Cahn

CAST: Glenn Ford (Dave the Dude); Bette Davis (Apple Annie); Hope Lange (Queenie Martin); Arthur O'Connell (Count Alfonso Romero); Peter Falk (Joy Boy); Thomas Mitchell (Judge Henry Blake); Edward Everett Horton (Hutchins); Mickey Shaughnessy (Junior); David Brian (Governor); Sheldon Leonard (Steve Darcy); Peter Mann (Carlos Romero); Ann-Margaret (Louise); Barton MacLane (Police Commissioner); Jerome Cowan (Mayor); John Litel (Inspector McCrary); Jay Novello (Cortega); Hayden Rorke (Captain Moore); Jack Elam (Cheesecake); Mike Mazurki (Big Mike); Ellen Corby (Soho Sal); Benny Rubin (Flyaway); Willis Bouchey (Newspaper Editor); Frank Ferguson (Newspaper Editor); Fritz Feld (Pierre); Gavin Gordon (Hotel Manager)

THE SATAN BUG

Hollywood's John Sturges directed many popular action movies. Scottish author Alistair MacLean wrote many popular adventure novels. However, neither Sturges nor MacLean is renowned today. Since Sturges' death in 1992, many film critics regard him as a director whose movies lack cinematic artistry and appeal primarily to blue-collar audiences. Since MacLean's death in 1987, many book reviewers regard him as a writer whose novels lack artistic merit and appeal to blue-collar readers. Despite such condescension, contemporary action film directors and current thriller writers owe a large debt to, respectively, Sturges and MacLean.

Alistair MacLean wanted to entertain readers and was intent on writing good novels. He avoided ostentatious literary tricks and only used distinctive craftsmanship to create exciting narratives. None of his books contain explicit violence or sex. His books celebrate machismo through a courageous male or a band of men engaging in various adventurous acts against nefarious evildoers. While he was criticized for relegating women to the background, his female fans did not object.

John Sturges wanted to entertain filmgoers and was intent on making good movies. He did not utilize flamboyant directorial techniques and avoided elaborate camera tricks. None of his films depict graphic violence or sex. His most famous films emphasize masculinity and male-bonding through action and character development. Though he was accused of using female characters only in secondary roles, his films appealed to women as well as to men.

During World War II, Alistair MacLean joined the Royal Navy and served aboard various ships, including the HMS *Royalist* which assisted in the evacuation of Changi Prison, the notorious Japanese prisoner of war camp in Singapore. After the war, he studied to be a teacher and, in 1955, wrote his first novel, *HMS Ulysses*, based on his wartime experiences and the first of numerous worldwide best sellers. To date, there have been 14 film versions of Alistair MacLean's 28 novels, including the blockbuster hit, *The Guns*

Alistair MacLean, c. 1930

of Navarone (1961). In 1968, two major MacLean-based films were released: *Ice Station Zebra* and *Where Eagles Dare*, which MacLean initially wrote as a screenplay and subsequently novelized. Other film versions of the author's novels include *When Eight Bells Toll* (1971), *Fear Is the Key* (1972) and *Breakheart Pass* (1976).

John Sturges directed film versions of two of MacLean's novels. *Ice Station Zebra* is a Cold War thriller and features major stars, including Rock Hudson, Patrick McGoohan, Ernest Borgnine and Jim Brown. It was an expensive production which MGM premiered in exclusive engagements in selected cities. Three years earlier, Sturges had filmed another MacLean novel, *The Satan Bug*, a thriller about biological terrorism. It was a relatively small-scale production with no major stars and United Artists dumped it on the market.

MacLean wrote *The Satan Bug* in 1962 under the pseudonym of Ian Stuart. The setting of the novel is England. Pierre Cavell is a private investigator with a reported history of insubordination who has allegedly been fired from a top secret government laboratory. In reality, Cavell is working undercover for "The General," a military officer in charge of national security. When criminals break into the laboratory and kill the head of security, The General recruits Cavell to solve the crimes. Upon inspection, Cavell discovers that several flasks of a deadly botulinus toxin have been stolen. More alarmingly, he learns that a lethal virus called the Satan Bug, which has the power to destroy all life on Earth, is also missing. Cavell's unorthodox methods uncover guilty parties inside the lab but the plot's mastermind, whose identity remains unknown, threatens to unleash a vial of botulinus if the laboratory is not destroyed. The mastermind's gang then captures Cavell and kidnaps his wife, Mary, who is also the General's daughter. After escaping, Cavell unmasks the guilty party who has been working at Morton as Dr. Gregori but actually is a master criminal by the name of Scarlatti. After Scarlatti reports secreting a flask in London and threatens to expose the Satan Bug, Cavell discovers that his gang intends to rob the major banks in London once the city has been evacuated. The climax of the novel involves a battle between Cavell and Scarlatti aboard a helicopter over London and Cavell's victory over the criminal chief with the Satan Bug safely in his possession.

This is a typically exciting MacLean novel. The author doesn't allow anything to impede the action and keeps readers captivated by the tempo of his narrative. It holds interest until the end, despite some lapses in logic. For instance, it seems dubious that a specialist like Cavell would involve his wife in his investigation. When Cavell is captured, it also seems unlikely that his captors would not search him, despite Cavell's explanation that investigators do not carry weapons. But this is escapist reading, and as such, contains occasional dubious plot developments.

The Satan Bug is fiction but the foundation of the story is factual. It is set during the Cold War when the development of biological weapons was a reality in many countries. Though government officials continue to conceal or have destroyed relevant documents on the history of the development of germ warfare, researchers have uncovered many significant facts. During World War II, both Japan and Germany developed and utilized biological weapons upon human subjects. In 1942, England used the Scottish island of Gruinard as a test subject for a germ warfare attack and rendered it inhospitable for half a century. In 1943, the United States government under President Roosevelt authorized the Biological Weapons Laboratory in Camp Detrick, Maryland. Throughout the war, the Soviet Union conducted analogous research on a wider scale. *A Higher Form of Killing: The Secret History of Chemical and Biological Warfare* by Robert Harris and Jeremy Paxman (Random House; 2002) is a comprehensive chronicle of the subject.

In 1942, Roosevelt authorized the creation of the wartime intelligence agency, the Office of Strategic Services, to engage in espionage activities within enemy territories. After the war, OSS agent Allen Dulles implemented Operation Paperclip which secretly brought to the United States more than 1,500 German scientists to work in laboratories, while the Soviet Union engaged in the same clandestine practice. Contrary to President Harry Truman's edict, Dulles brought over scientists who had conducted biological and chemical experiments upon a multitude of human subjects. The book, *Secret Agenda: The United States Government, Nazi Scientists and Project Paperclip* by Linda Hunt (St. Martin's Press; 1991) provides detailed information on this program. *Factories of Death: Japan's Biological Warfare 1932-1945 and the American Cover-Up* by Sheldon H. Harris (Revised Edition: Routledge; 2002) documents Japan's horrific experiments upon Chinese civilians and military prisoners at the infamous Unit 731 along with concealment of these war crimes by the United States in exchange for data for its own developing germ warfare program. In retrospect, these secret exploits that Dulles and his cronies concealed from the American people originated the shadow government that would eventually control and corrupt the nation.

Truman wanted to dissolve the OSS after the war, fearing its burgeoning power, but government officials convinced him of the necessity of a peacetime intelligence bureau to counter Soviet espionage activities. Thus, the OSS became the Central Intelligence Agency. During the Cold War, the U.S. and Russia both conducted long-range programs to develop biological and chemical weapons not only to kill people on a massive scale but also to manipulate human behavior. During the Korean War, reports that the Russians and Chinese were conducting mind control experiments on American prisoners received wide exposure. Simultaneously, the CIA implemented Project Bluebird in which psychiatrists conducted experiments utilizing drugs, chemicals, abuse and torture upon convicts in prisons and patients in psychiatric hospitals. Researchers at prestigious medical schools and hospitals participated in the CIA-funded program, often using unwitting patients and disabled children as subjects.

In 1952, President Dwight D. Eisenhower appointed Allen Dulles to be the director of the CIA. Bluebird evolved into Project Artichoke and, under Dulles's guidance, became MKULTRA. This covert program attempted to design techniques of so-called "brainwashing' and behavior-manipulation through chemical and biological experimentation on human subjects, including Cold War prisoners and unsuspecting Americans. Many books, including *The Search for the Manchurian Candidate: the CIA and Mind Control* by John Marks (W.W. Norton; 1991) have documented the Agency's atrocities.

In 1972, the Biological Weapons Convention mandated the dismantling of all such programs throughout the world. But there is no surefire way to monitor secret government laboratories. Since the CIA has been unaccountable to Congress or to presidents, it certainly had no intention of obeying the BWC. Indeed, in 1973, CIA director Richard Helms ordered the destruction of all MKULTRA documents in order to prevent disclosure of the extent of the Agency's illegal and inhumane activities in this area. Fortunately, the purge missed several thousand documents. The aptly titled *The Devil's Chessboard: Allen Dulles, the CIA and the Rise of America's Secret Government* by David Talbot (HarperCollins; 2015) is the definitive biography of Dulles as well as an extensively documented account of the heinous crimes of his Agency.

Thus, it is not by any means unbelievable that the setting of the film version of *The Satan Bug* is the United States. Nor is it incredible that the setting of the novel is England; according to a 2001 report by the Royal College of Physicians, during the Cold War, research on biological and chemical weapons expanded considerably in the United Kingdom. It is also not a stretch of the imagination that such weapons of mass destruction

John Sturges on the set of *The Satan Bug*

could target major cities. Indeed, relatively recent incidents such as the 1995 subway attack in Japan and the 2001 anthrax attack in Washington signify that access to such weapons is impossible to control. Considering the scientific advances in the biotech industry over the past four decades, a large scale bioterrorist attack in the future is a frightening prospect. And it is possible that a Satan Bug may be resting in some flask in some private or government laboratory somewhere in the world.

MacLean's novel obviously appealed to John Sturges since it included the type of action, suspense and forceful male protagonist that marked the best of his films. Sturges began his film career as an editor in the early 1930s. After the attack on Pearl Harbor, he joined the Army and directed numerous training films for the Army Signal Corps and the Air Corps. In Europe, he co-directed — with William Wyler — the acclaimed documentary, *Thunderbolt*. Upon his return to Hollywood in 1946, he started directing features at Columbia and initially earned recognition with above-average B movies, including *The Walking Hills* (1949). In 1950, he moved to MGM and graduated to A movies, proving to be adept in film noir with *Mystery Street* (1950) and in the suspense genre with *Jeopardy* (1953). He then established his natural aptitude for Westerns with *Escape from Fort Bravo* (1953). In 1955, he directed the classic modern Western, *Bad Day at Black Rock* which earned him his only Best Director Academy Award nomination. This was also the first movie in which he displayed his skilled use of the wide Cinemascope screen through his staging of key scenes with several characters as well as with the desert landscape.

Over the next several years, Sturges continued to display his versatility at a number of studios, with mixed results. He directed some good Westerns, including *Gunfight at the O.K. Corral* (1957), which became his biggest commercial success to date. *The Old Man and the Sea* (1958), a mostly one-character parable, has some interesting moments but has the burden of being based upon a story by a pretentious author. *Never So Few* (1959), a World War II adventure, emerged as disappointing due to studio-imposed script changes during production.

Wanting independence and control over his films, Sturges signed a contract with the Mirisch Corporation which released its films through United Artists. *The Magnificent Seven* (1960) was the first film that he produced as well as directed. Filled with marvelous set pieces and memorable characterizations, this film proved to be immensely influential. However, though it was popular in other parts of the globe, the movie was initially not a financial success in the United States. Because of this, his status in the film capital did not significantly rise.

Sturges worked for other producers for his next several films. *By Love Possessed* (1960) and *A Girl Named Tamiko* (1962) revealed that romantic melodramas were not his specialty. *Sergeants 3* (1962), with "the Clan" (Frank Sinatra, Dean Martin, et al.) indicated that comedies were also not his forte; this Westernized remake of *Gunga Din* (1939) is neither as exciting nor as amusing as the original, due in part to producer Sinatra's insistence that comedy predominate. But its box-office success convinced Sturges that he could direct another Western farce. This faulty assumption would have a direct influence upon *The Satan Bug*.

In 1962, the Mirisch Corporation approved Sturges' proposed project about a mass escape from a World War II German prison camp that he had been trying to make for over a decade. He produced and directed *The Great Escape* (1963), which was an enormous critical and commercial success. (Incidentally, James Clavell, who co-wrote the screenplay, spent three years in Changi Prison; he based his novel, *King Rat*, upon his experiences as a prisoner of war.) This film elevated Sturges to the level of top directors. But although many studios requested his services, he preferred to be in charge of his own productions and remained with Mirisch.

For his next film for Mirisch, Sturges chose *The Satan Bug*. He hired James Clavell to write the screenplay and brought in Edward Anhalt to re-write the script. Anhalt, who had begun his writing career by scripting training films for the Army Air Force during WWII, had written *A Girl Named Tamiko*, which had flopped. But he was an ideal choice for a story about a contagious virus since he and his wife Edna had won an Academy Award for the story basis for *Panic in the Streets* (1950), a movie about pneumonic plague. Anhalt had also just won his second Academy Award for *Becket* (1964).

Clavell and Anhalt transfer the location of the story from England to California but the story remains basically the same with some marked improvements. The hero, re-named Lee Barrett, is not married and his relationship with the only female character is not a major factor in the plot as the marriage was in the novel. More significantly, the motivation of the criminal genius behind the theft of the deadly viruses is more terrifying in the film. As a result, the threat of wiping out all existing life on Earth, instead of being a ruse by a grandiose bank robber, becomes far more frightening because a fanatical extremist is behind the plot.

The opening sequence of *The Satan Bug* is set in Station 3, the top secret microbiological laboratory in the California desert. Unlike the novel which opens with government agents informing the protagonist of the violation of security at the research station, the movie's initial scenes are at the top secret laboratory. The dangerous nature of the laboratory appears evident from the level of uneasiness that permeates the scientists, specifically Dr. Baxter and Dr. Ostrer. Already, there is a menacing tone in the movie because it is obvious that something is off-kilter. Adding to the tension is the manner in which Mr. Reagan, the chief security officer, watches everything and gradually develops the feeling that something may be amiss.

The film then introduces Lee Barrett, who is not the spurious private eye of the novel but a former intelligence officer whose insubordination and outspokenness on the immorality of war caused his dismissal

Lee Barrett (George Maharis) holds a deadly flask while Ann Williams (Anne Francis) looks on in fear.

from several positions, including that of security chief at Station 3. Unlike the novel, these dismissals are not a deception. Special Agent Cavanaugh informs Lee of the violation of the laboratory and that "The General" wants him to lead the investigation. At Station 3, Deputy Administrator Tasserly obviously has issues with Barrett but knows that he is the best man for the job. Barrett then learns the full extent of the danger posed by the breach. Two men are dead and six flasks of the deadly botulinus virus developed at the laboratory, any one of which could destroy an entire city, are missing. However, there is a far more serious danger. The scientists have also developed an indestructible, airborne virus which has the potential to destroy all forms of life on Earth. It is called "the Satan Bug" and it to is also missing.

Barrett leaves Station 3 to rendezvous with Ann Williams who takes him to meet the General, who is also her father. General Williams informs Lee that an anonymous person has sent him a telegram warning of the dangers to the world posed by Station 3 and threatening to unleash the Satan Bug upon the world if the government does not destroy the laboratory. As proof of the sender's resolve, he promises to expose one flask of the botulinus at an unknown location. Lee and the General realize that they are dealing with a madman and Lee also figures that the thefts had to have been an inside job. But, as the clock rapidly ticks away, the identity of the inside man is not easy to determine.

At a house in the desert, two men — Donald and Veretti — are waiting for a man named Ainsley. Meanwhile, Lee visits a suspect's home and finds a dead body in the pool. A telephone caller asks for Ainsley, whose name Lee recognizes as an eccentric millionaire involved with radical social causes. Ann then informs Lee of a disaster in Florida which has wiped out an entire community. Shortly thereafter, a man identifying himself as Charles Reynolds Ainsley calls General Williams and threatens that the next target will be Los Angeles. Lee, puzzled by the fact that Ainsley discloses his identity, pursues his own leads as the General and his men hasten to evacuate Los Angeles. Lee's suspicions increase when he hears a police report of a car having a flat tire on a desert road. He suspects that the incident is related in some way to the crimes and, accompanied by Ann, follows the clue. His suspicions lead to the discovery of the missing flasks but, before he can bring them to safety, Donald and Veretti capture him and Ann. Back at Station 3, Cavanaugh reports to the General that Lee and Ann are missing and informs him whose car Lee was investigating.

Ainsley reveals his deception when he joins Veretti and Donald. Veretti informs Ainsley that he has placed a second flask somewhere in Los Angeles. Unknown to Ainsley, the General has ordered agents to follow him but he cannot rescue Lee or Ann because he must allow Ainsley to remain free to learn the location of the flasks. As Donald and Veretti take Lee and Ann away, two agents follow them. Veretti uses one of the deadly flasks against his opponents and causes two horrible deaths. But the General has set a trap for Donald and Veretti and a shoot-out kills both men. However, one of the botulinus flasks is missing. In Veretti's motel room, Cavanaugh finds a clue that leads to Dodger Stadium and a frantic search for the missing flask. Meanwhile, the Satan Bug remains in the possession of Ainsley who is determined to use it unless his demands are met. This leads to a fierce battle between Lee and Ainsley aboard a helicopter careening wildly out of control. Lee desperately fights to save the world from destruction while Ainsley uses every ounce of his remaining strength to murder millions of innocent people. At the end of the film, humankind survives—at least until someone creates the next Satan Bug.

Sturges' expertise is evident throughout *The Satan Bug*. Aided immensely by the photography of Robert Surtees, he again displays a command of the widescreen, effectively utilizing the Panavision cameras to convey the isolation of Station 3 and the expansiveness of the surrounding desert. And yet, in the opening sequence, the same widescreen is used to convey the oppressiveness within the secret laboratory as an unknown menace bears down upon Reagan. This sequence also generates a feeling of escalating apprehension and sets the tone for the entire movie. As the story progresses, explanatory scenes occasionally interrupt the tension but even these quieter scenes contain their own share of edginess because of the provocative implications of the dialogue. There is no escape from the Satan Bug, not even in the furthest corners of the globe, and both the script and the direction slam home this fact.

The film contains many suspenseful sequences, including the one in Station 3 which reveals the object of Lee's investigation, though his true status as a maniac is not known by the other men in the room. There is the tense scene in the abandoned building in which Lee, facing probable death, asks Veretti to take Ann with him. Veretti stares at Lee and doesn't say a word but allows Ann to leave. His previous actions have made it clear that he does not take her out of mercy. And then, Lee and the two agents await almost certain death to be hurled into the building. The action sequences are also well-staged, including the one in which Lee and the two agents desperately try to stay alive after the flask of botulinus crashes at their feet. There is Lee's duel with the bogus agents which is particularly exciting because it happens so unexpectedly. Another highlight of the film is the scene in which Veretti and Donald drive into a trap along the highway. And the climactic fight sequence aboard the careening helicopter as the Satan Bug flask rolls back and forth is a tour de force of tension and action.

The deliberate irony contained within the film is that Ainsley's argument makes sense, despite his fanaticism. The scientists at Station 3 have created a weapon that has the potential to destroy all life on Earth. There can be no justifiable reason for such a weapon. So who is more insane? Is it Ainsley or the Station 3 scientists, and by implication, the government that delegates its employees to devise increasingly potent viruses with unconstrained carnage potential? The answer is obvious and the film makes a significant statement against the development of biological weapons of any kind.

Sturges experienced some frustration during production of the film. In Glenn Lovell's biography of the director, *Escape Artist* (University of Wisconsin Press; 2008), Sturges states that he intended to film thousands of frightened Los Angeles motorists jammed bumper to bumper on highways trying in vain to get out of the city. Such scenes of mass chaos would have conveyed the necessary sense of potential catastrophe to audiences. Unfortunately, city politicians would not allow him to stop traffic and he was forced to substitute glass-shot composites which he believed looked fake. He also laments not showing Ainsley falling from the helicopter to his death, which would have made the climactic fight more memorable. While he is correct on both points, he doesn't mention his own responsibility for other failings. If only he could have gotten that silly story called *The Hallelujah Trail* about a whiskey-filled wagon train out of his mind.

To play Lee Barrett, Sturges chose George Maharis who had co-starred (with Martin Milner) in the hit television series *Route 66* from 1960 to 1963. His portrayal of streetwise, rebellious drifter Buz Murdock brought him small screen stardom. During the third season, he left the series following widely reported disputes with the producers. Though the producers claimed that Maharis wanted more money, the actor asserted that he had to leave due to health problems. The following year, he began to pursue a film career. However, his first starring movie, *Quick Before It Melts* (1964), a dull comedy, had flopped and his second movie, *Sylvia*, was awaiting release. This was the third movie to try to elevate him to the status of a movie star.

The Mirisch Corporation's Walter Mirisch didn't want Maharis. In his book, *I Thought We Were Making Movies, Not History* (University of Wisconsin; 2008), Mirisch writes: "We were disappointed that we were not able to get a star to play the leading role; I felt the subject required a major action-adventure star." He does not name the stars that were unavailable but Charlton Heston writes in his book, *The Actor's Life* (E.P. Dutton; 1978), that he declined the starring role. In retrospect, Mirisch felt that he should have prevailed. He told Glenn Lovell, "John pressured us to cast Maharis; the movie suffered from the fact that we were not able at attract a front-line star." Sturges disagreed. "George had something," the director said, "he just never clicked." He may have insisted on going with a former television star because the two lead actors of *The Great Escape*

Lee and Ann locate the stolen flasks but they are not alone.

Lee is not fooled by the bogus agent.

(Steve McQueen and James Garner) had first achieved fame on the small screen. Actually, it was in *The Great Escape* that both actors "clicked;" prior to that film, their attempts to achieve film stardom had not been successful. (Garner's box-office failures include *Cash McCall*, *The Children's Hour* and *Boys' Night Out* while McQueen's include *The Honeymoon Machine*, *Hell is for Heroes* and *The War Lover*.)

In actuality, Maharis is quite convincing as the film's hero. Interestingly, he doesn't try to make Lee Barrett likeable. He is quick to anger, doesn't waste time or words and can be rude and abrupt. Once he agrees to do the job, he displays a single-minded tenacity to solve the case. Maharis conveys all of these traits with a straightforward performance. He is also quite believable in the fight sequences and, in general, exhibits the qualities of a good action hero. If this film had been a box-office hit, his screen career might have been more successful. He subsequently had one more starring role in *A Covenant with Death* (1967), the failure of which effectively doomed his chances of becoming a major motion picture actor. He then co-starred in several films before returning to television where he acted quite regularly until his retirement.

Richard Basehart, playing the villain, is an actor who consistently provided terrific performances, whether as a cop-killer in *He Walked by Night* (1948) or a heroic soldier in *Decision Before Dawn* (1951). He was superb as an Army officer accused of treason in *Time Limit* (1957). He also displayed his versatility in several European films, including *La Strada* (1954) and *Il Bidone* (1955), both directed by Frederico Fellini. Beginning in the mid-1950s, he acted frequently on television while still appearing in movies. After completing *The Satan Bug*, he began starring as Admiral Nelson in the television series, *Voyage to the Bottom of the Sea*, which would debut six months before the release of the Sturges movie.

Basehart could have played Ainsley as a raving lunatic but wisely underplays, providing his character with sanctimonious dignity. He convincingly conveys the feeling that Ainsley's self-righteousness is understandable and even, in a perverted way, correct in view of the monstrous weapon that has been created. However, the extent of Ainsley's madness soon becomes more evident as he reveals his atrocious plan. He gradually replaces his smug self-righteousness with an ominous expression and menacing tone. Fans of his heroic Admiral Nelson must have had a shock seeing him play a madman. The television series lasted for five years and Basehart then continued to act extensively on television with occasional film roles, including a fine supporting performance in Michael Winner's *Chato's Land* (1972). Among many prominent roles on the small screen, he excelled as the prison camp commander in *The Andersonville Trial* (1970).

Basehart and Maharis play extremely well against one another and their scenes together sparkle with tension. Ainsley's sophisticated demeanor against Barrett's relatively primitive behavior creates a genuine feeling of suppressed apprehension during their shared scenes, as though each man is sizing the other up and is waiting for an opportunity to get the better hand. It is a well-matched duel and the two actors make the best of it. In 1963, incidentally, Basehart guest-starred on an episode of *Route 66* but Maharis was not in the episode, his departure from the series being imminent.

Dana Andrews was one of the most underrated stars of the 1940s and 1950s and gave consistently great performances in a variety of genres, from film noirs to Westerns, from war movies to romances. By the mid-1960s, he was playing supporting parts but still provided his usual sincerity for the role of General Williams. Regardless of the size of his role, Andrews' commanding screen presence invites viewers to watch him and his earnest performance in *The Satan Bug* adds tremendously to the sense of urgency which propels the movie. By the way, this was one of eight movies released in 1965 in which Andrews appeared.

Anne Francis, who had co-starred in *Bad Day at Black Rock* as well as *The Scarlet Coat* (1955) for Sturges, gives an appealing performance as Ann Williams. However, she had some reservations about the completed film. In an interview with author Tom Weaver, she praises the script but is critical of Sturges and editor Ferris Webster, stating: "They were having meetings at lunch every day about another movie they were going to be doing, *The Hallelujah Trail*." As a result, she feels that "the pace was dragged out tremendously; the only thing I can consider is the fact that John and Ferris were pressed for time and that *The Satan Bug* suffered." Anne's powers of deduction are as perceptive as those of detective Honey West, though the damage to the film may not be as extensive as she believed. In 1961, she appeared with Maharis in two episodes of *Route 66*.

The supporting roles are all perfectly cast and are another indication of the director's instinct for choosing the right actors for each character (as he did so unforgettably in *The Magnificent Seven* and *The Great Escape*). However, instead of the distinctive personalities who provide colorful support in his more famous movies, Sturges chose average-looking actors that do not stand out in a crowd. Ed Asner projects quiet menace as Veretti, his malevolent stare suggesting a complete disregard for human life, while Frank Sutton complements him as the more edgy Donald. Two of Hollywood's most gifted character actors make brief but impressive appearances and contribute to the film's overall impact: John Anderson provides a solemn and sturdy portrayal of Reagan and Simon Oakland also stands out as Tasserly.

(Sturges believed that Frank Sutton's casting may have harmed the film, through no fault of the actor. Immediately after filming *The Satan Bug*, Sutton was cast in the comedy television series, *Gomer Pyle U.S.M.C.* By the time the movie was released, he had achieved fame as the frequently exasperated marine sergeant and, as a result, his appearance in the film elicited laughter from many audiences. Ed Asner, incidentally, would not become a television comedy star until 1970.)

It is informative that Ed Asner agrees with Anne Francis about the director's preoccupation with his next film. In Glenn Lovell's book, Asner reports that Sturges was frequently conferring with John Gay, the writer of *The Hallelujah Trail*, during filming of *The Satan Bug*. Asner is quoted as saying with some anger, "Obviously (his next movie) was where his heart and mind were; he wanted to get through our film as quickly as possible." Regrettably, the evidence against Sturges appears indisputable.

For the most part, the editing by Ferris Webster—who edited 15 of the director's films—keeps the film moving at a rapid pace which doesn't allow any respite from the tension. Alas, Anne Francis' judgments about the lack of concentration by both Webster and Sturges prove to be correct. There are some errors in continuity that are rarely found in a Sturges film. For instance, later in the film Veretti speaks with a lisp that is noticeably different from his former tone. According to Lovell, an earlier scene in the script in which Veretti was the recipient of a karate chop to the throat was not filmed. Similarly, Sturges was not as diligent about retakes, the result being that Maharis stumbles during one long speech but quickly

recovers. Actually, this makes his speech seem more natural but it apparently wasn't intended.

The score by Jerry Goldsmith sets the mood with a jittery main title theme that accompanies equally edgy animation of a deadly virus and its effect upon humanity. During the opening sequence, the music is especially effective in maintaining a level of suspense and, throughout the film, adds to the mood of apprehension. At times, there is an atonal quality to the music, in part due to a modular synthesizer, which unconsciously alerts audiences to an undercurrent of menace even in tranquil scenes. To enhance the sinister atmosphere of the story, Goldsmith avoids high strings, using instead an array of percussion and woodwind instruments. The dissonant and occasionally raucous quality of the score augments the action as well as the suspense and is a perfect complement to the film. (United Artists did not issue an LP soundtrack album at the time of the film's release. For years, the original stereo soundtrack masters were missing but, in 1999, music aficionados located some segments. In 2007, Film Score Monthly combined these stereo sessions with mono selections from the 1996 laser disc release of the film to produce a long-overdue soundtrack CD.)

Prior to the film's release in April, 1965, "Whit" in *Variety* gave it a favorable review. "This is a superior suspense melodrama and should

DOOMSDAY MESSAGE MISSES MARK
Sturges' Satan Bug Found Non-Communicable

By ALI SAR

Moviemaker John Sturges has been responsible for some solid productions — "The Magnificent Seven," "The Old Man and the Sea," "The Great Escape," et al.

However, his most recent, "The Satan Bug," fails to live up to the producer-director's reputation.

Sturges says most of his films have one common denominator — an examination of the behavior of men under stress.

Sturges' current production also focuses its cameras on such a project.

However, as soon as one starts recalling the suspense, action and highly charged drama created in "Great Escape," one quickly will discover "Satan Bug" never can generate such a reaction.

Of course, the story line and the cast do not measure up to that of "Great Escape" either.

The role of Lee Barrett, a young government investigator in "Satan Bug," is played by George Maharis, who makes his first major motion picture appearance.

Maharis won acclaim off-Broadway in Jean Genet's "Deathwatch" and Edward Albee's "Zoo Story." Later he zoomed to stardom in "Route 66" Television series.

Although he given a convincing performance in "Satan Bug," it is evident that he needs more practice.

Richard Basehart has the part of Dr. Hoffman, a scientist.

Anne Francis, who was seen earlier in Sturges' "Bad Day at Black Rock," has the leading feminine role in this film. She portrays the daughter of a security-minded general.

The general is played by veteran actor Dana Andrews, who is making his return to the screen after an absence of several years during which he has been appearing on Broadway and in television.

As the title suggests, the plot centers around "the satan bug," a virus which could kill the entire population of the world in a couple of months.

Maharis is selected for the job of finding out if the bug really exists.

If he is contaminated, they will have to shoot him. Maharis gives the instruction to a guard: "You'll have five seconds to pull the trigger as soon as I come out of that room."

Maharis himself is to give the signal.

The cast also has Ed-

The screenplay was penned by James Clavell and Edward Anhalt based on a novel by Ian Stuart, nom de plume for Alistair MacLean, author of "The Guns of Navarone."

A Mirisch Corp. presentation for United Artists release, "Satan Bug" was shot in Los Angeles, San Diego and Palm Springs.

This marks the third film produced and directed by Sturges for Mirisch. Their association will continue with two forthcoming pictures — "The Hallelujah Trail" and "The Law and Tombstone."

"Satan Bug" currently is showing at citywide release. Oh yes, the companion feature is "Great Escape," a great film.

SAT. MATINEE
OPEN 12:45—KIDS 50¢
'THE SATAN BUG'
plus
'THE GREAT ESCAPE'
Reg. Show Cont. Sun. 1 p.m.
Why not drop the kids off...
and shop in the reservations
Panorama City Shopping Center

NOW! REGULAR PRICES!
JOHN FORD'S
CHEYENNE AUTUMN

Laugh it up in Lootsville!
EMIL AND THE DETECTIVES

tempo
FILM CONCERT STAGE
MIKE MARTH, Tempo Editor

---

keep audiences on the edge of their seats," adding that "the film is packed with shock values suitable for strong exploitation and better than average box-office returns are indicated." However, when the movie opened in theaters, most of the reviews were negative. Bosley Crowther in *The New York Times* wrote: "This highfalutin drama has much the triteness and monotony of an average serial television show." *Newsweek*'s reviewer called it "an unpersuasive thriller [and] just harmless formula stuff." *Time*'s reviewer wrote that the movie "is full of fake moments which are supposed to create suspense but provoke only laughter." Unfortunately, such reviews may have influenced potential moviegoers.

In *Variety*'s chart of Top-Grossing Films of 1965, 85 movies earned more than the minimum of $1 million in domestic theatrical rentals. *The Satan Bug*, which opened in April, did not earn the minimum amount to qualify for inclusion on the list. George Maharis' second starring movie, *Sylvia*, in which he plays a private detective, opened in February and was Number 67 with $1.5 million; this movie inspired critic Judith Crist to write: "Maharis manages to suggest that he might be worth watching in a role worth acting in a movie worth making. *Sylvia* wasn't." *The Hallelujah Trail* opened in June and was Number 36 with $3 million; this was disappointing, considering that it featured big stars — Burt Lancaster and Lee Remick — and was in Cinerama; sadly, the attempts at madcap humor repeatedly fall flat and confirm Sturges' later description of the movie as an "epic folly."

Incidentally, though *The Hallelujah Trail* proved that Sturges was not suitable for comedy, United Artists opened it in first-run theaters with a huge promotional campaign. In contrast, UA didn't seem to have too much faith in *The Satan Bug*. In the Los Angeles area, it opened in neighborhood theaters without any pre-release publicity. It also opened city-wide in New York City and one theater tried to drum up interest by adding the word "Operation" to the title, as in *Operation Satan Bug*; (the World War II movie, *Operation Crossbow*, was concurrently playing a first-run engagement at the Radio City Music Hall). However, UA's decision to dump the movie on the market combined with the poor reviews doomed its chances and it was soon playing the bottom half of double bills.

Sturges directed seven more movies before retiring. *Hour of the Gun* (1967) is a sequel to *Gunfight at the O.K. Corral*, at least as far as the storyline is concerned. But the tones of the two films are quite different. This movie is a bitter depiction of the moral deterioration of Wyatt Earp and its effect upon his friendship with Doc Holliday; in *The Filming of the West* (Doubleday; 1976), John Tuska describes this film's predominant force as "the intangible substance of what links one man's fate with another's." This was the last film that Sturges personally produced.

Ice Station Zebra (1968) is a Cold War story about a race between the Americans and the Russians to retrieve a downed spy satellite in the Artic. MGM made the mistake of initially releasing it in Cinerama roadshow engagements which fans of action movies tended to avoid. However, it's frequent appearance on television has vastly increased its status and is now one of the director's most popular films. In his *Time Out Film Guide* review, Chris Petit writes: "It's not saying much but Sturges has been responsible for two of the more successful Alistair MacLean adventures, this and *The Satan Bug*."

Sturges took over the director's reigns for the space drama, *Marooned* (1969), after Frank Capra withdrew from

John Sturges prepares to film a scene with George Maharis.

Agents search Dodger Stadium for a stolen flask.

the project. This film is a disturbing exploration of heroism and frailties among astronauts. In the *Time Out Film Guide*, David Pirie calls it "one of Sturges better films in which the suspense builds remorselessly."

Joe Kidd (1972) is a substandard Western, due primarily to conflicts between the director and producer-star Clint Eastwood which led to inconsistencies in characterizations as well as the tone of the film. Glenn Lovell's book relates how Sturges' friendship with Ferris Webster ended on the set of this film because Webster reportedly betrayed Sturges to curry favor with Eastwood. The two men eventually retired to the same community but never spoke to one another again.

Chino (1973) is an Italian-Spanish-French co-production filmed in Spain and is predictably a mess, due in part to additional scenes filmed by an Italian director. The film's star, Charles Bronson, was in charge and he ensured that Sturges knew it; ironically, Sturges had helped Bronson achieve stardom by giving him prominent supporting roles in three movies.

McQ (1974) is an exposé of bureaucratic police corruption; in *Time Out Film Guide*, Chris Petit writes that it is "the first commercial film to show the indirect influence of Watergate" and the only film to show John Wayne as "an anachronism in a world of institutionalized crime." While the political theme may be subliminal, the action scenes show the director at the top of his game.

Sturges ended his career with *The Eagle Has Landed* (1976), an intriguing World War II adventure which would probably be better if not for post-production problems and difficulties between Sturges and the film's producer. This film, by the way, was based upon a novel by Jack Higgins, the best-selling author of adventure novels who called Alistair MacLean "one of the greatest page-turners in the business."

Some book reviewers have accused Alistair MacLean of writing unsophisticated novels to appeal to a popular readership. Such criticism didn't concern MacLean. He once said, "I know the day I start to satisfy readers of *The Times*, I'm finished." He sold himself short. In his best novels, he displayed a distinct command of plot and structure that keeps readers enthralled from one page to the next. However, even his fans believe that his formula wore thin with the passage of time. His last novels are disappointing, reportedly due to his inability to control his alcoholism. Nevertheless, his best novels remain uniquely exciting to this day.

Some film critics have accused John Sturges of directing competent action movies for undemanding audiences. Such criticism didn't concern Sturges. He once said, "I got into the film business to make a living, and I proved fairly good at telling a story." He didn't give himself enough credit. In his best films, he displayed a mastery of the art of filmmaking. His fans were disappointed that his later films lack the spark of his more famous films. However, this was probably due to the fact that his style of filmmaking became unfashionable and not because of reports of heavy drinking. Nevertheless, his best movies remain exceptionally entertaining to this day.

And more than four decades after its release, *The Satan Bug* remains a suspenseful and exciting motion picture. Its horrifying depiction of the dangers of biological warfare was way ahead of its time and its portrait of home-grown terrorists would sadly become a reality in the future.

The Satan Bug may have flaws but a flawed gem is still a gem.

CREDITS: Producer, Director: John Sturges; Screenplay: James Clavell, Edward Anhalt, Based Upon the Novel by Ian Stuart; Cinematography: Robert Surtees; Editor: Ferris Webster; Music: Jerry Goldsmith

CAST: George Maharis (Lee Barrett); Richard Basehart (Charles Reynolds Ainsley); Dana Andrews (General Williams); Anne Francis (Ann Williams); John Larkin (Dr. Leonard Michaelson); Richard Bull (Eric Cavanaugh); John Anderson (Reagan); Frank Sutton (Donald); Ed Asner (Veretti); Simon Oakland (Tasserly); Henry Beckman (Dr. Baxter); Harold Gould (Dr. Ostrer); John Clarke (Lt. Raskin); Hari Rhodes (Lt. Johnson); Martin Blaine (Agent posing as Martin); Harry Lauter (Ainsley's Henchman); James Hong (Dr. Yang); Tol Avery (Police Captain); Russ Bender (Mason)

A HIGH WIND IN JAMAICA

At the end of Richard Hughes' novel, *A High Wind in Jamaica*, the unnamed narrator watches a group of young girls playing together and is unable to determine which one of them is Emily Bas-Thornton. She should look different, he surmised, but she blended in perfectly with the other children, projecting the same demeanor of innocence that only comes with childhood. There was no way to tell Emily from the others, even though she had killed one man and sent many other men to the gallows for her crime. If the narrator doesn't hope with all of his heart that she will never remember what she did during her ill-fated voyage and beyond, then the reader surely does.

Richard Hughes was a British poet, playwright, screenwriter and novelist. He only wrote four novels but his first, published in 1929, is his most famous work. *The Innocent Voyage* was the novel's title in the United States and its appearance caused some debate. Though some critics praised it as a literary work of art, others condemned it for its heretical depiction of children and their behavior. *A High Wind in Jamaica* was the title in England (U.S. editions later adopted this title) and British critics similarly either praised or denounced it. Over the next several decades, the novel gradually achieved prestigious status. In 1998, the Modern Library named *A High Wind in Jamaica* one of the best 100 novels of the 20th century.

On the surface, the novel is an adventure story about pirates. Beneath the surface, it casually depicts a series of events that range from vicious to shocking. It is also about the corruption of innocence, but as much by adulthood as by the novel's presumed villains. Primarily, it is a novel about childhood, though it is not a novel for children. Hughes presented a markedly different portrait of children, whom prior literature had depicted as benevolent and loving. As Richard Perceval Graves points out in his biography, *Richard Hughes* (Andre Deutsch; 1994), Hughes did not envision children as bearers of original sin, as William Golding would later do with *Lord of the Flies*. "He accomplishes something more subtle and profound," Graves writes. "His central thesis is that children cannot be judged in terms of adult values [and that] a child's mind differs profoundly

from an adult's mind." In brief, children live in an entirely different world than adults; they are neither moral nor immoral but completely amoral.

The setting of the novel is Jamaica, one of the largest islands in the Caribbean. A brief history of the island's colonization by Europeans may be helpful to understanding the background of the story. In 1494, Christopher Columbus discovered Jamaica and annexed the island in the name of the King and Queen of Spain. In 1509, Spain officially colonized the island, despite the wishes of the native inhabitants who lived peaceful lives of fishermen and farmers. The Spaniards enslaved the natives, many of whom eventually died due to harsh treatment and a lack of immunity from European diseases. The Spaniards then imported slaves from Africa to replenish the labor pool and cultivate the land. In 1655, England captured the island from Spain and made it a British colony. The British considered the island to be a valuable addition to its empire because of its natural resources, especially sugar cane and cacao. They continued the tradition of transporting slaves from Africa to work on the plantations. The British government eventually abolished slavery in 1834, though the freed slaves still worked on the plantations; these included the Creoles who were descended from African and European ancestry. The British also continued to encourage English families to permanently settle in Jamaica by giving them valuable land grants. These families attempted to maintain some semblance of their native country's culture amidst the primitive island environment.

The time period of *A High Wind in Jamaica* is 1860. Fredrick and Alice Bas-Thornton live on their Jamaican estate with their five children: John, Emily, Edward, Rachel and Laura, whose ages range from three to 12 years. Alice has become increasingly concerned about their environment which includes dangerous weather and voodoo rituals practiced by a neighboring

Alice and Fredrick Thornton (Isabel Dean, Nigel Davenport) are concerned for their children after the hurricane.

On board the Clorinda, the children wave good-bye to their parents.

Creole family. After a hurricane damages their home, the parents decide to send their children to England to provide a proper education in a civilized society. Two Creole children accompany them: Margaret, age 13, and her younger brother, Harry. Fredrick and Alice feel relieved as they place the children aboard the *Clorinda* in the care of Captain Marpole. However, on the high seas, pirates led by Captain Jonsen and his first mate Otto raid the *Clorinda*. As the pirates search for booty, the children sneak onto the pirate ship. After sailing away with their swag, the pirates are stunned to find the children aboard. They take the children to Cuba, intending to leave them on the island which British ships regularly visit. However, an accident kills John. Since none of the Cubans want to be involved in the child's death, Jonsen is forced to sail the seas with the children who seem to enjoy their new surroundings. Though the children's behavior annoys the crew, Jonsen develops affection for 10-year-old Emily. When the pirates attack a Dutch ship, they take the captain prisoner and tie him up. They leave him in the cabin with Emily who is sick with a fever. As the captain struggles to reach a knife, Emily hysterically stabs him. After the children are safely in England, authorities charge the pirates with murder. The prosecutor finds that the younger children have forgotten details of the voyage and just want to find other games to play. Only Emily seems to have some knowledge of what happened. However, in court, she testifies that she saw the Dutch captain die but not that she killed him. Jonsen and his crew are convicted and hanged.

Nothing is really what it appears to be in this novel. On Jamaica, the Bas-Thorntons symbolize a pretense of nobility rather than genuine aristocracy. The supposedly bloodthirsty pirates are really ineffectual. The allegedly civilized citizens of England are thinly veiled savages. The figures of authority embody hypocrisy instead of honesty. And the dear children are deadlier than a hangman's noose. The children inhabit a world that is different than the world inhabited by adults. These two worlds can only co-exist because of an invisible truce by which the adults, perhaps unconsciously, refuse to acknowledge that their children are quite different than they are.

Throughout the novel, the emotions of the children remain obscure to their parents, as well as to the pirates. Alice has no understanding that the children enjoy the hurricane and are unaware of the danger. Afterward, the children are unconcerned over the death of a servant but grieve for the family cat. Alice worries about them traveling on their own, not realizing that they will take full advantage of the lack of parental control. Aboard ship, they quickly forget John after he dies and are only interested in playing games. By the end of the novel, the adults who comfort Emily never consider that she may be guilty of a terrible crime. But yet Emily is not really evil. Fear and hysteria cause her to kill the Dutch captain while intense pressure from an overzealous prosecutor precipitates her betrayal of Jonsen and his crew.

Prosecutor Mathias (Dennis Price) interrogates Emily (Deborah Baxter).

The zeal of the British authorities to execute the pirates was customary for the time period of the story. Historically, the so-called "Golden Age of Piracy" occurred during the early 18th century and was the scourge of the high seas. During this period, the British Empire controlled one-fourth of the world, including such territories as India, Canada, South Africa, Egypt, Australia and New Zealand. Piracy represented a grave threat to trade with these colonies. The British Empire was determined to make the oceans safe for commerce and had to eradicate piracy in order to preserve her supremacy of the seas and her global dominance. By the mid-19th century, the British Navy had turned the tide and was winning the war against the buccaneers.

(England's oppressive imperialism generated a spirit of insurgence in her colonies. The British military had crushed the Indian Rebellion of 1857, also known as India's First War of Independence, and was equally intent on winning the Second Anglo-Chinese War, also known as the Second Opium War. However, other European nations resented England's status as the foremost global power. Germany, flushed with victory in the Franco-Prussian War of 1870, founded the German Empire and enlarged its navy to compete with the British Empire. Nationalism and militarism spread across the continent as the various nations extended their colonial power throughout the world. To increase their strength, the European nations formed alliances for mutual defense in the event of war. In 1882,

Germany, Italy and Austria-Hungary formed The Triple Alliance against Russia and France. The balance of power vacillated as tensions escalated into the next century. Germany gradually became a highly industrialized nation and its status as a potential global power threatened England's supreme position. In 1907, England joined France and Russia to form The Triple Entente. Russia also had a close relationship with Serbia, a nation which had been bitter enemies with Austria-Hungary for over a hundred years. Austria-Hungary's conflicts with both Russia and Serbia steadily increased and, due to their alliances, threatened to pull the other nations into the fracas. In 1914, a Serb assassinated Austria's Archduke Franz Ferdinand and the First World War erupted.)

In view of the acclaim for *A High Wind in Jamaica*, Hollywood perceived its potential as a movie. However, though the novel's overt themes have the ingredients of a grand adventure story, the psychological themes contained within the subtext and the disturbing implications of the story presented problems. Nevertheless, in the mid-1930s, attempts to arrange a film production at MGM proceeded with Charles Laughton as Jonsen. However, trepidation from studio executives over possible controversy resulting from a faithful depiction of the children cancelled the project. In the early 1940s, Warner Bros. took a stab at the novel but eventually also passed, realizing that it didn't fit in with the kind of family friendly pirate and adventure films that the studio was producing during this period.

(In 1943, playwright Paul Osborn adapted the novel to the Broadway stage as *The Innocent Voyage* with Oscar Homolka as Jonsen and Abby Bonime as Emily. Osborne had some highly publicized problems with the play's original director and eventually took over the directing reigns himself. The playwright excised some of the troubling inferences of the story and toned down the children's amorality; in this version, Emily confesses to the crime but no one believes her. Upon opening, the play received mostly negative reviews which criticized the uneasy mixture of humor and drama; the reviewer for *Billboard* called it "dull and disappointing" while the reviewer for *Time* wrote that Osborn missed the novel's "subterraneous horror." The play ran for 40 performances before closing.)

Hollywood studios continued to periodically express interest in filming the novel but problems in adapting it to the screen seemed insurmountable. However, one man at Britain's Ealing Studios had definite ideas on how to film it. Alexander Mackendrick, though born in Boston, was raised in Scotland and established his film career in England. In the early 1930s he was an art director in the advertising industry and, by mid-decade, was scripting commercials. When the government awarded contracts to his advertising agency during World War II, he wrote animated shorts and shot newsreels. Following the war, the British film industry stagnated except for the efforts of producers such as Alexander Korda and J. Arthur Rank who were injecting quality into their films. Michael Balcon, the new chief of Ealing Studios, was determined to be a part of this revival and, in 1946, hired Mackendrick as a scriptwriter. Mackendrick had aspirations to be a director—and he had always loved Hughes' novel.

As if designed by fate, in 1948, Balcon also hired Richard Hughes as a scriptwriter. Among other projects, Hughes worked on a script for a proposed film called *The Herring Farm* that Mackendrick was scheduled to direct, though it was never filmed. Perhaps it was the close contact with Hughes that awakened Mackendrick's dream to make a film of *A High Wind in Jamaica*. He informed Balcon of his desire but the Ealing chief did not think the novel

Richard Hughes

was a suitable project for his studio and rejected the idea. Mackendrick went onto other assignments and directed his first film, *Whiskey Galore* (1949; U.S. title: *Tight Little Island*), which was a hit. He then directed four more movies at Ealing, including the acclaimed comedies *The Man in the White Suit* (1951) and *The Ladykillers* (1955).

These films, in which he utilized dark humor to criticize sacred British traditions, brought Mackendrick praise in England. Since they also were surprise successes in the United States, Hollywood studios courted the director. This was timely in view of the fact that the BBC had just purchased Ealing, which left him without a contract. Mackendrick arrived in Hollywood in 1956 to direct *Sweet Smell of Success* for United Artists. It was also in 1956 that 20th Century Fox acquired the film rights to *A High Wind in Jamaica*. James Mason, who had just signed a contract with Fox, expressed an interest in playing Jonsen. But studio boss Darryl F. Zanuck did not approve the project, in part because writers were unable to craft an acceptable script. So the plan to film the property was put on the back burner.

In 1957, *Sweet Smell of Success* became a critical success but commercial failure (due in part to the repeated disparagement of the movie in his daily column by the influential journalist Walter Winchell, whom many perceived as the model for the film's main character.) Mackendrick proved that he could direct a major production with big stars—Burt Lancaster and Tony Curtis—but he did not have the independence he had been accustomed to at Ealing and had sporadic clashes with the producers, one of whom was Lancaster. The following year, on his next film for Lancaster, *The Devil's Disciple*, he again had problems with the actor, which led to his dismissal from the film. In 1960, Carl Foreman hired him to direct *The Guns of Navarone* for Columbia but, after six months of planning and pre-production, disagreements with — once again — the film's producer led to his departure. After directing a Broadway play that failed, he directed an episode of a U.S. television series, which signified a humiliating comedown. In 1962, his former Ealing boss Michael Balcon hired him to direct a film called *Sammy Going South*. His Hollywood career apparently over, he returned to England.

However, Hollywood had not given up on either *A High Wind in Jamaica* or on Mackendrick. Specific details are vague but, according to some reports in trade papers at the time, producer Jerry Wald, who had produced many successful films at Fox, accepted the challenge of bringing Hughes' novel to the screen and, in 1962, offered Mackendrick the opportunity to direct the film version. But fate seemed to be against the director. When Wald died suddenly, the studio again postponed the project. It remained in limbo until 1963 when Peter Ustinov expressed interest in directing and starring in a film version. However, Darryl Zanuck didn't have much faith in Ustinov because of the box-office failure of *Billy Budd*, another seafaring adventure that the actor had starred in and directed the previous year. Then Zanuck signed Nunnally Johnson to write a new script. The studio chief wanted a family tale of adorable children outwitting wicked pirates, similar to Disney's *Swiss Family Robinson*, a huge hit in 1960. In fact, Zanuck actively sought Disney favorite Hayley Mills to play Emily. Accordingly, though Johnson's script deviated from the novel and had a happy ending, it pleased Zanuck. He offered the director's job to Mackendrick who quickly agreed. But, though he was finally realizing his dream, if Mackendrick believed that smooth sailing was ahead, he could not be more mistaken.

Andrew Mackendrick

In his book, *Lethal Innocence: The Cinema of Alexander Mackendrick* (Methuen; 1991), author Philip Kemp details the numerous problems that plagued the film. To begin with,

Mackendrick hated the script. Anthony Quinn, who signed on to play the pirate chief, also disliked Johnson's screenplay. Through Quinn's leverage and under Mackendrick's guidance, Ronald Harwood wrote a new screenplay which pleased both the director and Quinn but displeased Zanuck. Nevertheless, Zanuck reluctantly approved production because the studio had already spent a great deal of money on pre-production. But he hired Stanley Mann to do another revision of the script to strengthen the relationship between the pirate chief and his mate and build up the part of Rosa, the brothel madam. Unhappy with the changes, Mackendrick brought in Dennis Cannan, who had written *Sammy Going South*, to also work on the script. Finally, the production started filming in the Caribbean in the summer of 1964.

As filming proceeded, the problems continued. Mackendrick still visualized the film as a faithful adaptation of the novel while Zanuck saw little commercial potential in such a film. Mackendrick prevailed but the studio executives became increasingly dissatisfied with the production as it progressed. Consequently, though Mackendrick was able to complete the film, Zanuck dismissed him during post-production and the studio subsequently edited more than a half-hour from the director's version of the movie. According to Philip Kemp, most of the deleted scenes concerned the children while occasional narration by Emily was also cut out. Other deleted scenes involved the complicated relationship between Chavez and Rosa, who is actually his partner-in-crime in the original script. Mackendrick was quite bitter about his removal from the film and the ensuing changes, believing that the version that Fox released in June 1965 was a betrayal of the novel.

A High Wind in Jamaica begins in Jamaica as a raging hurricane destroys the home of Fredric and Alice Thornton and their five children, the eldest of which are 12-year-old John and 10-year-old Emily. This is the last straw for the Thorntons who decide that they have to send the children to England, not only because of the physical danger on the island but because of the increasing influence of the superstitious natives upon the children. The Thorntons believe that a proper Victorian upbringing in England will save the children from the decadence of their environment. Two children from a neighboring Creole family, the adolescent Margaret and her younger brother Harry, will accompany the five Thornton children. The Thorntons place the seven children aboard the *Clorinda* in the care of Captain Marpole.

En route to England, pirates led by Captain Chavez and his first mate Zac board the *Clorinda*. While Chavez and his crew force Marpole to reveal the location of a small fortune noted in the log, the children play aboard the pirate ship. After sailing away with their plunder, the pirates discover the children aboard. Chavez is furious, not only because of the

Chavez (Anthony Quinn) faces a rebellious crew.

children's presence but because the crew claims that they will bring bad luck. This is proven true after mishaps involving the ship's figurehead and the dropping of the anchor frighten the superstitious crew. The exasperated Chavez decides to leave them in their home base of Tampico with Rosa, the madam of a brothel. Once in Tampico, John wanders about unsupervised and, excited by the action of a cockfight, accidentally falls to his death. Since the angry Rosa now wants nothing to do with the remaining children, Chavez has no alternative but to again take them on his ship.

The children quickly adjust to their new environment, playing games and scaring the crew with their antics. Despite his initial resentment, Chavez gradually grows fond of Emily. However, the crew is becoming restless since the British Navy is scouring the seas for the children. During one of her games, Emily receives a gash on her leg which leads to an infection and a fever. Chavez's concern for her gradually takes precedence over obligations to his men, which causes resentment among the crew. When a Dutch ship is sighted, the crew wants to raid it but Chavez wants to put the children aboard the ship. The men mutiny and Zac knocks Chavez unconscious to protect him and locks him in his cabin with Emily. As Chavez tries to comfort Emily, Zac leads the men in the seizure of the ship and the kidnapping of the captain. But upon sighting a British military ship. Zac releases Chavez who angrily refuses to resume command of the crew. After Chavez leaves, the captured Dutch captain staggers into the cabin. Struggling to untie himself, the captain tries to give Emily a knife to free him. Unable to understand him, the feverish Emily panics and stabs the Captain with the knife.

After the children reunite with their parents in England, British authorities charge the pirates with the deaths of the Dutch captain and John. Mr. Mathias, the prosecutor, has no direct evidence against the pirates and, without such proof, knows that Chavez and his men will escape a death sentence. Mathias senses that the vulnerable Emily is the weak link and puts her on the stand. His aggressive questioning forces the frightened child to implicate Chavez in the killing. As Emily is rushed out of the courtroom by her parents, the stunned Chavez and his men know that they will now face the hangman. Zac can only take out his anger on Chavez who, rebounding from the shock, assumes a fatalistic attitude.

The differences between the film version of *A High Wind in Jamaica* and the novel are not as radical as Mackendrick believed. The most obvious changes are the names and nationalities of the pirate captain and his first mate, from the Danish Jonsen and Austrian Otto to the Mexican Chavez and the American Zac. The characterizations are similar, though the friendship between Chavez and Zac is more pronounced in the movie. More significantly, the novel is told primarily from the perspective of Emily. The film, to some degree, is also told from Emily's viewpoint. But some scenes are seen from the perspective of Chavez, which serves to illuminate some of the events that in the novel are limited in scope due to Emily's narrow vision.

The manner in which the children leave the pirate ship is also different. In the novel, Jonsen becomes worried for the children's safety because of the crew's growing anger toward them. When his crew sights a steamship, he concocts a plan with the children to tell the steamship captain that Jonsen found them on an island. A poignant scene in the novel occurs when Emily hugs Jonsen and tells him that she doesn't want to leave him. In tears, she agrees to go but innocently asks Jonsen to come and visit her in England. However, once the children are aboard the steamship, the ship's officers coax Emily into telling the truth which leads to the capture of the pirate crew by the British Navy. The movie eliminates this steamship episode but this is beneficial to the story since, although it again reveals the capricious nature of the children, the events tend to be superfluous.

The movie strengthens the relationship between the pirate chief and his first mate. While Jonsen and Otto have common goals, Chavez and Zac are close friends. Until Chavez becomes enchanted with Emily, his friendship with Zac may have been his only meaningful relationship. Due to his affection for Chavez, Zac restrains the crew and keeps an increasingly delicate situation under control. In view of this, the end of their friendship is distressing, especially since Chavez doesn't seem to care that Zac hit him to save his life. Chavez only feels that his friend has betrayed him. As a result, he refuses to resume command of the pirate crew when Zac asks him to, an incident that is also not in the novel. The lost friendship between the two men makes Zac's final angry words to Chavez in the courtroom agonizing because he knows that he didn't betray Chavez but was only protecting him.

Similarly, Chavez's relationship with Emily assumes an even deeper level in the film because he is still suffering from what he perceives as

In the courtroom, Chavez and his crew await their fate.

his only friend's treachery. All Chavez has now is Emily which is why the scenes they share in the cabin are so touching. When Emily asks him to tell her a story, it is heartbreaking, particularly because it symbolizes the child's inherent innocence. After the killing of the Dutch captain, Chavez's attempt to shield her from the truth of her own actions by telling her that she had a bad dream achieves a level of poignancy that is missing from the novel.

The reaction of the pirate chief to his death sentence is also different in novel and film. Jonsen subsequently tries to commit suicide by cutting his throat, only to have his life saved for the hangman. In contrast, Chavez quickly accepts the consequences of Emily's betrayal. His expression of resignation contrasts with Jonsen's panic. In the novel, during Emily's courtroom testimony, she only sights Jonsen for a brief instant before being hastened out of the courtroom. But in the movie, Emily repeatedly looks at Chavez in the dock, her eyes almost pleading for help. It becomes increasingly clear from his sympathetic expressions even as she is unwittingly condemning him that the love he feels for Emily is worth his life. This dramatic highpoint of the film is very important because Chavez displays the self-sacrificial act of which Jonsen is incapable.

Despite Mackendrick's assessment of his film, *A High Wind in Jamaica* captures most of the complex themes of the novel. As a result, the movie leaves audiences with disturbing thoughts similar to those that troubled readers. Just as incidents and passages of the novel linger in the mind, scenes and images from the movie are similarly memorable. Mackendrick uses his camera to highlight the amorality of the children in ways the novel cannot do. As they prepare to board the ship, they appear so innocent that no one would suspect them of being a source of unpredictable danger. These children view lust and brutality as entertainments while death becomes just another game. Yet it is made clear that they are not deliberately malevolent but just unable to comprehend the ramifications of their behavior. The director conveys this basic amorality in a myriad of ways, from the manner in which they delight in teasing the superstitious crew to their incessant quest to find new games to play.

Mackendrick directs the sequence involving the killing of the Dutch captain with particular finesse. As Chavez tries to comfort Emily, they can hear the seizure of the Dutch ship by the pirate crew. The attack on the pirate ship by the British Navy, which occurs just as the Dutch captain has his fateful encounter with Emily, immediately follows. Chavez's discovery of the dying captain near the hysterical Emily happens concurrently with the boarding of the ship by the British. Even though Mackendrick keeps his camera inside the cabin during all of these events, the sounds of the action above sufficiently increase the level of tension and hysteria down below.

Mackendrick also displays an unassailable knowledge of proper use of the widescreen. The multi-masted ships were fortunately completed before the studio slashed the budget and give the movie a visual grandeur that otherwise would have been missing. Despite the impressive spectacle, however, the director doesn't lose sight of the fact that this is primarily a story about people. His children are believable because they are so genuinely natural and free of affectation while the pirates are depicted not as either bloodthirsty or fun-loving rogues but human beings who are simply trying to make a living the only way they know how.

The only real villains in the film are the acerbic Mathias and the cultured British citizens whose angry calls for blood resonate through the courtroom. It is ironic that this self-righteous prosecutor and the allegedly civilized members of Victorian society want only to kill the pirates while the pirates never killed anyone. Indeed, this cultured lawyer terrorizes Emily in a way that the pirates never considered doing. It is also revealing that Mathias suspects the worst when the children disclose that Chavez used the word "drawers," when he was actually admonishing the children to be modest when playing games. After the trial is over, Chavez establishes his moral superiority over the Victorians with his insightful statement to Zac: "Well, they've got to hang somebody."

Some critics have commented that the emotional feelings Chavez develops for Emily may include an unnatural sexual element. However, his expressions at key sequences clearly illustrate

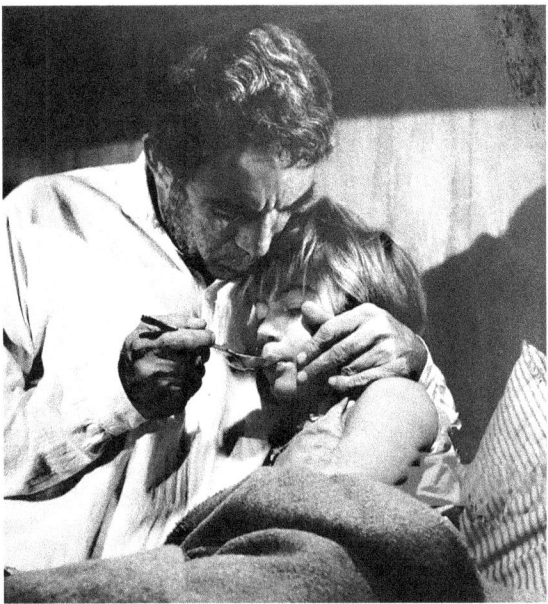

Chavez tries to nurse Emily.

that his feelings are primarily paternal but that his emotions are confused due to his inadequacy in such a role. There is a sexual undercurrent in both novel and film but it does not involve Emily. And it is in this regard that Margaret's presence on the ship serves a specific purpose. When the inebriated Chavez and crew members step down into the hold in search of Margaret, Emily asks with some annoyance, "What do you want?" This innocence makes them laugh and Emily remains oblivious to the crew's desires. Indeed, she is so annoyed at the violation of etiquette that she bites Chavez's thumb which gives him the excuse he needs to angrily order the men to leave. This scene also indicates the basic benevolence of the pirates who do not even think of forcing themselves upon Margaret once she refuses to accompany them.

This sequence is taken directly from the novel but Margaret's subsequent actions are different in the movie. In the novel, she will eventually have sexual relationships with some of the crew, including Otto, which will traumatize her; it is Margaret's innocence that is destroyed, not Emily's. In the film, flirtatiousness replaces her initial fear of the pirates. If anything else occurs, the film doesn't depict it. (In the film, Margaret is played by an 18-year-old actress who looks that age, thus making a clear distinction between her and Emily.) Thus, some of the pirates in the novel deserve culpability while the pirates in the film do not. Zac, due to his deference to Margaret, is deserving of far more sympathy than Otto who does not hesitate to take advantage of the adolescent.

There is one scene in the movie that is suggestive concerning Chavez and Emily. As the children tease Chavez by playing with his hat, the pirate chief angrily chases them. After he catches Edward, Emily jumps upon him to protect her brother. Chavez irritably wrestles with her and as he pins her to the deck, for one brief moment, he stares at her with a strange expression. Zac, who was laughing at his friend's exasperation, senses that something is amiss and sits up. But Chavez quickly releases the girl, an expression of embarrassment on his face. As Emily furiously berates him, his confusion appears to increase and he goes to his cabin. Whatever feelings — whether emotional or physical — he may have experienced during that brief moment, he immediately feels ashamed of them.

Concerning this sub-theme, Richard Graves writes that Hughes chose the original title of his novel for a specific reason. "By portraying what has happened to Margaret, the author has increased the emotional range of the novel and can portray more truthfully the nature of the strong affection which grows between Emily and Jonsen and which remains innocent despite containing a strong sexual undertone. It was this innocence at the heart of the story which led Hughes to the title for which he had been seeking: *The Innocent Voyage.*" The filmmakers, with the contentious wrestling scene, made the undertone slightly more overt. (When the ABC network televised the movie, censors cut out those few controversial seconds.) Nevertheless, the innocence contained in the novel's original title is translated to the film, despite several seconds. The love that Chavez develops for Emily is as innocent as the love she develops for him.

Mackendrick fortunately had the assistance of terrific actors. Anthony Quinn started his film career in the mid-1930s. During World War II, he was exempt from military service because he was a Mexican citizen; (he became a U.S. citizen in 1947.) As a result, he played many important supporting roles in war movies which brought him attention. Nevertheless, it took him about 20 years to become a major star. He was the recipient of two nominations for the Best Actor Academy Award and won two Best Supporting Actor Awards. As Chavez, he successfully submerges his familiar personality and provides an introspective and multifaceted performance quite unlike his effusive one-note interpretation of *Zorba the Greek* the previous year. Underneath the debauched exterior, Quinn doesn't overtly convey warmth but, as the story progresses, suggests a gradual awareness of tenderness that is as much a surprise to him as it is to Zac. His expressions of puzzlement in the presence of the children imply that he is initially unaware of his deep-seated emotions and desires. It is only when Emily is hurt and suffering that he allows his emotions to finally rise to the surface.

Chavez threatens Captain Marpole (Kenneth J. Warren).

However, it is Quinn's ability to express so many conflicting and repressed emotions through his demeanor that makes his portrayal so extraordinary. During many key scenes, such as the moment when Emily apologizes for biting him or when he discovers the Dutch captain's body, it is obvious that the affection inside Chavez is steadily increasing. During the courtroom sequence, he doesn't say a word as Emily testifies but his expressions convey the truth of his feelings. When he realizes that Emily has just condemned him to death, Quinn's exemplary skill is particularly evident. As he stares at her, his expression conveys a mixture of shock, understanding, compassion and, most of all, love. This is an unappreciated but superb performance from Quinn.

First mate Zac (James Coburn) and Chavez.

Mackendrick disapproved of Quinn's portrayal, believing that his comical hat and frequent laughter made him into a Disney character. But Chavez is an inadequate pirate and Quinn plays the role as if he realizes this, using the hat to conceal his failings. This awareness makes his character susceptible to Emily's innocence, particularly since he knows — just as the novel's Jonsen knows — that the days of the buccaneers will soon be over. Chavez doesn't *want* to be a pirate and this is obvious from his initial appearance when he boards the *Clorinda* and sees Emily for the first time, turning away from her gaze as if embarrassed. His experiences with her create within him a longing for the kind of life he never thought he would want and Quinn's portrayal reflects this desire. With due respect to the director, Quinn's interpretation of the role was the correct one.

James Coburn served in the Army in the early 1950s as a disc jockey and narrator of training films. Following his discharge, he studied acting. In 1957, he made the first of about 70 appearances in episodes of television series. Though he worked steadily, he seemed to be stuck in television guest shots until his role in John Sturges' *The Magnificent Seven* (1960) brought him initial recognition. After more television appearances and a couple of failed series, Sturges called on him again for *The Great Escape* (1963), which further increased his profile. He subsequently had more prominent supporting roles in films which led to his first co-starring role as Zac. The actor's distinctive smile, which he displays in Captain Chavez's presence, initially reflects Zac's close relationship with his friend. But as events unfold, changes in his demeanor gradually reveal growing concern while his expressions perfectly convey increasing exasperation over Chavez's unusual behavior. After the mutiny, his pained response to Chavez's refusal to forgive him illustrates his total distress over the loss of his only true friend. In the climactic sequence, the range of emotion he displays flawlessly reflects his anger, fear and sense of injustice. Coburn's performance in this film directly led to his first starring role as *Our Man Flint* the following year.

Deborah Baxter is perfect as Emily, a complex character that had to be difficult for the 10-year-old to convincingly portray. This was her first movie and she gives an engaging performance as a precocious girl who initially looks upon the world as a playground. But then she is placed in circumstances that she is incapable of controlling due to her youth. Her baffled expressions often convey the impression that her inability to comprehend the strangeness of events leads to increasing frustration. She then becomes besieged by incidents which no child should have to experience. Despite the terrible nature of Emily's actions, she emerges with sympathy due to the depth of emotion that young actress brings to two important sequences: her terror during the killing of the Dutch captain and her increasing hysteria in the courtroom as she becomes as much a victim of her hypocritical society as Chavez and the pirates.

Deborah Baxter didn't appear on screen again until 10 years later when she appeared in *The Wind and the Lion* (the director of which requested her because she made such a vibrant impression upon him in her first movie.) In addition to two television episodes in the 1970s, she has appeared in only one more film and that was in 2000 when she had a part in a movie entitled *The Calling*. Nevertheless, she made an indelible mark upon cinema history and will always be remembered as Emily Thornton.

Incidentally, Mackendrick's resentment seems to have spread to any facet of the film that was against his wishes. His disapproval even extended to the music score by Larry Adler and especially to the ballad that Fox executive Elmo Williams insisted accompany the beginning and the finale. Actually, the score is quite appropriate to the mood of the film and the beautiful ballad that Mike LeRoy sings perfectly complements the sense of sadness and loss that is reflected in Emily's face in the last sequence.

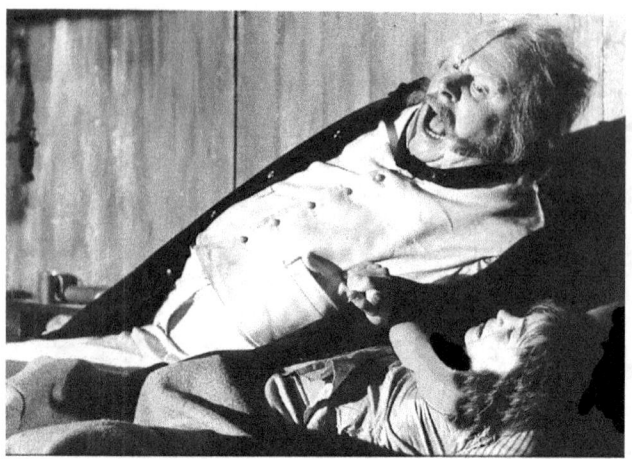
Emily has a fatal encounter with the Dutch captain (Gert Frobe).

Mackendrick, gifted though he was, perhaps should have lightened up a bit. (The ballad was not released on record, though it would have been good publicity for the movie. Since the film's release, the song has developed a loyal following of people who love it because of its association with the movie or due to its own merits. In 2010, four and a half decades after the film's release, fans started a petition to persuade 20th Century Fox to allow Mike LeRoy, who was still performing, to re-record the ballad.)

Reviews for *A High Wind in Jamaica* were all over the map. The reviewer for *Newsweek* called the movie "a stunning piece of work [and] one of those rarities that is all things to all ages, delightful as pure escapism and impeccable as a morality play that never moralizes. It is that most horrible of horror films, a changeling [that initially] seems a cheerful, predictable affair [but then] takes a swerve into madness." *Time*'s reviewer also liked it, calling it "a family picture with a ferocious theme; on the surface, it is a conventional tale of piracy, kidnapping and adventure [but] like the corrosive novel, its deeper purpose is to fathom the psyche of children whose innocence is only skin deep." A.H. Weiler in *The New York Times* didn't like the movie. "It is merely a breezy adventure ruffled by some confusing ill winds," he wrote, adding that "a good deal of the philosophy and insight into the human condition for which the book was lauded appears to be missing on screen." Hollis Alpert in *The Saturday Review* wrote that the movie lacks the novel's "sense of irony, its imaginativeness and its subtlety," concluding that "the net effect is a lackluster one [that] is never fully fascinating or stirring."

The fact that some reviewers could detect underlying themes which eluded others is perhaps an indication of the intricacy of the script as well as the direction. Indeed, this divergence of interpretation is perhaps most illustrative of the film's faithful adaptation of the equally complex themes of the novel. In support of this, Martin Amis, the future novelist who plays John, reported that Richard Hughes visited Pinewood Studios during filming of interior scenes and was delighted with the production.

Zac, Chavez and the pirate crew with the children.

In fact, Hughes must have liked the completed film because, according to Richard Graves, he personally introduced a screening while on vacation in Kampala, East Africa a couple of years later.

A High Wind in Jamaica did not earn the minimum of $1 million in domestic theatrical rentals to earn a place on *Variety*'s annual list of Top-Grossing Films of 1965. This is particularly aggravating since such awful movies as *I'll Take Sweden* and *Get Yourself a College Girl* are on the list. 20th Century Fox deserves at least partial blame for the commercial failure. Since the movie did not fit in with its expectations, Fox unloaded it on the market without the special promotion it needed. The primary poster for the movie depicted a smiling Quinn and Coburn flanked by children looking at them with awe. The tag line read: "20th Century Fox Recreates the Fantastic World of Piracy and High Adventure on the High Seas!" Unsuspecting audiences expecting a *Treasure Island*-type adventure for children of all ages must have been disappointed and possibly angered by the film's themes.

Since Alexander Mackendrick had more or less disowned the film, he probably didn't care about its commercial failure and may have perhaps interpreted such failure as vindication for his unseen version. Due to his recurrent dissatisfaction with the studio system and with various producers, he only directed one more film in 1967, a comedy called *Don't Make Waves*, which is a far cry from his Ealing comedies. In 1969, he accepted a position as Dean of the Film Department at the California Institute of the Arts. He held that position for several years, then became a professor in 1978 and had a rewarding career until his death in 1993.

Regardless of its fate at the box office, *A High Wind in Jamaica* is a superb motion picture that is both entertaining and provocative. If the

Even today, pirates still fascinate children.

footage that was edited out by 20th Century Fox exists anywhere in the studio's vaults, it would be a wonderful discovery to see Mackendrick's original version of the film. However, the released movie is still a splendid achievement.

The last sequence of *A High Wind in Jamaica* is heartrending. In Hyde Park, Mr. Thornton joins his wife and children following the execution of the pirates. Sitting silently on the bench, Fredric and Alice both appear anguished as they watch Emily playing with the other children. Clearly, they suspect that Chavez may have been innocent of the murder but are afraid to consider any alternative since Emily was the only other person in the cabin when the Dutch captain died. Emily seems to be enjoying herself, totally unaware of the fate of the pirates or of her parents' distress. But then she sees a toy boat moving slowly across a pond and stares at it, her expression suggesting a combination of purity and confusion. Unlike the novel, in which Emily seems to have re-captured her innocence, the film's Emily appears more haunted by her experiences. The disturbing memories buried deep within her mind are perhaps struggling to rise to consciousness. As in the novel, it is hoped that she will never remember everything that has happened to her.

Unfortunately, in all probability, that is not very likely.

CREDITS: Producer: John Croyden; Director: Alexander Mackendrick; Screenplay: Stanley Mann, Ronald Harwood, Dennis Cannan, Based Upon the Novel by Richard Hughes; Cinematographer: Douglas Slocombe; Editor: Derek York; Music: Larry Adler, conducted by Philip Martell; Lyricist: Christopher Logue; Singer: Mike LeRoy

CAST: Anthony Quinn (Captain Chavez); James Coburn (Zac); Deborah Baxter (Emily Thornton); Nigel Davenport (Fredrick Thornton); Isabel Dean (Alice Thornton); Dennis Price (Mathias); Kenneth J. Warren (Captain Marpole); Vivienne Ventura (Margaret Fernandez); Lila Kerdrova (Rosa); Gert Frobe (Captain Vandervort); Benito Carruthers (Alberto); Brian Phelan (Curtis); Martin Amis (John Thornton); Roberta Tovey (Rachel Thornton); Jeffrey Chandler (Edward Thornton); Karen Flack (Laura Thornton); Henry Beltran (Harry Fernandez); Charles Laurence (Tallyman); Kenji Takaki (Cook); Phillip Madoc (Guardia Civile); Trader Faulkner, Dan Jackson, Charles Hyatt (Pirates)

SOL MADRID

"We're going to turn you into a junkie."

Mafia underboss Dano Villanova is speaking to Stacey Woodward, his former mistress, and he is sadistically enjoying her terrified reaction. With these words, Stacey realizes the fate that Villanova has ordained for her. She struggles but Villanova's thugs are holding her down on the bed. She can scream but no one will help her. She watches in horror as heroin is injected into the needle that will soon pierce her skin. It is the beginning of a nightmare, one that will get more terrifying and painful with each injection.

This is a horrifying sequence from the 1968 MGM movie, *Sol Madrid*, a solid and vigorous thriller about an Interpol agent who is determined to bring a drug kingpin to justice by any means at his disposal. The film contains excitement, action, thrills and a touch of romance. It is also quite startling, not only in the sequence in which Stacey excruciatingly suffers her fate, but in the scene in which the hero exposes a traitor among his colleagues and enforces his own brand of justice. Such scenes would probably induce yawns today among jaded audiences who are accustomed to gratuitous brutality but, in the late 1960s, they were very disturbing.

The review of *Sol Madrid* in *Variety* by "Whit" was favorable though not enthusiastic and predicted some degree of box-office success. "Hard-hitting action compensates for certain confusing story elements," Whit wrote, "and plotting is sufficiently exciting and suspenseful to warrant interest." In actuality, the story isn't confusing but is quite clear in its progression. The film moves quickly from one encounter to another, each scene advancing the story and the characterizations, expertly balancing scenes of exposition with scenes of action.

Nevertheless, *Sol Madrid* failed commercially, despite its quality as well as star David McCallum's popularity (due to his co-starring role in the television series *The Man from U.N.C.L.E.*). In New York City, the movie didn't earn a first-run opening and was a supporting feature to an Elvis Presley movie, *Speedway*. Despite this, Renata Adler in *The New York Times* gave it a favorable review. "The plot is old-fashioned and solid," Adler wrote, "the tricks are mean and the ending for McCallum and [Stella] Stevens might have been happier but they were good and so was [Ricardo] Montalban." She concluded by writing that "the audience which was sold out all day yesterday cheered a lot and it was like a great episode in a first-class television series." The packed theater must have been due to Elvis because audiences elsewhere were uniformly sparse.

The response from the New York City audience is an illustration of the kind of popularity *Sol Madrid* could have obtained if the studio had spent more time on promotion and publicity. Even though the patrons probably bought tickets to see the Elvis musical, they wholeheartedly approved of the crime drama and this type of appreciation would doubtless have occurred everywhere else due to the inherent quality of the movie. But it didn't have a chance. MGM apparently had no faith in the movie and dumped it on the market for quick play-offs. Most major magazines did not review it in and it rapidly vanished from theaters.

On *Variety*'s list of Top-Grossing Films of 1968, there are 90 movies but *Sol Madrid* did not earn the required minimum amount of $1 million in domestic theatrical rentals to qualify for inclusion. In the police-crime genre, *Bullitt* with Steve McQueen (and Robert Vaughn, McCallum's partner from *U.N.C.L.E.*) was the biggest hit with $19 million; this movie has a forceful central performance but is marred by an inept professional killer and an unnecessary romantic sub-plot. *The Thomas Crown Affair* with a miscast McQueen is a far-fetched caper film but it earned $6.5 million. *The Detective* with Frank Sinatra, an effective depiction of moral decay and bureaucratic corruption, also earned $6.5 million. *Point Blank*, featuring Lee Marvin's memorable portrayal of Richard Stark's ruthless thief Parker, called Walker in the film, earned $3.2 million. The brutally realistic and underrated *Madigan*, with Richard Widmark and Henry Fonda, earned just enough — $1.1 million — to make the bottom of the list.

Sol Madrid is based upon the novel, *Fruit of the Poppy*, by Robert Wilder (Putnam & Sons; 1965). Wilder was a novelist, screenwriter, playwright and journalist. All of his novels give the impression that he has direct knowledge of his topics. *Flamingo Road*, which he adapted for the screen in 1949, breathes realism in its depiction of the corruption of Southern politics while the decadent oil-rich characters of *Written on the Wind*, the basis for the 1956 movie, emerge not as caricatures but real people. *Fruit of the Poppy* contains this same authenticity that was absent from so many other novels that flourished in the 1960s about the illicit drug traffic.

The following may help to provide a background for the novel and the movie based upon it. Heroin, a major component of the illicit drug trade, is synthesized from morphine which is derived from the opium poppy. The poppy flower is cultivated in mountainous areas in such regions as Southeast Asia, Afghanistan, Columbia and Mexico. A British research chemist created heroin in 1874 but the medical establishment did not realize its dangers and addictive elements for several decades. In 1924, the United States Congress prohibited the sale, importation and production of heroin. This led to illegal trafficking, particularly by the Mafia in Italy.

Robert Wilder

Following its creation during World War II, the Office of Strategic Services developed relationships with Mafia leaders in Italy to gain information prior to an allied invasion and to restrain the increasing influence of the Italian communist party. The OSS knew that the Mafia was also the prime purveyor of the illicit drug trade but didn't consider this a hindrance to their association. After the war, the Central Intelligence Agency continued this relationship. The CIA utilized clandestine operations and paramilitary actions to sustain anti-communist factions, including the Sicilian Mafia, in threatened nations. As the profits from illegal heroin trafficking increased enormously during peacetime, the CIA and the Mafia found their relationship to be mutually beneficial.

Alfred McCoy's *The Politics of Heroin: CIA Complicity in the Global Drug Trade* (Lawrence Hill Books; 2003) thoroughly documents the extent of this relationship; this is the revised and expanded edition of the author's groundbreaking book, *The Politics of Heroin in Southeast Asia* (Harper & Row; 1972). Much of the information detailed in McCoy's book is set during the 1960s. Lyndon Johnson was president, the Cold War was beginning its third decade and the Vietnam War was raging. During this period, U.S. foreign policy supported corrupt governments that were engaged in drug trafficking because they were anti-communist. The CIA's assistance to the Chinese Nationalists helped to create the Golden Triangle, an area in Southeast Asia in which much of the world's illicit opium was grown. This assistance transformed the area—which was not too distant from where American soldiers were fighting and dying—into a major supplier of heroin to the world. The book proposes that such covert operations by the CIA counteracted the efforts of the law enforcement agents who were fighting the drug traffickers.

Compelling evidence indicates that the CIA's collusion with mafia drug lords was responsible for the scourge of illegal narcotics in the United States beginning in the mid-1960s. Air America, which the CIA covertly owned, was a major transporter of narcotics. If Lyndon Johnson was not aware of this CIA connection to the drug trade, then he must have been as ignorant as he was corrupt. His successor, Richard Nixon, must have been equally aware, even as he was popularizing the fraud known as the "War on Drugs." *Cocaine Politics: Drug Armies and the CIA in Central America* (University of California Press; 1991) by Peter Dale Scott and Jonathan Marshall documents the complicity between the CIA and drug traffickers during several administrations. This book, among others, authenticates the financial support that the Ronald Reagan–George H.W. Bush administrations gave to Latin American fascist regimes as well as to insurgents who were fighting to overthrow democratically elected governments, all in the name of anti-communism. These regimes and insurgency groups subsequently murdered thousands of innocent people who wanted freedom from dictators and foreign imperialism. Scott and Marshall suggest a clear correlation between these illegal CIA operations and the smuggling of drugs into the United States.

In 1996, journalist Gary Webb published a series of articles in the *San Jose Mercury News* on the CIA's involvement in the smuggling of cocaine into the United States by the Contras, the right-wing militia group in Nicaragua that the Agency supported. In his series, entitled "Dark Alliance," Webb claimed that the CIA had knowledge that the Contras were using the drug profits to overthrow the leftist Sandinista government. Webb's investigative articles brought upon him the wrath of the Agency and their mass media toadies, resulting in attacks upon his integrity in such newspapers as *The New York Times*, *The Washington Post* and *The Los Angeles Times*. Eventually, his own newspaper withdrew their support of him. Webb persevered and expanded his research into his full-length book entitled *Dark Alliance: The CIA, the Contras and the Crack Cocaine Explosion* (Seven Stories Press; 1998). But the smear campaign succeeded in ending his career. *Kill the Messenger: How the CIA's Crack-Cocaine Controversy Destroyed Journalist Gary Webb* by Nick Schou (Nation Books; 2006) chronicles the events that led to Webb's death in 2004 which was determined to be a suicide. The ongoing collusion between the Agency and the national mass media extended to the 2014 film version of Schou's book entitled *Kill the Messenger*. Promotion for the movie's release was noticeably deficient and, after its debut, the film quickly disappeared from theaters.

Sol Madrid (David McCallum) deals his own justice to Emil Dietrich (Telly Savalas).

This rather sordid history gives an indication of the deep politics involved in the alleged War on Drugs. The type of law enforcement agents depicted in *Fruit of the Poppy* had to fight not only the drug traffickers but their clandestine allies in official positions of power. The novel begins on the Super-Chief train from Chicago to Los Angeles. Sol Madrid, a treasury agent assigned to the Bureau of Narcotics, watches three people. Harvey Mitchell, a former Mafia accountant, has stolen a quarter of a million dollars from his boss, Dano Villanova. Dano's mistress, Stacey Woodward, has also run away from him and wants a share of the stolen money. Roy Gaines, a contract killer, is after both Mitchell and Stacey. Mitchell outwits Gaines and travels to Mexico to meet with local drug kingpins. In Chicago, Villanova vows to get Stacey and Mitchell while Madrid is assigned to go to Mexico and convince Harvey to testify against the mob.

In Mexico, Mitchell seeks shelter from Batuc, a drug merchant whom the Mafia has forced out of the business. Madrid arrives and meets with Lieutenant Ortega who arranges for his incarceration to give him a cover story. In jail, he meets Lieutenant Mendoza, who works undercover as a guide called Jalisco. Together, they arrange a plan to convince Batuc that Madrid can safely smuggle drugs across the border. Madrid also intends to use his entry into Batuc's home to persuade Mitchell to return to the U. S. Meanwhile, Villanova has sent a killer to Mexico to silence Mitchell.

He has also tracked Stacey to Los Angeles and orders a nurse and her henchmen to kidnap her. They repeatedly inject heroin into her and, once she is totally addicted, throw her out into the streets to prostitute herself to feed her habit.

Back in Mexico, Madrid tricks the drug cartels into fighting one another and persuades Batuc that Mitchell represents a danger to him. Without protection, Mitchell agrees to return to Los Angeles. Madrid also sets a trap for Batuc with a phony drug operation. Back in Los Angeles, Madrid learns that Mitchell has apparently committed suicide which ruins the case against Villanova. When Madrid hears of Stacey's fate, he angrily resigns from the Bureau to exact his own personal revenge against Villanova. He uses illegal means to frame Villanova who, upon being informed of a contract upon his life by the Mafia, agrees to testify just as Mitchell would have done. Madrid's supervisor then informs him that he burned his resignation letter and Sol returns to work.

When MGM purchased the rights to Wilder's novel, studio executives may have seen the potential for the hero as a series character. In the midst of the James Bond phenomenon, all of the major studios were looking for a character that had the potential to be the basis of a lucrative film series. Since attempts to emulate Bond had met with either limited or no success, studios were looking for a different kind of hero to attract audiences. MGM executives perhaps figured that the espionage genre itself was overly familiar by this time and hoped that the subjects of international drug trade and Mafia crime lords would be different enough to appeal to audiences.

Sol Madrid is a Jerry Gershwin and Elliot Kastner production in association with Hall Bartlett Productions. Bartlett, who is credited as producer of the film, was also a director, screenwriter, documentarian, novelist and occasional actor. He usually directed films about social issues and they tend to be preachy, whether about prison reform (*Unchained* in 1955), racial prejudice (*All the Young Men* in 1960) or mental health (*The Caretakers* in 1963). Bartlett was apparently an earnest humanitarian but he may have immersed himself too deeply within the counterculture of the 1960s that he eulogizes in *Changes* (1969). This seems evident from his dedication in his film version of *Jonathan Livingston Seagull* (1973) to "the real Jonathan Livingston Seagull who lives within us all." (Clue: he is an alumnus of Yale.)

However, for *Sol Madrid*, the message about the evils of the drug trade emerges without sermonizing and is secondary to the film's entertainment value. This seems to indicate that Kastner and Gershwin, who were more oriented toward making movies than sending messages, may have been more involved with the production aspects of the movie than Bartlett. It also seems likely that Kastner and Gershwin chose Brian G. Hutton to direct the movie. According to some accounts, Gershwin and Hutton came from the same New York neighborhood. And this film would be the first of several collaborations between Kastner and Hutton.

Fruit of the Poppy contains interesting characters and situations but the plot is very complex. David Karp's screenplay is a vast improvement. Karp served in the U.S. Army Signal Corps during WWII. He wrote several novels, including the 1953 futuristic thriller, *One*, which he adapted for television in 1955 for an American anthology series and which was also the basis for two additional adaptations in 1956 and 1957, one for British television; this novel was out of print for half a century until Westholme Publishing issued a new edition in 2010 as part of its "Rediscovered Fiction" series. Karp started writing for television in the early 1950s and wrote episodes of numerous series, attaining a reputation for exploring controversial social issues during what is now referred to as the "Golden Age of Television". In 1964, he won an Emmy for a two-part episode of the series, *The Defenders*. His first film credit is as co-writer of the script for *Cervantes* (1967; U.S. title: *Young Rebel*), an undistinguished Italian-Spanish production. He achieved sole credit for *Sol Madrid* the following year.

Karp retains the basic plot of the novel for the screen but constructs additional scenes, revises events and creates composite characters. He based his conception of Madrid upon Wilder's character but embellishes him with other qualities to make him more distinctive. He keeps the film's focus on Madrid and excludes much of the extraneous information in the novel that tends to detract from the main storyline. Karp also provides a more brutal and more satisfying denouement for the main villains. In addition, he enhances the relationship between Madrid and Stacey, in effect making his hero more ruthless while increasing the depth of their liaison. As a result, the last scene of the movie elicits a poignancy that is missing from the novel.

Sol Madrid was re-titled The Heroin Gang in England.

The first shot of *Sol Madrid* is of a beautiful poppy flower growing in a field in a foreign country that is not identified. The flower is sliced open to reveal a flowing white liquid which will be transformed into heroin. Underneath the credits, assorted means of transportation (Air America?) convey the heroin to various parts of the world, including New York City. A group of addicts in an apartment are getting high when police break down the door. One man tries to escape but the cops roughly apprehend him and take him into custody. He looks like a clean-cut college student who should be studying in a campus library. He doesn't look like an addict but he also doesn't look like an undercover cop, which is what he is.

The man is Sol Madrid, an Interpol agent who is a specialist in infiltrating the opposition. Interpol Chief Danvers informs him that Harry Mitchell, a Mafia accountant who knows all of the secrets of the crime family led by Capo Riccione, has absconded with $500,000. Also missing is Stacey Woodward, mistress of Dano Villanova, Riccione's underboss. Madrid's job is to track down Mitchell and persuade him to testify against the Mafia. Simultaneously, at Mafia headquarters, Riccione berates Villanova for his carelessness in trusting both Mitchell and Stacey. But Villanova responds furiously that he will find and kill them both.

However, Madrid finds Stacey first and persuades her to reveal that Mitchell is in Acapulco to meet a drug dealer named Emil Dietrich. He then forces her to accompany him and another agent, Joe Brighton, to Acapulco. Once in Acapulco, he meets Jalisco, an agent working undercover, and Captain Ortega of the Mexican police. Ortega informs Madrid that Mitchell is in Dietrich's home and that his department has never been able to get proof of Dietrich's drug-dealing. Because the Mafia forced Dietrich out of business, he is willing to shelter Mitchell. Madrid devises a plan to give Ortega the evidence he needs on Dietrich while compelling Mitchell to testify.

Madrid poses as a drug trafficker and arranges a meeting with Dietrich who would like to resume his heroin traffic but is cautious. Meanwhile, after she is almost killed, Stacey emotionally collapses and her vulnerability elicits some humanity from Madrid. But the agent remains primarily interested in ensnaring Dietrich. When he transports fake drugs across the border in a ruse that Danvers has arranged, Dietrich agrees to harvest a new batch of heroin. Villanova, having tracked both Stacey and Mitchell to Acapulco, arrives with a lust for vengeance. While Madrid is away, Villanova's thugs kill Brighton and kidnap Stacey. Villanova sadistically exacts his revenge against Stacey by turning her into a heroin addict. Madrid hopes that Jalisco will be able to learn where Stacey is being held prisoner while he continues his plan to ensnare Mitchell. After he persuades Dietrich that Mitchell's presence is hindering the drug deal, Dietrich throws Mitchell out. Madrid's plan backfires because someone kills Mitchell before the agent can take him into custody. Madrid then sets a trap for Dietrich, leading to a police raid and a gun battle in which Madrid deals his own justice to Dietrich.

Upon reflection, Madrid can only conclude that there is a traitor on the side of the law, someone who betrayed the location of both Stacey and Mitchell. He doesn't have any direct proof against the person he suspects but confronts him anyway. When he offers immunity to the suspect in exchange for information on Stacey's whereabouts, the suspect provides information without legally implicating himself. But this is enough for Madrid who promptly breaks his promise and executes the traitor. Only Villanova remains at large and he will feel the full fury of Madrid's personal sense of justice in a vicious battle in the Mexican swamps. Madrid's reunion with a damaged Stacey is bittersweet but reveals that the intimacy he briefly shared with her was an aberration in his behavior.

Unlike many genre movies in which both the heroes and villains tend to be superficial, *Sol Madrid* credibly develops all of the major individuals. Madrid initially appears to be a typical film hero in the tradition of numerous undercover cops of previous decades. However, it quickly becomes clear that he possesses a steely self-righteousness that borders on fanaticism. He is merciless in his pursuit of justice and is intent on destroying anyone who damages his moral universe. And unlike so many film heroes of his era, he is not a clone of James Bond—he is neither charming nor debonair. While Bond's world is partly one of fantasy, Madrid's world is a corrupt cesspool. He is satisfied to put a dent in that corruption by taking down one crook at a time. He achieves this with a ruthlessness that makes him unpredictable and dangerous. At one point, Stacey asks him directly, "Can't you ever be nice?" His answer is direct. "No," he says, and it is obvious that he cannot be anything but what he is.

In a scene with Ortega, Madrid succinctly expresses his personal code. "We're right and they're wrong," he states quite simply. When he gets the drop on Dietrich, he exposes the depth of his moral anger. "Yes, guns are stupid," he tells the drug lord. "Ours is a stupid world, full of liars, cheats and traitors. But now and then, there is a flash of justice and seeing you spend the rest of your stupid life in a Mexican prison is going to fill my taste for justice." On the surface, he may seem like other contemporaneous police heroes. Steve McQueen's *Bullitt* of the same year and Clint Eastwood's *Dirty Harry* three years later both share Madrid's disdain for established procedures in their pursuit of criminals. They all believe in traditional morality and realize that, in the modern world, extreme methods are often necessary to defeat evil. Madrid differs in the

David McCallum tries to help the drug addicted Stella Stevens return to her normal way of life.

degree of emotion he displays; while Frank Bullitt and Harry Callahan are somewhat detached, Madrid is passionate. But his passion does not extend to the compassion that Bullitt and Callahan exhibit. As a result, he sometimes appears as unsavory as his adversaries, particularly in his exploitation of people to achieve his ends.

Madrid cannot display compassion toward the people he encounters because the decadence of his environment is so pervasive. This makes his relationship with Stacey more complex and edgy than it otherwise could have been. It would have been more in sync with the libidinous protagonists of the '60s if the relationship was more sensual, but this would have been a concession to commercialism that the movie refuses to make. It is obvious from their initial encounters that they have no use for one another and the angry words they exchange indicate their mutual scorn. She even ridicules his name. Fortunately, the manner in which they draw closer is devoid of the usual clichés. But the events that follow quickly terminate the warmth they briefly share. And, in view of the resolution, even the romantic implications leave a bitter taste. Indeed, in the final scene, when Stacey contemptuously tells Madrid that he got what he wanted, he knows that she is right. He only cares that he has restored some justice to his world and is satisfied that he has completed another mission. And beneath his slight smile is the implication that he has used his badge as a cover for his vigilantism against a corrupt world.

Stacey Woodward is given more depth than is usually provided for a typical gangster's moll. Initially, she appears to be a materialistic, self-centered woman who has sold herself to a crime boss for a life of luxury. But she reveals her true character when she tells Madrid, "I never knew a man who didn't use me or want to." When she breaks down after an attempt is made upon her life, Madrid discerns vulnerability beneath the hard surface. She is so hungry for any bit of kindness that she warmly responds to Madrid when he offers her token words of regret for placing her life in jeopardy. But she evokes the most sympathy when Villanova forces her into an excruciating dependency that reduces her to a pitiful wreck. At the end of the film, there is not much hope for Stacey. As she feared, Madrid has used her and it is symbolic that she is last seen lying despondently in a clinic bed.

Jalisco similarly displays enough individual traits to make him totally believable as an intrepid officer. He comes across as a generally nice fellow with a warmth that makes him appealing as an ally for the hero. When he saves Stacey's life, his skills make him even more admirable. He appears to be a devoted family man as well as a valiant agent. He looks forward to retiring with his wife and children and, in view of the deadly aspects of his profession, this seems like a reasonable ambition. It is this apparent normalcy and genuine congeniality that makes his fate so lamentable.

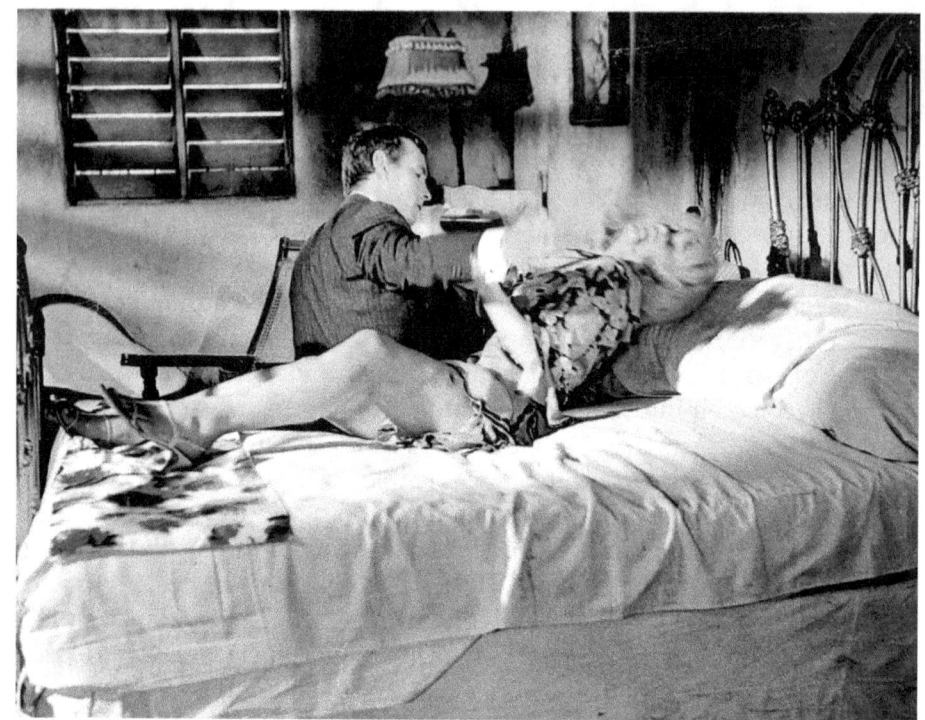

Dano Villanova (Rip Torn) enjoys inflicting pain upon Stacey Woodward (Stella Stevens).

Villanova is more than a scorned and sadistic lover. One brief line spoken by Danvers to Madrid in his introductory scene reveals that he had an emotional attachment to Stacey. This sets the stage for the degree of personal vengeance he directs toward her. Dietrich also possesses more than the usual requirements of a standard villain. On the surface, he appears to be a cultured gentleman but that superficial veneer is gradually exposed to reveal a supercilious drug merchant and murderer. And then there is Mitchell whose educated background somehow makes his sliminess more reprehensible. The depth of all of these characterizations makes *Sol Madrid* intriguing and memorable.

Director Brian G. Hutton began his film career in 1954 as an actor and attained small roles on television and in movies, including two for John Sturges: *Gunfight at the O.K. Corral* (1957) and *Last Train from Gun Hill* (1959). He was quite believable as twins in a 1961 episode of *Have Gun Will Travel* and as a beatnik in a 1962 episode of *Alfred Hitchcock Presents* entitled "The Big Kick." But his career didn't appear to be making any headway and this may be why he switched careers and became a director. According to a Universal press release in 1964, the studio was implementing a program to develop new talent through small-scale inexpensive films. One of these films was the first that Hutton directed, *Wild Seed* (1965), about a drifter who befriends a teenage runaway in search of her father. It was not a commercial success, despite some good reviews and, though it is obscure today, it has attracted something of a cult following among the few people who saw it. His second film for Universal, *The Pad and How to Use It* (1966), featured a kind of love triangle between a sensitive young man, his lothario friend and the woman who has no trouble choosing between them. This equally obscure film was quite impressive but failed at the box office, undoubtedly due in part to the terrible title, not to mention the downbeat but realistic ending. However both movies signified that Hutton's proficiency was behind the camera. He moved to MGM for *Sol Madrid*, which showed that he could handle a crime thriller with as much finesse as an "arty" film.

Hutton did not have a high opinion of *Sol Madrid*. In 2012, he told Lee Pfeiffer of *Cinema Retro* that the movie was a "total disaster both as a film and as an experience (because) everything that could possibly go wrong on a picture went wrong." Shortly before finishing the movie, he had to replace a major actor, thus necessitating the re-shooting in Hollywood of many scenes that he had previously filmed in Acapulco. He also states that he had to change the tone of the film because David McCallum, unhappy over the break-up of his marriage, was unable to do romantic scenes that conveyed Madrid's sexual manipulation of Stacey. However, Hutton's memory may be faulty since Madrid does have a sexual interlude with Stacey and he does exploit her. In actuality, since the cynical tone of the completed film is part of what makes it so memorable, the changes that occurred during production may have benefited the film. In essence, while these problems undoubtedly affected the director's attitude toward the production, they may have impaired his objectivity to assess the film's qualities.

Sol Madrid is the first film to demonstrate Hutton's expertise with action sequences. He depicts the attempt on Stacey's life and the vicious fight that follows in a frenetic manner, rapidly and repeatedly cutting between Madrid's fight with one assassin and Stacey's increasingly hysterical attempt to escape from the other one. Madrid's final confrontation with Dietrich is equally exciting as the tension of the verbal confrontation escalates steadily and eventually explodes in gunfire. But the most brutal sequence is the final fight between Madrid and Villanova which begins inside the villa and ends in a swamp with both men struggling in a literal fight to the death. This scene exposes Madrid as a ferocious animal. The fact that he was fighting an even more brutal beast only partially detracts from the taint that accompanies him because it is clear that this is what Madrid has wanted to do from the beginning. He never had any intention of bringing Villanova to justice. He wanted to kill him with his bare hands.

Madrid deceives Dietrich upon their first meeting.

Hutton displays equal expertise with his actors. The director's first two movies were character-driven vehicles that gave the principle actors opportunities to shine which they did under his firm guidance; Brian Bedford, in particular, in *The Pad and How to Use It* gives an excellent, unappreciated performance while Michael Parks seemed destined for stardom after his role in *Wild Seed*. Though *Sol Madrid* is primarily action-driven, Hutton still elicits uniformly fine performances from the entire cast.

David McCallum was born in Glasgow, Scotland in 1933. His family moved to London when he was a child and he subsequently attended the Royal Academy of Dramatic Art. In 1951, he fulfilled his obligation for National Service, the British term for compulsory military service, by serving in the British Army in the Gold Coast Regiment when the Gold Coast, now Ghana, was a colony of Great Britain. He started his acting career playing juvenile roles in British films in the 1950s and first attracted international notice in a supporting role in *The Great Escape* (1963). In 1964, MGM offered him a secondary role in the studio's new NBC series, *The Man from U.N.CL.E.* But his appearance elicited so much fan mail that he was quickly elevated to a full-fledged co-starring role, thus precipitating his fame. MGM then took advantage of his small screen celebrity by starring him in the romantic comedy, *Three Bites of the Apple* (1967), which appeared in theaters while the series was still on the air. This lightweight vehicle wasn't really a good test of his box-office appeal but its quick fade at the box office didn't help him. NBC cancelled the television series in January,

1968 because of lower ratings which were due to the asinine decision of the producers to make it campy, thus alienating many of its fans. Consequently, it was the commercial fate of McCallum's second starring movie, *Sol Madrid*, that would determine his future as a movie star.

McCallum's performance as Sol Madrid is essential to the film's impact. While he fulfills the requirements of an action hero, it is the subtle nuances he brings to other scenes that make Madrid memorable. The soft smile on his face when Stacey tries to insult him is just one example. His sanctimonious anger at Ortega's office and the snarling satisfaction he displays when he tells Dietrich what he plans for him add immeasurably to his character's portrait. His expression after he has killed Dietrich is outwardly one of satisfaction but is more complex because he doesn't look directly at Ortega, who clearly suspects that Madrid never had any intention of bringing his quarry in alive. But it is in the concluding scene with Stacey that he reveals his true feelings, or lack of them. Stacey is smart enough to see through his insincere apology and, when she confronts him with it, he smiles slightly and turns from her. He knows that she knows that he doesn't care about her or anyone; he only cares about his job. All of these complex emotions are evident in McCallum's terrific portrayal of Sol Madrid and it is unfortunate that he never got the opportunity to play him again.

As Stacey Woodward, Stella Stevens initially appears heartless and perhaps too hard-edged. But this cleverly sets the stage for her credible transformation into a perennial victim which validates the reasons for her bitterness. In the scenes which follow her addiction, she is particularly fine. She actually gives the impression that her skin is burning from the inside out. Devoid of make-up, pale and haggard, she lacks all of the glamour and attractiveness she displayed in the earlier scenes and becomes truly pathetic. In the final scene, she perfectly communicates her contempt for Madrid through her expression and tone. The bitterness and despair that she exhibits makes her character heartrending. It is a very intelligent performance and probably Stevens' best.

In any thriller or crime movie, the actor who plays the villain has to be a worthy antagonist for a dynamic hero or the movie suffers. In this film, there are two excellent performances that bring Madrid's opponents to brutally realistic life. Rip Torn is chillingly terrifying as Villanova, projecting sadism that oozes from his voice and a ferocity that glistens in his eyes. He is so frightening in his cruelty that it is difficult to imagine anyone else in the role, including the actor who originally played it. Torn projects such malevolence that, when the film was initially screened in theaters, his fate elicited applause from audiences. In contrast, Telly Savalas as Dietrich initially projects a smooth sophistication with even a trace of effeminacy. But his true nature emerges when Madrid impugns his integrity and he unleashes his suppressed fury. (Six years earlier, actor Brian Hutton had a small role in *The Interns*, which co-starred Savalas.)

Ricardo Montalban as Jalisco projects his natural likeability and warmth into his character yet there is always a suggestion of hardness beneath the amiable surface. His skill is particularly evident in his final scene with Madrid when he initially registers a variety of emotions, from convincing disappointment and chastisement to acceptance and disbelief. It is to Montalban's credit that he leaves viewers with a mixture of emotions as he exits the story. Pat Hingle also provides an indelible portrait of a wretched character whose criminal ambitions exceed his capabilities. There is absolutely nothing likeable about Harry Mitchell but yet Hingle still manages to make him pitiable. Veteran actor Paul Lukas makes the most of his single scene as Don Riccione and Michael Ansara is a convincing Captain Ortega. (Nine years earlier, Hutton had played a role in an episode of Ansara's television series, *Law of the Plainsman*.)

Lalo Schifrin's music is also an asset. Shifrin's film scores often combine aspects of pop and jazz along with some offbeat elements into a cohesive whole. For this film, the composer fuses Mexican-flavored tunes with jazz to create a dynamic score that occasionally mimics various sound effects, thus enhancing the effectiveness of many scenes. His main title provides an ironically pleasant melody to accompany the creation of heroin; the

utilization of the same theme for the romantic interlude conveys a suggestion of sorrow which will reach its apex in the conclusion. He also utilizes the talents of Brazilian classical guitarist Laurindo Almeida whose guitar solo both contradicts and highlights the immorality of the intricate drug scheme hatched by Madrid to trap Dietrich. (In 1968, MGM Records released an LP soundtrack album which contained re-recorded excerpts from the score. In 2010, Film Score Monthly issued the complete soundtrack as part of a five-CD set entitled *Lalo Schifrin Film Scores*.)

Though Brian Hutton didn't like *Sol Madrid*, producers Jerry Gershwin and Elliott Kastner must have been pleased with it because they signed Hutton to direct their next movie, a large-scale expensive World War II adventure story. *Where Eagles Dare* (1969) starred Richard Burton and Clint Eastwood (with whom Hutton had appeared in a 1961 episode of the television series, *Rawhide*). Based upon an Alistair Maclean screenplay, Hutton created an exhilarating action/adventure epic that was a huge box-office success and remains to this day enormously popular. In contrast, his next film, *Kelly's Heroes* (1970), also with Eastwood, suffers from an uneven tone that shifts from comedy to action and there's nothing funny about WWII or about the Vietnam War which it alludes to with an anachronistic hippie character. (In fairness to Hutton, the movie's faults appear to be due to studio-imposed changes to which the director objected.) After directing two more movies, *X, Y and Zee* and *Night Watch*, both with Elizabeth Taylor and both mediocre, he semi-retired in 1973. Seven years later, Elliott Kastner lured him back to Hollywood for *The First Deadly Sin* (1980) with Frank Sinatra. Three years later, he directed his last feature, *High Road to China* (1983) with Tom Selleck. Hutton only directed nine movies and his last films are unremarkable, which perhaps reflects his lack of interest. In 2011, he told Lee Pfeiffer, "I was bored by it. To me it was always just a hobby. I didn't start out to be a film director. I didn't start out to be a film actor. I just started out to make a living and do what I wanted to do. There was just no rush anymore. There were other things I wanted to do."

Despite the excellence of the script for *Sol Madrid*, David Karp did not write any more theatrical films, except for co-writing the story basis for *Che* (1969). He then returned to television to write and produce for the next two decades. In 1975, incidentally, he produced the short-lived series, *Archer*; among the cast for one of the episodes is an actor named Brian Hutton.

The undeserved failure of *Sol Madrid* ended MGM's attempts to develop David McCallum's feature film career. Away from the studio, he starred

Telly Savalas, Stella Stevens, Pat Hingle and David McCallum in a publicity photo.

in programmers like *Mosquito Squadron* (1969) and an Italian film called *La Cattura* (also 1969), both of which made little impression. Subsequently, though he occasionally starred in minor movies such as *The Kingfisher Caper* (1975) and *Dogs* (1976), McCallum worked more extensively in television. He starred in three additional series, two of them British, as well as many television movies, while making guest appearances in episodes of numerous other series. In 1983, he reunited with Robert Vaughn for a television movie, *The Return of the Man from U.N.C.L.E.* He also made several appearances on stage and, in 1984, received a Drama Desk Award nomination for Outstanding Actor for his starring role in the off-Broadway play, *The Philanthropist*. In 2003, he began co-starring in the U.S. series *NCIS*, a role which he has continued to play for 15 years. In 2016, at the age of 82, he wrote his first novel, *Once a Crooked Man* (Minotaur Books), a crime caper.

Sol Madrid failed at the box office in part because of the circumstances of its release. To begin with, the choice of title was an unwise one since the name of Sol Madrid was not familiar to the majority of potential ticket-buyers and had no drawing power. The average moviegoer probably thought the title as well as the movie had something to do with the capital of Spain. The British title, *The Heroin Gang*, was not much better and sounded like a standard crime programmer. The title of the original novel would have been the best title for the movie. *Fruit of the Poppy* has a poetic ring to it and would have appealed to audiences.

Furthermore, MGM released *Sol Madrid* in the U.S. one month after *The Man from U.N.C.L.E.* had been cancelled. The series had been on the air for four years and the public still identified McCallum as Ilya Kuryakin, his character in more than 100 hour-long episodes. MGM did not publicize the fact that he was playing a different kind of role and released the film with very little promotion. The studio further handicapped it by releasing it after it had distributed several episodes from the television series as theatrical features. These "movies" were either expanded versions of single episodes or two-part episodes. They played in second-run theaters in the U.S. but were main features internationally. Two of these features were released in England in 1968, the year that *Sol Madrid* was released and their generic titles (*The Karate Killers*, *The Spy with My Face*, etc.) were similar to the equally generic British title, *The Heroin Gang*. Increasing the appearance of familiarity was the fact that two of the *U.N.C.L.E.* movies featured, respectively, Telly Savalas and Rip Torn in supporting roles.

Madrid comforts Stacey after she is almost killed.

Additionally, Ricardo Montalban had appeared in two episodes of the series while Michael Ansara and Paul Lukas had each appeared in one episode. Thus, potential ticket-buyers may have perceived *Sol Madrid* as another television show masquerading as a theatrical feature.

Nevertheless, *Sol Madrid* is a terrific movie that deserves re-discovery.

CREDITS: Executive producers: Jerry Gershwin, Elliot Kastner; Producer: Hall Bartlett; Director: Brian G. Hutton; Screenplay: David Karp, Based Upon the Novel, Fruit of the Poppy, by Robert Wilder; Cinematographer: Fred Koenekamp; Editor: John McSweeney; Music: Lalo Schifrin

CAST: David McCallum (Sol Madrid); Stella Stevens (Stacey Woodward); Telly Savalas (Emil Dietrich); Ricardo Montalban (Jalisco); Rip Torn (Dano Villanova); Pat Hingle (Harry Mitchell); Paul Lukas (Riccione); Michael Ansara (Captain Ortega); Perry Lopez (Hood #1); Michael Conrad (Scarpi); Robert Rockwell (Danvers); Ken Del Conte (Joe Brighton); Henry Escalante (Hood #2); George Sawaya (Hood #3)

THE STALKING MOON

Salvaje, in Spanish, means "savage."

Salvaje is the Apache warrior whose name strikes fear in the hearts of everyone, friend and foe alike. He has a reputation throughout the territory of being a fearless and powerful killer. And he is on a rampage. Nothing can stop him from finding his son and punishing the boy's mother for taking his son away from him. And no one will stop him from killing the man who would dare to take his place as the boy's father. As he trails after them, he leaves in his wake bloodshed and death.

This is the story of a Western movie entitled *The Stalking Moon*, which National General Pictures released in 1968. It is not only a Western but a suspense movie. It is an action film and it even has a hint of romance. In some respects, it is a horror film. It is also an allegorical story about the Vietnam War. The setting is the Apache Wars, a series of conflicts during the latter half of the 19th century between the Apaches and the United States Army which lasted for over three decades. (The Apache Wars were just one of numerous conflicts known as the American Indian Wars. Other conflicts included the Navaho Wars, the Mojave Wars, the Yuma War, the Dakota War, the Great Sioux War, the Paiute War, the Black Hawk War, the Modoc War, the Nez Perce War, etc.)

The history of the Apaches, which consisted of several sub-tribes, is naturally difficult to chronicle. However, some archaeologists believe that the Apaches migrated from (what is now) the Alaskan and Canadian regions sometime between the 11th and 14th centuries. They lived a nomadic existence and occupied various regions of what would later be the American West. Historical as well as anecdotal evidence indicate that the Comanches, who may have migrated to the region earlier, drove the Apaches further southwest to the mountains and plains of (what is now) Northern Mexico and the Southwestern United States. In the 16th century, the Spaniards invaded Mexico and conquered the Aztecs, who were that region's native inhabitants. They subsequently established Mexico as a Spanish colony. As the Spaniards attempted to extend their colonization northward, they encountered the Apaches and began decades of tense co-existence, marked by frequent clashes. These clashes steadily increased as Spanish explorers surged further northward following the discovery of silver lodes.

The Apaches had other enemies besides the Spaniards. At various times, they continued their war with the Comanches and waged hostilities with other tribes, including the Utes and the Navajos. Although the Apaches settled in the New Mexico and Arizona regions, they also attempted to inhabit parts of Texas that both the Comanches and the Spaniards claimed as their territory. The Comanches, who had also migrated further south shortly before the Spanish invasion, resisted such encroachment and expanded into Apache territory. The two tribes continued to wage intermittent war against one another and, in the 18th century, the Comanches often joined forces with the Spaniards against the Apaches. As an old Arabian proverb says: "The enemy of my enemy is my friend."

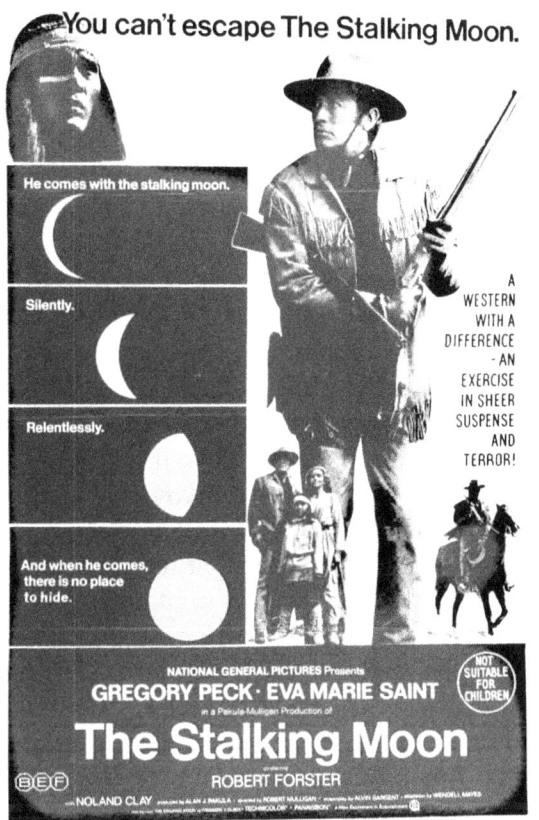

(Despite revisionist Westerns, Indian tribes were generally not peaceable nature-lovers living in harmony with their environment. Most of the tribes were in a continuous state of warfare with one another as they fought for arable land, for material goods, to avenge blood feuds and to take captives. Long before the white settlers started expanding westward, Indian tribes had an extensive history of conflict and bloodshed, not unlike the Americans and their European ancestors.)

The Apaches eventually realized that they could not win wars against both the Spaniards and the Comanches. This led to a peace treaty in the late 18th century and many Apaches subsequently accepted Spanish control. However, by the beginning of the 19th century, the Mexicans — which included Spaniards born in the colony and people of mixed blood — were intent on achieving freedom from Spain. In 1810, the Mexicans declared war against the Spanish colonial authorities, beginning the Mexican War of Independence. In 1821, the Mexicans achieved sovereignty. Subsequently, after Spanish soldiers left Mexico, the Mexican population became vulnerable to both the Comanches and the Apaches who wanted their own independence. The Comanche-Mexico War lasted for almost three decades at a cost of thousands of lives. During the same period, the Apache-Mexico War escalated as the Mexicans unsuccessfully attempted to drive the Apaches out of the northern territories.

In 1845, the United States annexed Texas which led to the Mexican-American War of 1846-1848. During this war, the Apaches assisted the Americans against the Mexicans. (The enemy of my enemy…) Following the American victory, the U.S. acquired the New Mexico territory and the Arizona territory. The ensuing westward expansion of settlers into these territories precipitated increasing tension with the Apaches. Some of this intrusion into Apache territory was unintentional. Other encroachments were deliberate due to the government's belief in Manifest Destiny which maintained that the Americans were ordained to expand across the new land.

Americans who had waged war to achieve freedom from British colonialism now began to do their own colonizing. In fact, the U.S. government used the same Discovery Doctrine that the Europeans used to justify their confiscation of lands occupied by indigenous natives. Many government officials further justified the removal of Indians from their lands by viewing them as savages who would learn peaceful ways from American civilization. (This was before and after the Civil War which, according to revised 2012 figures, killed more than 750,000 Americans.)

Many of the settlers, who had escaped European oppression, wanted to live in peace and many of the Apaches were willing to accommodate them. But hostile factions on both sides had their own agendas. Miners in search of gold and silver routinely broke treaties and murdered Apaches, who retaliated against all whites by killing the men and abducting their women. Reports of such bloodshed and of atrocities perpetrated upon white captives gave Washington bureaucrats the rationale to use military force to crush the Apaches into submission. These same bureaucrats earned popular support for the use of military force by exploiting the barbarism of the Apaches, as well as of other Indian tribes, while concealing the barbarism of the Americans.

In 1851, the U.S. Army officially declared war against the Apaches. Years of fierce fighting and savagery on both sides followed. Due to superior numbers and weaponry, the Army had the advantage. One by one, the tribes surrendered and moved to reservations. By 1868, the Army had subdued most of the tribes, except for the Chiricahua Apaches who continued fighting until 1872 when Chief Cochise signed a peace treaty. Nevertheless, half of his tribe, led by Geronimo, remained defiant. In 1886, Geronimo's surrender ended the war. By the following year, all of the Apaches were either on reservations or in prisons.

The Stalking Moon is set during the twilight of the Apache Wars. It is based upon the novel of the same title by Theodore V. Olsen (Doubleday; 1965). Olsen was a popular writer of Western fiction and wrote almost 50 novels as well as numerous short stories. He published his first novel in 1956 but he wrote his best novels in later decades. If he had written many of his books — such as *Rattlesnake* (1979) and *Blood Rage* (1987) — twenty years earlier, they probably would have had a better chance of being filmed. However, since traditional Westerns had lost much of their popularity by the 1970s, Hollywood filmed only one other Olsen novel. *Arrow in the Sun* (1969) was the basis — though a remote one — for *Soldier Blue* (1970), a terrible movie in which references to atrocities in Vietnam are supposed to justify nauseating violence.

The setting of *The Stalking Moon*, the novel, is 1881 Arizona. Army scout Sam Vetch has one last mission before retiring to his ranch in New Mexico with Evangeline, the woman he intends to marry. Sam and fellow scout Nick Tana, who is half Indian, are leading a cavalry patrol on the trail of Apaches when they find a group of women and children who have been left behind. One of the women is white captive Sara Carver, who has an eight-year-old son, Jimmie Joe, and a baby. Major Kinship, the company commander, arranges for her to travel East to live with a Quaker family and asks Sam to escort her to the Silverton train depot. Since Evangeline lives in Silverton, Sam agrees and bids farewell to Nick and the Army.

In Silverton, Evangeline rejects Sam's offer of marriage while Sara realizes the problems her children will have living in a society plagued by prejudice. When she also hears that someone has slaughtered a family at a stage depot they passed through, she mentions one name: Salvaje. She eventually confesses that the legendary Salvaje is the father of her children and Sam realizes that the Apache warrior is on their trail. Believing that Salvaje will not be able to find them in New Mexico, Sam asks Sara to marry him and live on his ranch. At the ranch, Sam's two hired hands, Ned and Hilario, are wary of Sam's new family but stay on. Though Sam tries to make Sara and Jimmie Joe feel comfortable, Sara is emotionally distant, while hatred consumes Jimmie Jo. When her baby becomes ill

Sarah Carver (Eva Marie Saint) and the boy (Noland Clay) among the Apaches taken captive.

and dies, Sara mourns but becomes closer to Sam due to his attempts to save the infant.

Soon Nick arrives and tells Sam that Salvaje has killed anyone who may have helped to take his family from him. After finding the murdered bodies of his neighbors, Sam rushes home and comes upon Salvaje standing over his baby's grave. Before Sam can shoot him, Jimmie Joe warns his father who disappears into the woods. At the ranch, Sam finds Sara unconscious. Upon awakening, Sara tells him that Salvaje intends to mutilate her and kill Sam but he intends to do it slowly to increase their suffering. Sam and Nick see traces of their foe everywhere but cannot find him. Despite their skills at tracking, the warrior constantly outsmarts them. One night, Salvaje leaves Ned's severed head next to the house. Sam tries to outwit Salvaje by setting a trap for him but Jimmie Joe once again aids his father who escapes into the night.

The next day, Salvaje kills Nick and Sam survives Salvaje's bullet only by accidentally falling. Regaining consciousness, Sam races back to his ranch and finds Salvaje carrying Jimmie Joe as Sara tries to hold on to the boy. When Salvaje is about to disfigure her, Jimmie Joe grabs his rifle and cries out for him to stop. As Salvaje turns back to his son, this gives Sam the opportunity he needs to fire and he hits Salvaje. Sam allows Salvaje to die thinking that Jimmie Joe cried out to help his father and not to save his mother. Embracing Sara, Sam also knows that Jimmie Joe no longer hates him.

The Stalking Moon is a good novel but it has faults in the characterizations of Sam and Sara. Sam recovers quickly from Evangeline's rejection and almost immediately asks Sara to take her place, suggesting that he would be satisfied with any woman as his wife. Sara initially lies to Sam by telling him that Salvaje's deceased brother was her husband. If she wanted to keep her relationship with Salvaje a secret, whether out of fear or shame, she should simply have said nothing. There are also errors in the plotting. It is difficult to believe that Sam is able to surprise Salvaje at his baby's grave since the warrior, based upon his reputation, would have been able to detect anyone approaching him. The explanation given for Salvaje's knowledge of his baby's death and place of burial seems contrived while Sam's hesitancy to shoot him doesn't make sense. And the long-awaited duel between Sam and Salvaje is disappointing, considering the build-up to it. However, the novel had definite potential as a movie.

Alan J. Pakula started his Hollywood career in the late 1940s in the Warner Bros. cartoon division. He spent his spare time stage-managing and directing plays at the Circle Theater where he worked with many young actors, including future writer Alvin Sargent. An MGM producer eventually hired him as his apprentice and then brought him to Paramount as his assistant head of production. His first film as a producer was *Fear Strikes Out* in 1957. Robert Mulligan began directing in the 1950s for television anthology series and achieved a reputation as a skillful director of quality drama. During this period, out of several dozen shows, he directed one Western, "The Death of Billy the Kid," a 1955 episode of *Philco Television Playhouse*. In 1957, he directed his first feature film, *Fear Strikes Out*, for producer Pakula before returning to television. In 1959, Mulligan won an Emmy for his direction of *The Moon and Sixpence*. He then returned to feature films and, after directing four movies, reunited with Pakula. In 1961, they created Pakula-Mulligan Productions.

Pakula-Mulligan's first film was *To Kill a Mockingbird* (1962), which was their biggest success. Horton Foote won an Academy Award for his screenplay and Gregory Peck won an Oscar for Best Actor, though he admitted that the role wasn't overly taxing. Although celebrated upon its release, many critics today consider it contrived and simplistic since it focuses on the white liberal hero instead of the black victim. Two movies with Steve McQueen followed: *Love with the Proper Stranger* (1963), about pre-marital pregnancy, is a tedious soap opera but was another box-office hit; *Baby the Rain Must Fall* (1965), about an ex-convict's readjustment to society, is a disappointing adaptation of a Horton Foote play which Mulligan had directed for television eight years earlier. *Inside Daisy Clover*

(1965), an exposé of Hollywood, is their worst film with an embarrassing performance by Natalie Wood trying to act half her age. After these two box-office flops, they had another critical and commercial success with *Up the Down Staircase* (1967) featuring Sandy Dennis as an inner-city schoolteacher.

Gregory Peck brought *The Stalking Moon* to Pakula and Mulligan. They liked the idea of doing a Western that was both traditional and unusual and agreed that Peck would be ideal as the veteran scout. National General Pictures agreed to distribute the film. (National General was a semi-major studio formed in 1967 that courted prestigious filmmakers to develop its status as a major studio. The company produced nine movies and distributed several dozen more, including some profitable films, but not enough to prevent it from closing its doors in 1973.) Pakula and Mulligan had already decided that this would be their last film together because Pakula wanted to start his own directing career. Thus, they may have felt that it would be appropriate to work again with the actor who had starred in their first film. But unlike their initial collaboration, this role would require Peck to fully utilize the skills that he had developed over almost three decades.

In 1939, after appearing in a few plays at the University of California at Berkeley, Gregory Peck left school to pursue an acting career. He studied at the Barter Theater in Virginia and, in 1942, made his Broadway debut. After appearing in two more plays, he attracted the attention of a Hollywood producer. In 1944, he appeared in his first film, *Days of Glory*, a World War II film produced when the Soviet Union was an ally and in which he played a Russian guerilla fighter. Although the film was not a success, it was obvious that he had star quality. And since a spinal injury exempted him from military service, he was able to obtain starring roles in major motion pictures due to the shortage of leading men in Hollywood.

By 1968, Peck had starred in over three dozen films. Only six of these were Westerns and included such fine movies as *The Gunfighter* (1950), *The Bravados* (1958) and *The Big Country* (1958). *The Stalking Moon* would be his first Western in over a decade — excluding his small part in the all-star *How the West Was Won* (1962) — and it would provide him with his most challenging role since *Cape Fear* (1962). Actually, this would be Peck's first *released* Western in over a decade; he had just filmed *Mackenna's Gold* but, due to extensive post-production problems, it did not appear in theaters until after *The Stalking Moon*.

Eva Marie Saint accepted the role of the abused frontier woman. Saint had started her career in television, performing in numerous episodes of anthology series until she was cast in her first movie, *On the Waterfront* (1954), for which she won an Academy Award for Best Supporting Actress. Subsequently, she appeared in numerous motion pictures but never

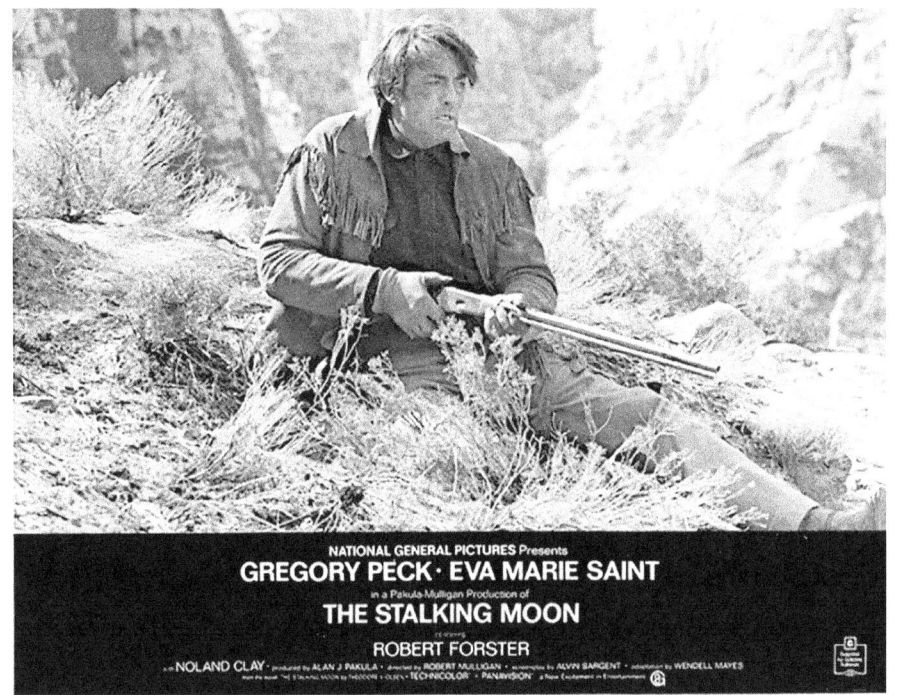

Sam Varner (Gregory Peck) is ready for Salvaje.

ventured out West. The closest she came to a Western was the Civil War drama, Raintree County (1957). She had not appeared on screen for two years when she signed on to play Sarah (spelled with an "*h*" in the film's credits) Carver.

In his book, Alan J. Pakula: His Films and His Life (Back Stage Books; 2005), Jared Brown provides an account of the development of the script for The Stalking Moon. Wendell Mayes, who wrote the adaptation, achieved initial acclaim for his scripts for television anthology series during the 1950s. Prior to The Stalking Moon, he co-wrote the scripts for two Westerns, From Hell to Texas (1958) and The Hanging Tree (1959). To write the screenplay, Pakula and Mulligan once again enlisted the services of Horton Foote but problems developed. Foote stated, "They didn't like my script and I didn't agree with the changes they wanted to make." As a result, Foote withdrew. Pakula and Mulligan then signed Alvin Sargent to write a new script. After making little headway as an actor, Sargent started writing for television in the mid-1950s. His first film script was Gambit (1966) and The Stalking Moon was his second movie. Sargent states that, "Alan and Bob made it clear that they liked Foote's script but needed another approach." He read neither the novel nor Foote's script because they needed a new screenplay in a hurry. "They told me the story and I wrote on my own with their guidance."

Cavalry major (Frank Silvera) and doctor (Richard Bull) wonder why Sarah is so anxious to leave.

The resulting screenplay improves upon the novel in part because it eliminates all extraneous details that detracted from the main storyline. While the basic plot outline and the most important characters are retained, the film eliminates Sara's baby and Evangeline as well as Hilario. Of equal significance is the fact that the dialogue gradually decreases during the course of the story to the point where there is practically none. Other changes will be apparent from a summary of the film version.

The Stalking Moon begins with the capture of a group of Apaches by a detachment of cavalry troopers. Major Kinship is in command of the company, which includes Army scouts Sam Varner and Nick Tana, who is a half-breed. Among the prisoners are a white woman and her nine-year-old son who is obviously the son of an Apache. She has difficulty speaking English but says that her name is Sarah Carver. Sarah was the only survivor of an attack upon the Carver family that had occurred 10 years earlier. Sam looks at her with pity but places her out of his mind. This has been his last mission and he plans to retire to his small ranch in New Mexico.

When the troopers return to their base, they find that someone has killed all of the soldiers. The signs indicate that there was only one murderer, whom Sam and Nick suspect must be the legendary Apache, Salvaje. Sarah registers this information in silence, her expression reflecting fear.

Back at company headquarters, Sarah frantically tries to explain that she has to leave as soon as possible but Kinship cannot spare any men, particularly since Sam is leaving the next day. After Sarah pleads with Sam to take her with him to Silverton, he reluctantly agrees to take her as far as the Hennessy stage depot where she can get a train to Silverton. That night at Hennessy, when the boy runs away, Sam and Sarah trail him into the desert and have to take shelter from a sand storm. The next morning, they return to the stage depot and find everyone butchered. Her fear steadily increasing, Sarah finally confesses that her son is also Salvaje's son.

Sam now just wants to put Sarah and the boy on the stage and be free of the responsibility for them. But when the stage driver asks him to protect the stage on the way to Silverton, he once again cannot ignore a plea for help. At Silverton, Sam purchases tickets for Sarah and the boy to return East but he quickly realizes that they will be helpless in the big city. After some deliberation, he offers to take Sarah to his ranch to cook for him and his hired hand, Ned. Since New Mexico is so far away, there seems to be little chance that Salvaje will ever find her. Sarah gratefully agrees and they make the long journey by train and buckboard, finally arriving at his ranch. Though the relationship is initially strained, Sarah slowly appears to adjust. However, Nick Tana soon arrives to tell Sam that Salvaje has been tracking them all the way from Arizona, leaving a trail of death and destruction behind him.

The next day, Sam visits a neighboring Mexican family to warn them but discovers that he is too late. He races home to find Sarah missing. Tracking signs, Sam and Nick find her bloody and unconscious in the woods. It is clear that Salvaje didn't kill her because he wants to enjoy taking his revenge upon her and Sam by prolonging their agony before they die. The Apache's brutality and terror tactics increase with each confrontation. First, he kills Ned's dog and then kills Ned. Despite their tracking skills, Sam and Nick cannot find Salvaje who keeps outwitting them. Sam devises a plan to entice Salvaje out into the open but, once again, Salvaje outwits them and kills Nick.

Sam is now determined to fight Salvaje one-on-one in a duel to

Sam and Sarah return to the stage depot to find everyone butchered.

Sam leads a raid upon an Apache stronghold.

the death. This leads to a brutal fight in which only one man can survive. On the surface, it is a duel for the boy and perhaps even for Sarah. But in reality it is a ferocious battle between two antagonists who are equally determined to prove that he is the better man. Sam, bloody and wounded, emerges triumphant and, with Sarah's help, returns to the cabin and to his new family. On a more symbolic level, the battle has been between two civilizations for a land and a country. But the resolution signifies not the triumph of one culture over another but the union of both cultures as represented by the boy, formerly the son of Sarah and Salvaje but now the son of Sarah and Sam.

The Stalking Moon contains fully developed and credible characterizations, beginning with the hero. Though Sam Varner has a reputation for being an excellent cavalry scout, he now just wants to live a peaceful life. He has no idea that he is about to face the biggest challenge of his life, one that will force him to utilize all of his capabilities if he is going to survive. Sam displays his true character initially in small ways as various incidents illustrate his compassion for others. First, he changes his plans because of the desperation in Sarah's eyes and takes her to Hennessy. Then, because of the pleas of the stage driver, he goes further out of his way to accompany the stage to Silverton. Finally, when it is apparent that Sarah and her boy don't have a chance alone, he offers to take them to his ranch. This offer is more logical than in the novel, since there is no suggestion of romance or marriage. Besides providing a home for her and the boy, he hopes that having a cook on the ranch will allow him and Ned to do more work.

Upon Sarah Carver's first appearance, she appears to be frail and cowed with even her voice quaking with fear. But as the details of her 10-year ordeal are revealed, she attains a certain degree of dignity. And as the threat of Salvaje looms increasingly closer, she achieves strength of character. Sarah's palpable fear and desperation also makes her silence about her relationship with Salvaje more comprehensible. In the movie, she doesn't tell an outright lie by saying that Salvaje's brother was her husband as she does in the novel. She doesn't say anything until it becomes apparent that Salvaje is on her trail. Her silence becomes more understandable when she reveals the extent of her shame. Though she is still suffering from the trauma of 10 years of captivity, she also has the burden of guilt. She therefore becomes less culpable for the bloodshed that follows her rescue. Her confession adds vastly to her characterization and also serves as a more believable impetus for the first sign of affection between her and Sam.

Sarah lives in fear from Salvaje.

Salvaje is the film's third major character. It is testament to the film's power that Salvaje as a character is the equal of Sam and Sarah, even though he has very little screen time until the final battle. Despite this, his prowess as a warrior and the results of his rampage are brutally evident. As a result, his presence pervades the entire film. Because Salvaje's rampage occurs sooner than in the novel, the apprehension begins more quickly. Though he is not seen for the first part of the movie, it quickly becomes clear that Salvaje has extraordinary skills because he is able to slaughter anyone who stands in his way. As the eventual confrontation between Sam and Salvaje draws closer, the outcome is certainly in doubt. Although he has committed unspeakable acts which invite repulsion, he elicits some begrudging admiration.

Nick Tana (Robert Forster) has something in common with the boy.

Nick Tana is not only Sam's friend but he symbolizes the kind of life that Sarah's son will have in white society. Nick is a scout for the Army but yet he is apart from the men, except for Sam. He knows that he is different and he accepts this fact in a stoic manner. It is a lonely life, which explains why he travels so far to help Sam, who has always accepted him as a friend, regardless of his ancestry. It also explains why he goes out of his way to befriend the boy whose problems, he knows, will mirror his own. Sam's total disregard for the fact that Nick is a "breed" also signifies the fact that Sam will accept the boy as his son if given a chance.

The boy doesn't have a name since he has not reached the required age in Apache culture to be given one. Though he rarely speaks, he is always next to his mother or nearby. Mostly, he just watches everything that happens, his pensive eyes suggesting deep thought. In the film, he does not display the excessive loyalty toward his father that he has in the novel. In fact, the script deliberately doesn't clarify his emotions toward his father. While this excludes a main plot point which would have had dramatic impact on the screen, it accentuates his devotion to his mother. Moreover, in the novel, Jimmie Joe's loyalty to his father, along with Salvaje's grief at his baby's grave, evokes some sympathy for the warrior. By decreasing the boy's allegiance to his father and eliminating Salvaje's grief, the screenplay decreases the warrior's humanity, which is appropriate to the film's presentation of him as an almost supernatural force.

The climactic sequence, in which Sam and Salvaje finally meet in a duel to the death, is particularly exciting. In the novel, Sam's ultimate victory is due only to the fact that Salvaje does not administer the final death blow. This is not believable since the novel repeatedly demonstrates Salvaje's mercilessness. But instead of killing Sam he leaves him unconscious for no rational reason. The film jettisons this illogical behavior for a more realistic finale in which Salvaje doesn't display any uncharacteristic behavior. In the climactic duel with Sam, he is intent on killing his enemy. Even when Sam has the advantage of reaching his rifle and fires repeatedly at Salvaje, the Apache still summons extraordinary strength to get his hands on Sam to strangle the life out of him. There is little doubt that if Sam hadn't reached the rifle, he would have lost the battle. Salvaje remains the supreme warrior until the end.

Sam and Salvaje (Nathaniel Narcisco) fight to the death.

Robert Mulligan's direction brilliantly elicits all of the strengths of the script. With the aid of cinematographer Charles Lang, Mulligan realizes the screenplay in strong visual terms. There are no extravagant directorial touches and the director tells the story in a severe style that reflects its harshness. Throughout the film, the emphasis remains on the characters, with the landscape itself almost becoming a character. The opening sequence, in which the troopers encircle the band of Apaches, focuses on Sam. The camera pans across the vast landscape with the silhouette of the film's hero moving effortlessly over rock and through canyon. He seems intrusive to the vast surroundings, as though he doesn't belong there. In contrast, once Salvaje appears, the countryside seems to become treacherous because of the many possible shelters it offers to the warrior. Unlike Sam, Salvaje inhabits the surroundings so naturally that he seems to blend in with them. He merges in so completely with the trees and rocks that the terrain itself seems to become his ally. The only refuge for Sam and Sarah is seemingly within the cabin, but even that sanctuary is soon invaded by Salvaje.

While suspense dominates, Mulligan injects some welcome comic touches amidst the tension. When Sam attempts to buy a train ticket for Sarah, the station manager makes the simple purchase so complicated that

Sam looks like he wants to throttle the man. During their first night at the ranch, Sarah is obviously nervous while the boy seems uncomfortable. To relieve the stress, Sam tells them that that they should feel free to talk about anything. But then he can't think of anything to talk about except passing the butter. The scene in which Nick tries to teach the boy to play cards and smoke cigars is a model of gentle comedy. However, even the few lighthearted scenes occur with an undercurrent of anxiety. Behind all of these scenes lurks the unseen but threatening shadow of Salvaje. The tension steadily and inexorably increases until Salvaje arrives at the homestead. Suspense and action then take precedence and build quickly from one violent encounter to another until the much-anticipated duel and its cathartic climax.

The performances of the major actors are central to the film's success. Gregory Peck brings his usual dignity and sincerity to the role of Sam Varner. While he initially underplays, correctly sensing his character's natural reticence, he gradually gives full reign to his feelings as circumstances change. He perfectly conveys his shifting sentiments regarding Sarah through subtle changes in his expression. As anger and eventually sympathy replace pity and apathy, his expression and tone clearly indicate his internal conflict. Peck also initially projects self-confidence in his portrayal, though his antagonist gradually shatters this poise. And when Salvaje kills Nick, Sam totally loses his self-control not only because of the loss of his friend but because his enemy has again smashed his assurance of his capabilities, this time with fatal consequences. The fury in his eyes as he goes out to face Salvaje suggest a steely determination to show his enemy that he may have lost the battles but he will win the war. Peck's superb performance reflects all of these emotions.

As Sarah Carver, Eva Marie Saint is not afraid to look unglamorous. From her vacant eyes to her bland complexion, it is obvious that hardship and pain consumed the previous 10 years for Sarah, as evident from her submissive manner and the trembling in her voice. When she speaks English, her halting attempts at communication suggest that she has difficulty forming words and then putting them together correctly. The fear in her face when she pleads first with Major Kinship and then Sam clearly gives an indication of the threat from which she is trying so desperately to escape. And her confession to Sam is extremely poignant in its simplicity because of the emotion with which she invests her words. Saint's performance is a perfectly realized one and both complements and contrasts with Peck's more assertive and dominant role.

The supporting players are all fine. As Nick Tana, Robert Forster creates a likeable character. His delivery of words, frequently accompanied by a twinkle in the eye, suggests a person who has come to terms with prejudice and sees it as society's problem, not his. The scenes at the beginning of the movie are very important because he must establish Nick's affection for Sam to pave the way for his willingness to travel so long and eventually to give his life for his friend. Forster conveys this feeling through discreet glances toward Sam and a minimum of words prior to his mentor's retirement. And, although his role is a brief one, Frank Silvera makes his usual compelling appearance as Major Kinship. Silvera was black but he could convincingly play black, white, Indian, Mexican, Tahitian, Italian, virtually anything.

Sarah and the boy face an uncertain future.

Noland Clay, an actual Apache youth, plays the boy with a welcome avoidance of the usual sugary cuteness displayed by so many Hollywood child actors. Indeed, he doesn't even smile but correctly projects the confusion he is experiencing. This absence of any attempt to endear himself to Sam (or to viewers) brings a welcome credibility to the role. As Salvaje, Nathaniel Narcisco doesn't have too much of an opportunity to make an impression as an actor since he has to be a ghost-like presence for the majority of the film. But when he does make his long-awaited appearance, it is with a ferocity that still manages to have a powerful impact. Apparently, neither Noland Clay nor Nathaniel Narcisco ever appeared in another movie.

All of the production qualities of the movie are first-rate. Throughout the film, little touches add to the authenticity. The stagecoach is so rickety that it conveys just how uncomfortable it must have been to travel by such means in the Old West. The makeshift cavalry base lacks any modicum of romanticism and suggests only a thankless way of life for the soldiers. The interior of Sam's cabin looks like the kind of dwelling that people actually lived in and gives an indication of how few comforts were available in the not-so-distant past. The stage depot and the train station also look like they are straight out of photographs of the real West. This realism pervades the film and adds to the believability of the story.

Fred Karlin's haunting musical score is a perfect complement to the story, conveying the emotion of the human drama, the suspense of the conflict and the excitement of the action sequences. The main title theme, featuring a solo whistler (Muzzy Marcelino) and a guitar (Al Hendrickson), is a perfect representation of Sam Varner, suggesting both nobility and loneliness. Sarah's musical accompaniment, on the other hand, conveys agony and frailty. However, just as Salvaje dominates the movie, he also dominates the score. Karlin uses soft string and woodwind instruments to convey the warrior's formidable attributes. Throughout the entire film, even during some of the quieter scenes, the suitably eerie and chilling theme suggests Salvaje's probable but concealed presence and conveys the fear that he might be lying in wait just out of sight. This theme pervades

the entire score, thus adding immensely to the sense of foreboding that permeates the film. (No soundtrack album was available at the time of the film's release; in 2002, Reel Music Down Under, an Australian label, released a compact disc of the complete score.)

Some critics gave *The Stalking Moon* terrible reviews. "Murph" in *Variety* couldn't find enough negative adjectives to describe the movie, calling it "a dull suspenser [with] ineffective stars, a poor script, clumsy plot structuring and limp direction which produces tedious pacing." Murph must have had his mind on surfing instead of watching the movie because the review is totally off the wall. But he was not alone in his criticism. Joseph Morgenstern in *Newsweek* wrote that the film is "painfully long on meaningful glances and pregnant silences and strives too hard to be a classic." And Vincent Canby in *The New York Times* called it "a pious, unimaginative suspense film."

Fortunately, other reviewers were more perceptive. *Film Daily*'s reviewer wrote that, "The picture is an exceptionally fine one and sets the screen ablaze with action and excitement." Arthur Knight in *The Saturday Review* called it a "good, old-fashioned story, excitingly told," adding that "this is Pakula-Mulligan's first Western and with the aid of a notably laconic script, they have pulled it off beautifully." *Time*'s reviewer praised Gregory Peck and wrote that "the suspense winds as taut as leather." Richard Schickel in *Life* Magazine called the film "an experience in sheer terror that transcends the externals of the Western genre to become one of the great scare films of all time."

Such reviews didn't help the film's performance at the box office. On *Variety*'s list of Top-Grossing Films for 1969, 90 movies earned more than the minimum amount of one million dollars in domestic theatrical rentals. *The Stalking Moon* is Number 38 with a disappointing $2.6 million. *Butch Cassidy and the Sundance Kid* with Paul Newman and Robert Redford was the highest-grossing Western of the year and is 4th on the list with $15 million (this figure doubled after the film's re-release in 1974); this overpraised movie has an ostensibly modish appeal, due to its incongruous score and dialogue, but it lacks genuine drama and is trivial. Two superior Westerns are also on the list: *True Grit* with John Wayne is 6th and earned $14.5 million and *The Wild Bunch* with William Holden is Number 23 with $5.2 million. Other Westerns include a diverse selection of oaters. *Support Your Local Sheriff*, an amusing spoof with James Garner earned $5 million. *The Undefeated* with John Wayne made $4.5 million. *100 Rifles* with Jim Brown was the first major-studio Western with a black hero and made $3.5 million. *Mackenna's Gold* finally opened, though not as a Cinerama roadshow presentation as originally planned and with its running time considerably shortened; it earned $3.1 million.

(Incidentally, though *Mackenna's Gold* was a commercial disappointment domestically, it was immensely popular in many foreign markets. In the Soviet Union, it was extraordinarily successful and today is still the 4th top-grossing foreign movie. In India, it played in cinemas for several years and was the all-time top Hollywood grosser for decades. The article in the 2014 inaugural issue of *The Indian Quarterly* entitled "Old Is Not Just Gold, It's Mackenna's Gold" is a detailed account by writer Kaushik Bhaumik of why this movie had such a tremendous impact upon the population of India as well as Indian filmmakers. In 2015, the Todd-AO 70mm Festival at the Shauburg Cinerama Theater in Germany presented a rare Super Panavision 70 mm print of the film.)

Gregory Peck, Eva Marie Saint Star in Film, 'The Stalking Moon'

CHILD ACTOR Noland Clay doesn't want to be rescued by U.S. Army and flees from troopers in this scene from "The Stalking Moon."

Valley of Fire Now Hollywood-in-the-Desert

By LOIS PERKINS

"The Stalking Moon" Theodore V. Olsen's best-seller, became a real live pulsing drama under the expert hands of title screenwriters Horton Foote and Alvin Sargent, and the sensitive direction of Robert Mulligan, assisted by his partner and producer Alan Pakula.

The period of the Pakula-Mulligan Production is in the 1800's, with the beginning of the dramatic story being filmed in the northern part of the scenic Valley of Fire State Park, 15 miles from Overton Sarah Carver (Eva Marie Saint) is rescued from a band of Apache Indians by U.S. Army troopers, after having been a prisoner for ten years. She has a nine-year-old son, whose father is a fierce renegade killer by the name of Salvaje. (This star had not yet been found at the time the crew was moved from the Overton area to their next location set near Las Vegas)

Eva Marie Saint brilliantly plays the part of the exhausted, bewildered young woman, who after so many years had almost given up hope of being rescued. Her son, played by Noland Clay (a new star) is resentful over being rescued, and tries to escape from the U.S. Army.

Sarah Carver and her son, along with a band of Indians, are brought to the U.S. Army Post under the direction of Sergeant Rudabaugh (Henry Beckman), where she is greeted by Major Winfield (Frank Silvera). She requests an immediate escort to return to her home, but is told that this is impossible.

Gregory Peck, who takes the important role of Sam Varner, a professional scout is at the post on Sarah Carver's arrival. Varner has worked with the detachment of Army Troopers for many years, helping to restrain Apache Indian outbreaks from the reservations of Arizona and New Mexico. He has trained as a scout, and leaves the "breed" Nick to fill his position as Scout, quitting his position with the Post. He agrees (after much persuasion) to take Sarah and her son to Silverton to catch a train east.

Enroute to Silverton, a narrow escape from Salvaje, who is determined to recover his son at any cost, changes the mind of Sam Varney. He takes Sarah and the boy to his New Mexico ranch, where he feels they will be safe.

Sarah recovers from her lengthy years of trouble under the thoughtful care she receives, but her son remains sullen and rebellious, missing his father. Nick, the good friend of Varney, travels to the ranch to warn Sam that Salvaje has left death in his path tracking down his son and that indications are the killer is close at hand.

'SUPER-HUMAN FOE'

A Mexican family living near the Varney ranch is ruthlessly murdered, and the "stalking" begins. Sam, leaving old Ned (Russ Thorson) to watch Sarah and her son, accompanied by his friend and scout, Nick, starts on the lengthy search for the renegade killer. Salvaje. Nick states "Salvaje is super-human." After days of tracking and finding nothing, they discover Sarah, whom Salvaje had had been brutally raped and left unconscious and bleeding beside the trail.

Returning Sarah to the ranch, Sam and Nick once again start on their search, a search that uses the best way they have learned in their many years of being scouts. They are up against an expert, a "super human" evasive enemy.

Publicity Manager Art Wilde states, "Producer Alan Pakula and Director Robert Mulligan have planned their motion picture, 'The Stalking Moon' to be made without artifice; a suspense drama with built-in universal appeal, panorama of a rocky wasteland seldom seen in a theatrical film and a warm, sympathetic look at an attractive child's first attempt to grope toward identification. A large order, but with a tight visual-oriented screenplay, a topflight technical staff, Gregory Peck and Eva Marie Saint as stars, a distinguished cast of supporting players and the sensitivity expressed by the producers in their past films, a distinct possibility."

Robert Mulligan, Alan Pakula and Gregory Peck made seven history with "To Kill a Mockingbird" and most recently, again with Pakula-Mulligan producing and directing "Up the Down Staircase"

The team of Pakula-Mulligan dates back to simultaneous entry into filmmaking with "Fear Strikes Out," co-starring Anthony Perkins and Karl Malden in the story of baseball star Jim Piersall. Fourteen years ago Mulligan was a messenger boy at CBS in New York and Pakula was a production apprentice at MGM Studios in Hollywood.

"The Stalking Moon" is the second blue chip film production to be distributed by National General Pictures. Late in 1967, this company pooled the talents of the country's top theater distribution brains to film only on a limited basis of 12 maximum per year. Its first film, also in production at this time, is the Debbie Reynolds-James Garner color comedy, "How Sweet It Is."

Cinematographer on "The Stalking Moon" is the veteran movie lenser Charles Lang, winner of many Academy Awards for his spectacular photography. For some time, Lang's ambition has been to document south western United States in a manner that will be of geographical (Continued on Page 5)

4 LAS VEGAS SUN

Sunday, January 28, 1968

Lower on the list, *Once Upon a Time in the West* is Number 47 with $2.1 million; this elephantine would-be epic with Henry Fonda at the nadir of his career has to be the most infantile, the most tedious, the most soporific, the most pretentious, the most overrated and the most unintentionally laughable Western of the decade; the opening segment is one of many that is guaranteed to cure insomnia. *Charro* with Elvis Presley and the modern Western *Smith!* with Glenn Ford were Numbers 68 and 69 with $1.5

GREGORY PECK, comfortably costumed in buckskins, reviews lines for his next scene with script supervisor Meta Rebner.

YOUNG co-star Robert Forster chats with sound supervisor Jack Solomon. Maintaining sensitive sound and camera equipment in primitive location settings is one of the challenges of movie production units.

Western Films Universal Favorites, and Hollywood Supplies the World

Behind the Scenes As New Pakula-Mulligan Production Bivouacs in Nevada

(Continued from Page 4)

and anthropological value as well as pleasing to the eye. In that regard, "The Stalking Moon's" locations at Nevada's Valley of Fire, Tule Springs and Pine Creek have never before been photographed by movie crews.

Film Editor Aaron Stell marks "The Stalking Moon" as a good luck venture. He won Academy Award nominations working with Pakula and Mulligan on "Mockingbird" and "Inside Daisy Clover." He, most recently, finished editing "Fade-In" for Paramount. Stell and his assistants have set up a complete film editing workshop in a still uncompleted supermarket at Echo Bay, Nevada—the first such elaborate cutting room and Panavision projection room ever devised while a movie company worked on an extended location. The camera assistants have a place in the market, also. They use the walk-in deep freeze compartment in the butcher department to load and unload Technicolor film into their camera's magazines. The refrigeration unit has not been completed yet, fortunately.

Russ Saunders, Unit Production manager, coordinates the movement and work of over 110 members of Pakula-Mulligan's staff and crew, as well as the hundreds of extra atmosphere people who appear as Army troopers and Indians in the movie. Russ was a star quarterback for the University of Southern California and pivot back for the Green Bay Packers. Saunders began his movie career in 1932 at Warner Bros. Studio as a second assistant director, rose to first assistant director and for the past ten years has been production manager and second unit director for top quality films. His latest credit is as production manager for Warren Beatty's "Bonnie and Clyde."

SPECTACULAR SETS

The sets for "The Stalking Moon" are as spectacular as any used for films. Along with using the natural terrain in southern Nevada, art director Roland Anderson has used a box canyon in the Valley of Fire to recreate a U.S. Army outpost exactly as documents proved it actually was in 1881. No stockades or blockhouses here. According to the novel and screenplay, the action takes place in an area considered remote even in the '80's. With towering rock of every hue disemboweled from the earth and etching their gigantic, jagged figures against a cobalt blue skyline, the New York skyline gone berserk, forming the background, Anderson has constructed dozens of tents, wagons, corrals and cooking sites and decorated them with authentic armament, surgical supplies, cooking utensils, cots and saddlery exactly of the period. There are even rough-hewn chopping blocks, piles of firewood, a blacksmith working and a man turning the large stone for sharpening of knives and swords.

The set is magnificent. You can feel the drama of the story, almost visualize the finished production.

EVA MARIE SAINT is readied for next shot by team of "Nannies". In rear, Naomi Cavin, hairdresser; left and right, makeup artists Del Armstrong and Frank Prehoda.

Sunday, January 28, 1968

LAS VEGAS SUN 5

million. Several Westerns that did not earn the million dollar minimum include *Young Billy Young* with Robert Mitchum, *Death of a Gunfighter* with Richard Widmark, *Sam Whiskey* with Burt Reynolds and *Heaven with a Gun* with Glenn Ford.

One factor that may have impacted upon the box-office reception of *The Stalking Moon* was the time of its release. The movie premiered in Los Angeles on Christmas Day in 1968, not the best time to open a Western

Good Movies...Evil Wars 199

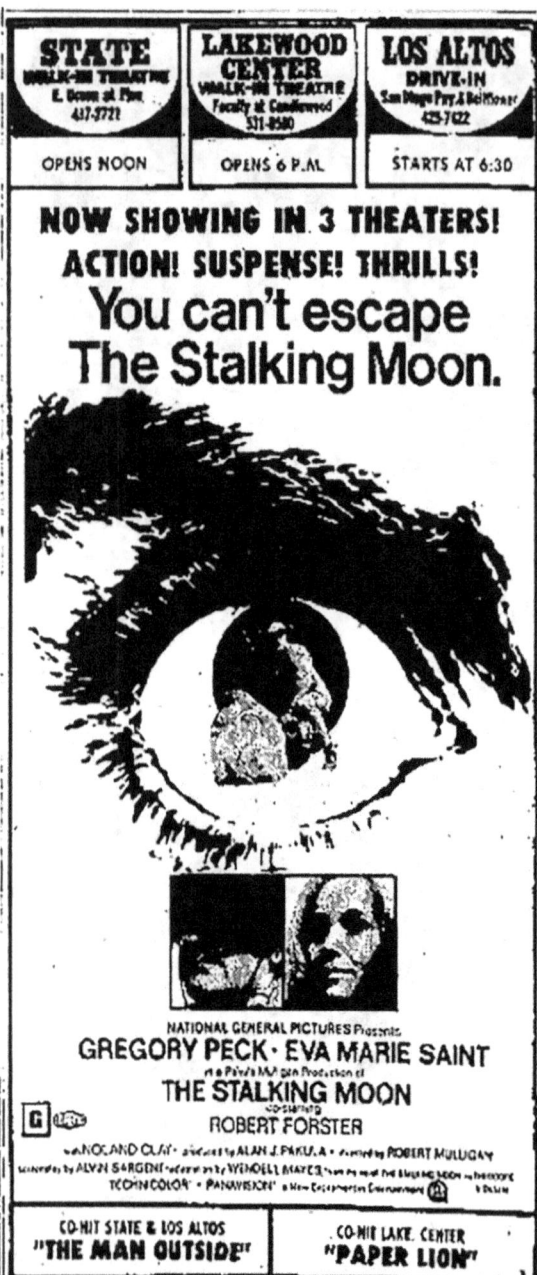

about terror and carnage. In many other major cities, it opened in January 1969, one week after Richard Nixon's inauguration as president. There was a general feeling of discontent about Nixon's ascendancy to the presidency, due in part to the knowledge that he would not have been elected if President John F. Kennedy and his brother Robert Kennedy had not been assassinated. The fact that Chief Justice Earl Warren, nominal author of the infamous tissue of lies known as the Warren Report which totally suppressed the truth of JFK's assassination, administered the oath of office to Nixon added to the mood of hostility.

Many American citizens knew that something was seriously wrong with the country. In their judgment, the United States had transmuted from a bastion of democracy and freedom into an imperialistic regime intent on oppressing other nations; and in Vietnam, it was sacrificing the blood of young Americans to achieve that objective. (Historical and political details of the Vietnam War are included in the next chapter.) Although public discontent and rage over the Vietnam War had forced Lyndon Johnson out of office, it was already obvious that Richard Nixon had no intention of ending the war. In this type of environment, many potential moviegoers seethed with resentment and patronized only counter-cultural movies.

Another significant factor in the film's commercial failure was the status of the Western genre at the time of its release. By the late 1960s, traditional Westerns were losing their appeal for the general public. For a Western to be successful at the box office, potential ticket-buyers had to perceive it as being different or having something unique. Furthermore, anti-Westerns were particularly fashionable with younger audiences that snobbishly considered themselves too sophisticated for conventional Westerns. Such audiences would applaud the politically correct revisionist Westerns of the 1970s which displayed contempt for the genre.

Pakula and Mulligan did not want to appeal to these audiences. They intended to make a different kind of Western but not a radical one and certainly not an anti-Western. They were intent on maintaining but not mythologizing the folklore of traditional Westerns. While the movie paints a picture of the Old West that differs from the idealized vision, it still respects the basic ingredients of the genre. The environment that the film depicts may be harsh but there still exists the time-honored Western hero who is faced with a test of fortitude to match any traditional hero of the classic Westerns. Furthermore, these classical Western elements merge with the type of suspenseful traits associated with thrillers, or even with some supernatural films. This mixture works brilliantly.

Nevertheless, biased critics despised *The Stalking Moon* because of its traditional aspects. They scorned it because the hero is a white man and the villain is an Indian. Thus, the political correctness of the period hurt it with Pauline Kael in *The New Yorker* exemplifying this position. "For years, Westerns have tried to be respectful and sympathetic toward Indians," she wrote as if lecturing to the ignorant masses, "and now *The Stalking Moon* goes back to the most primitive movie image of the vicious savage." On and on she babbled sanctimoniously, implying that the movie was racist and censuring other critics who liked the movie. This is the same person who once wrote that, "I don't believe that there ever were the great works in the (Western) genre that so many people claim for it." This is such an absurd statement that, besides exposing her obvious bias against Westerns, it connotes an appalling ignorance of cinema history.

However, this view was chic among critics who fancied themselves as elitists and today the movie still incurs the wrath of revisionist historians who refuse to comprehend that there were good Indians and bad Indians just as there were good whites and bad whites. These revisionists also criticize the film for its denial of a natural father's rights toward his son. They don't seem to have any complaint with the fact that Salvaje massacred Sarah's family and held her prisoner for 10 years. Like Kael, they have a myopic vision which distorts their opinions and blinds them to any other view. Also like Kael, they have bitsighaa tazhii, which means—roughly translated from Apache—the brains of a turkey.

Sarah and Sam know that Salvaje is getting closer.

The Stalking Moon has been subject to recent analysis from a political perspective. In *Hollywood's Frontier Captives* (Garland; 2000), Barbara Mortimer writes: "The film conveys a new form of cultural anxiety from the war in Vietnam: a disquieting sense that American cultural self-confidence and moral rectitude rest on a facile ignorance of non-industrialized societies." Mortimer equates "the Indians and the Vietnamese as resilient, resourceful non-white native populations ultimately at the mercy of American weaponry" and concludes: "The film suggests unmistakably that, were it not for having plenty of guns and plenty of people, Anglo-Americans would definitely have lost their war for land with the Indians; the relevance of this point to the escalating war in Vietnam during the late 1960s seems obvious, at least in retrospect."

(Gregory Peck, incidentally, opposed the Vietnam War. However, he was supportive of the military, especially since his son was in the Marine Corps in Vietnam. In 1972, Peck produced *The Trial of the Catonsville Nine*, about nine protestors who burned hundreds of draft records and were convicted of destruction of Selective Service files and interference with the Selective Service Act. Peck officially earned a place on Richard Nixon's "Master List of Political Opponents," a supplement to his "Enemies List.")

In addition to its possible allegorical messages, *The Stalking Moon* can now be judged more objectively. In the history of movies, time often corrects past offenses. In their book, *50 Years of American Cinema* (Omnibus; 1995), authors Jean-Pierre Coursodon and Bernard Tavernier call *The Stalking Moon* "Mulligan's masterpiece." In March 2009, the Film Society of Lincoln Center presented a festival of the director's films, including *The Stalking Moon*, which Associate Director of Programming Kent Jones called "Robert Mulligan's unsung masterpiece of moral suspense." At the conclusion of the film, the audience spontaneously applauded. If Pauline Kael could have heard that applause, smoke signals would have burst out of her ears.

Nick tries to befriend the boy.

The Stalking Moon entertains, excites and frightens. It is Pakula-Mulligan's best film and is a notable achievement in the careers of all of its artists. Alan J. Pakula subsequently established a career as a director; he never directed a Western but his films include the superb thriller, *The Parallax View* (1974), which is fiction but contains more truth about the political assassinations of the 1960s than the official government versions. Robert Mulligan never directed another Western. Alvin Sargent never wrote another Western. Wendell Mayes wrote one more Western, *The Revengers* (1972), which was unremarkable; he also wrote the compelling Vietnam War movie, *Go Tell the Spartans* (1978). During the rest of his five-decade career, Gregory Peck starred in two more Westerns, *Shoot-Out* (1971) and *Billy Two Hats* (1974), both undistinguished, as well as the Mexican Revolution-era *Old Gringo* (1989). His second and last association with the team of Pakula and Mulligan stands out as a superlative example of the Western genre.

The Stalking Moon is an exceptional movie.

CREDITS: Producer: Alan J. Pakula; Director: Robert Mulligan; Screenplay: Alvin Sargent; Adaptation: Wendell Mayes, From the Novel by Theodore V. Olsen; Cinematographer: Charles Lang; Editor: Aaron Stell; Music: Fred Karlin

CAST: Gregory Peck (Sam Varner); Eva Marie Saint (Sarah Carver); Robert Forster (Nick Tana); Noland Clay (Boy); Nathaniel Narcisco (Salvaje); Russell Thorson (Ned); Frank Silvera (Major Kinship); Lonny Chapman (Purdue); Lou Frizzell (Stationmaster); Henry Beckman (Sgt. Rudabaugh); Charles Tyner (Dace); Richard Bull (Doctor); Red Morgan (Stage Driver); Joaquin Martinez (Julio); Sandy Wyeth (Rachel); James Olsen (Cavalry Officer)

THE BRIDGE AT REMAGEN

The soldier feels tired and depressed. Dead bodies are everywhere. He feels guilty to be alive. As the tanks roll victoriously across the bridge, he walks recklessly alongside, almost hoping a bullet will crash into him. And then he hears his name called out in the darkness. The voice is familiar. But the man that voice belonged to is dead. He looks toward the sound of the voice and can't believe his eyes. It is his friend; his closest friend. And he is alive. The soldier runs to him as his friend smiles warmly at him. They are so happy to see one another that tears well up in their eyes. Out of the horror of war has been born a friendship that is as deep and true as either one of them had ever known.

In March 1945, U.S. Army Lieutenant Karl Timmermann wrote to his wife, "There's no glory in war. Maybe those that have never been in battle find that certain glory and glamour that doesn't exist. Perhaps they get it from movies or comic strips." They wouldn't get it from a movie based upon a World War II battle in which Timmermann played a major part. In 1969, United Artists released a film based upon that battle. The title is *The Bridge at Remagen*. Despite its merits, it became a casualty of the turbulent era in which it appeared. It was a time of political assassinations, civil unrest and the Vietnam War. A brief review of the roots of the Vietnam War and the war's impact on American society may explain why the movie failed at the box office.

In 1883, France colonized Vietnam. In 1930, Ho Chi Minh, a Marxist revolutionary, created the Vietnamese Communist Party to oppose French colonialism. During WWII, the Japanese invaded Vietnam. Ho formed the Viet Minh to fight the Japanese as well as the French. The United States provided military aid to Ho's guerilla forces and President Roosevelt promised Ho that the U.S. would recognize an independent Vietnam following the war. After the war ended, Ho established his government in the north and France established a government in the south. Ho appealed to President Truman to honor Roosevelt's pledge of independence but Truman refused.

When France attacked the Viet Minh forces in 1946 to regain control of the nation, the First Indochina War began. Truman recognized the French regime as the legitimate government while the Soviet Union's Joseph Stalin recognized Ho's regime. Truman sent financial aid to the French military while Stalin sent aid to the Viet Minh. In 1952, President Eisenhower inherited this quandary. Eisenhower favored colonial domination because he believed it would suppress communism. At the urging of his Secretary of State John Foster Dulles, he increased financial aid and

Japanese poster for *The Bridge at Remagen*

military supplies to the French; estimates are that, by this time, the United States was paying for approximately 75% of the Indochina war. He also provided military supplies, including 10 bombers. More significantly, he sent the first American military personnel, called advisors, to Vietnam.

After Ho's forces defeated the French at Dien Bien Phu in 1954, the Geneva Accords divided Vietnam into two countries with the provision that free elections in 1956 would unify north and south. With France no longer a player, both the United States and the Soviet Union wanted to control Vietnam. Because Ho espoused nationalism, he was popular among the Vietnamese people who wanted to be free of foreign intervention. Dulles and his brother, CIA Director Allen Dulles, feared that Ho would win in an election and, with Eisenhower's blessing and without consulting the Vietnamese people, chose anti-communist Ngo Dinh Diem to govern in the south. (The Dulles brothers rationalized such intervention by proclaiming that nationalist leaders in colonized countries were tools of Stalin and, thus, enemies in the Cold War. Consequently, they justified interfering in those nations and, whenever possible, the CIA instigated coup d'états as well as assassinations.) Only the supreme arrogance of the Dulles brothers can explain, to some degree, American entrance into Vietnam affairs to fill the void left by the French. *Hell in a Very Small Place* by Bernard Fall (Lippincott; 1966, Da Capo Press; 2002) is the definitive account of the French defeat at Dien Bien Phu and should have been a forewarning to the United States to stay out of the country. But American imperialists thought they could succeed where French imperialists had failed and were ready to shed American blood, though not their own, to replace French blood.

While Eisenhower was cautious in his dealings with the behemoths of the Soviet Union and China, he tended to be more aggressive in Third World countries and sent additional military advisors to South Vietnam. His loathing of communism made him susceptible to the Dulles brothers who repeatedly pressed for military intervention in not only Vietnam but Laos and Cambodia. Meanwhile, the leaders of the two Vietnam regimes tightened their dictatorial reigns and drew increasingly closer to war. Diem discarded his promise of democracy and began a despotic reign that killed an estimated 75,000 people. Ho discarded his promise of nationalism and implemented a Stalinist-type land reform policy that killed more than 600,000 people. During this period, the CIA conducted covert paramilitary operations to undermine Ho while the KGB, the Soviet equivalent of the CIA, trained South Vietnamese villagers to create the National Liberation Front, also known as the Viet Cong, to undermine Diem.

In 1960, Vice-President Richard Nixon promised the CIA that he would support its Vietnam war policy if he was elected president in November. But two obstacles impeded the Agency's plans for war. First, Eisenhower planned a peace summit in May in Paris with Soviet Premier Nikita Khrushchev, much to the displeasure of the CIA. (Perhaps Eisenhower regretted allowing the CIA to overthrow elected governments in Guatemala and Iran; perhaps Khrushchev regretted being known as "the Butcher of Budapest.") On May 1, a CIA U-2 spy plane crashed in Russia, thus effectively scuttling the summit. Though Eisenhower didn't publicly express his suspicions about who had sabotaged his peace plan, he did find a forum in which to articulate his viewpoint. In his farewell address, he warned the nation about the growing influence of the military-industrial complex, an amalgamation of military and business interests; he cautioned that this group's covert power could threaten the nation's democracy.

The second obstacle to war was the election of John F. Kennedy to the presidency. As congressman and senator, Kennedy had criticized the CIA's support of the French in Vietnam because he saw the conflict not as a battle between democracy and communism but between nationalism and colonialism. In 1957, Senator Kennedy had proclaimed to Congress that it was vital for America to signal to the world that it was going to separate itself from European colonialism. Kennedy's anti-colonialist views infuriated the industrialists who had made fortunes exploiting third world countries. Those same views enraged the CIA and the Dulles brothers whose worst fears were realized when JFK was elected president. Within weeks of his inauguration, Kennedy enraged the CIA by not sending military forces to support the Bay of Pigs invasion into Cuba, which had been a colonial prize until Fidel Castro overthrew the corrupt CIA-installed government; as Vice President, Nixon had promised the CIA he would send in American troops at the Bay of Pigs to install another puppet dictator. JFK further infuriated the Agency and the imperialists by refusing to wage war over the Cuban Missile Crisis. And when he subsequently initiated rapprochement proposals to Castro who responded positively, the Agency and their imperialistic colleagues went ballistic.

However, Cuba was only one part of President Kennedy's determination to end his nation's support of colonialism. During his administration, he implemented programs to support nationalism throughout the world, including Southeast Asia, Latin America, the Middle East and Africa. *JFK: Ordeal in Africa* by Richard D. Mahoney (Oxford University Press; 1983) demonstrates how Kennedy combated powerful colonialist forces within his own country, including the corporate powerbrokers of Wall Street, as well as European imperialists in his effort to support independence for the newly developed African nations. More recent scholarly books such as *Kennedy, Johnson and the Nonaligned World* by Robert B. Rakove (Cambridge University Press; 2012), *Betting On the Africans* by Philip E. Muehlenbeck (Oxford University Press; 2012) and *The Incubus of Intervention* by Greg

Pouligrain (Strategic Information Research Development Center; 2015) provide incontrovertible evidence of how radically dissimilar his policies were from those of his predecessors (except FDR) as well as those of his successors. John F. Kennedy represented a grave and unprecedented threat to the rabid imperialists who despised him and his nationalist policies.

And in no other area of the world was there so much at stake for the CIA and the military industrial complex as there was in Vietnam. Too many powerful forces were banking on an American war in Vietnam. President Kennedy repeatedly and adamantly repelled those forces. Though he increased the number of advisors to train the South Vietnamese Army, he believed that the best way to defeat communism was through political and economic policies, not by involving American troops in a war. He knew that committing troops to Southeast Asia would be an unmitigated disaster. In October 1963, he signed National Security Action Memorandum 263 which mandated that the withdrawal of all U.S. personnel from Vietnam would begin in December 1963 and be completed by 1965. On November 22, 1963, he was assassinated

Many books have since documented the relationship of his assassination to the Vietnam War, including *JFK and Vietnam* by John Newman (Warner Books; 1992), *JFK: The CIA, Vietnam and the Plot to Assassinate John F. Kennedy* by Fletcher Prouty (Birch Lane Press; 1992) and *American Tragedy: Kennedy, Johnson and the Origins of the Vietnam War* by David Kaiser (Belknap Press/Harvard University Press; 2000). These scrupulously researched books substantiate the following facts: the policies that led to the war were developed by the Dulles brothers during Eisenhower's administration, with the endorsement of Vice President Nixon who planned to continue those policies if elected president; the CIA forcibly transported over one million refugees from North Vietnam to the south to instigate a civil war that would require American involvement; JFK repeatedly resisted his military and civilian advisors who coveted American intervention in Vietnam and adamantly refused to commit ground troops to Southeast Asia; JFK was the only impediment to realization of the Agency's plans and his elimination paved the way for the war; Lyndon Johnson reversed Kennedy's policies and continued the policies initiated by the Dulles brothers, Eisenhower and Nixon.

Shortly after Kennedy's funeral, President Johnson exhibited the hubris that equaled that of the Dulles brothers, now represented only by Allen Dulles (Foster died in 1959). He authorized NSAM 273 which cancelled JFK's directive to withdraw from Vietnam and sanctioned covert operations against the North Vietnamese Army. In March, 1964 Johnson authorized NSAM 288 which prepared for the mining of harbors, a naval blockade and air attacks upon military and industrial sites in North Vietnam. In August, 1964 Congress passed the Gulf of Tonkin Resolution which gave Johnson authorization for the use of total military force in Vietnam. In March, 1965 Johnson (who, during his 1964 campaign for election, promised not to send "American boys" to Vietnam) sent the first American ground troops to Vietnam. Thus, the Vietnam War—the Second Indochina War—officially began. Soon thereafter, the anti-draft movement began.

By 1966, U.S. troops in Vietnam numbered 200,000 and steadily increased to over 400,000. Johnson's massive and horrific bombing campaign succeeded only in killing far more civilians than enemy combatants. Meanwhile, on the ground, Americans continued to die and be maimed in increasing numbers. As hundreds and then thousands of American troops came home in body bags, hostile resistance to the draft steadily amplified. This antagonism fully exploded in the year 1968. In February, the Selective Service System drafted 48,000 men, the second highest number since the beginning of the war. On February 18, the military posted the highest casualty rate of the war for a single week—542 killed and 2,547 wounded.

The assassinations of Martin Luther King in April and Robert Kennedy in June, both of whom opposed the war, increased animosity toward the government. Anti-war protests increased as young men burned their draft cards and echoed the refrain: "Hey, hey, LBJ, how many kids have you killed today?" Due to his unpopularity, Johnson abandoned his plans for re-election. At the Democratic National Convention in Chicago in August, more than 10,000 protestors, including members of the National Mobilization Committee to End the War in Vietnam, demonstrated and were confronted by over 27,000 police and National Guardsmen. (*Chicago Eyewitness* by Mark Lane, published by Astor-Honor, is a personal account of the riots, violence and excessive police brutality that occurred.) During Johnson's last year in office, over 540,000 U.S. troops were in Vietnam. During his administration, over 37,000 Americans died in Vietnam.

In 1968, Richard Nixon campaigned for the presidency on a promise to end the war. However, after he was elected president, he expanded the war into Cambodia and Laos. *Nixon's Nuclear Specter: The Secret Alert of 1969, Madman Diplomacy and the Vietnam War* by William Burr and Jeffrey Kimball (University Press of Kansas; 2015) reveals that Nixon and his Secretary of State Henry Kissinger attempted to end the war by convincing the North Vietnamese and Russia that he was so unstable that he would use nuclear weapons to achieve victory. This tactic did not work and the war continued, becoming increasingly more barbaric and unwinnable. In 1969, the American public learned about the My Lai massacre of the previous year in which a U.S. Army unit murdered over 500 villagers, including women and children; this was just one atrocity of the CIA's Phoenix Program which slaughtered an estimated 26,000 civilians suspected of being communists. The North Vietnamese Army had a similar policy

SMILES OF TRIUMPH
The Nixon family members stand together in New York after Richard Nixon's election as president. Left to right are David Eisenhower, Julie, Tricia, Nixon and Mrs. Nixon. The President-elect holds an emblem Julie made.

toward villagers that they suspected of being American sympathizers; the Hue massacre is one example of the NVA carnage which killed more than 160,000 civilians. During Nixon's administration, more than 21,000 Americans died in Vietnam.

And those Americans, like those under Johnson's reign, need not have been sacrificed. *Fatal Politics: The Nixon Tapes, the Vietnam War and the Casualties of Reelection* by Ken Hughes (University of Virginia Press; 2015) reveals that, in the initial years of his presidency, Nixon and Kissinger had concluded that the United States could never win the war in Vietnam. Nevertheless, he prolonged the nation's military involvement because he knew that early withdrawal and admission of defeat would destroy his chances for re-election. In 1973, the year after his reelection, American forces withdrew from Vietnam.

In retrospect, it is understandable that the 1960s exploded in rebellion and violence. Under Presidents Johnson and Nixon, the United States had ostensibly become the kind of imperialist nation that it had defeated in World War II. This perception infiltrated the production and the reception of Hollywood movies. Just as WWII had a pervasive impact upon the films of the 1940s and 1950s, the Vietnam War had a similar impact upon the films of the 1960s and 1970s.

Prior to the Vietnam era, war movies glorified democracy and patriotism with an underlying message that war was abhorrent but necessary when defending freedom and fighting totalitarian nations. By the late 1960s, this type of war film was no longer popular. The costly *Anzio* (1968) failed at the box office while low-budget movies such as *Attack On the Iron Coast* (1967) and *Submarine X-1* (1968) played the bottom half of double bills. In contrast, anti-military and anti-establishment war films—in which militarism and the government replaced totalitarianism as the enemy— were fashionable. *The Dirty Dozen* (1967) earned $18 million in domestic theatrical rentals but its tremendous success was due to its anti-authority theme and its depiction of a callous military bureaucracy—with obvious allusions to the Vietnam War. *The Devil's Brigade* (1968) was somewhat imitative but still earned a respectable $4 million.

(John Wayne's 1968 Vietnam War movie, *The Green Berets*, bucked this trend. Wayne believed in the evils of communism and wanted to make the kind of patriotic war movie that Hollywood produced in abundance during WWII. Despite negative reviews by liberal critics and protests by radicals, the movie earned $10 million. But without the Duke, it never would have been made. Incidentally, Wayne originally commissioned a screenplay that would have conveyed some of the war's complexities but he had to modify the script to obtain Pentagon approval and assistance.)

It was within this cultural environment that United Artists released *The Bridge at Remagen*. Advertisements for the film made it appear to be a traditional World War II movie. In reality, the movie's premise was in accord with the prevalent feelings of the 1960s since it attacked the military mindset as epitomized by the commanders on both sides of the conflict. But since promotion for the movie did not convey this theme, draft-age moviegoers with a hatred for the military stayed away in droves. It is not coincidental that in October 1969, while the movie was in theaters, the largest anti-war protest in the nation's history occurred with hundreds of thousands of people demonstrating against the Vietnam War in Washington D.C. and in cities across the nation.

Reviews for *The Bridge at Remagen* were not very encouraging.

Howard Thompson in *The New York Times* liked the film's action sequences which he called "tense, properly chaotic and colorful" and he gave praise to stars George Segal, Ben Gazzara and Robert Vaughn; but he criticized the "obviousness" of the script and concluded that the movie "runs too long and rambles downhill." Judith Crist in *The New Yorker* called it "viable viewing if explosions and clichés are your shtick and exciting if you're not sure who won the war." *Variety*'s review was more positive; "Whit" called the movie "a colorful World War II melodrama," praised the direction and performances and forecast "good box-office potential for the general market." He would be wrong.

The Bridge at Remagen failed at the box office. On *Variety*'s annual list of Top-Grossing Films of 1969, it ranked 66th with domestic theatrical rentals of only $1.6 million. Other World War II movies were equally disappointing. *Battle of Britain*, about the first major battle of the war to be fought completely in the air, was one of the most expensive British movies ever filmed; this traditional war movie was Number 57 with $2 million. The allegorical *Castle Keep* was so bizarre that it even confused its intended audience of nihilists; it was Number 61 with $1.8 million. Brian Hutton's *Where Eagles Dare* was in 13th position with $6.5 million and was the only successful war movie of the year, primarily because it is an exciting adventure film that shuns realism and starred Richard Burton and Clint Eastwood. Though Disney's family comedy, *The Love Bug*, was at the top of the list with $17 million, anti-establishment movies were beginning to make an impact upon the box office. *Midnight Cowboy* was 7th with $11 million and *Easy Rider* was 11th with $7 million; the earnings for these two films would increase the following year.

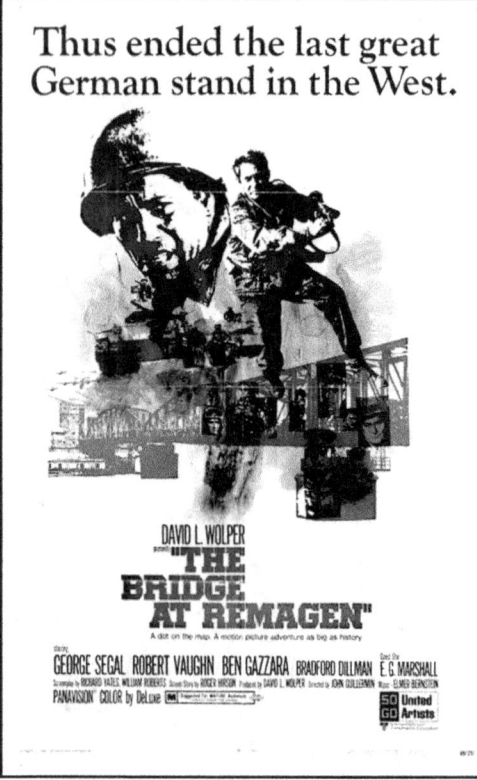

In addition to United Artists' ill-conceived advertisements, *The Bridge at Remagen* had another obstacle to commercial success. Specifically, many moviegoers of 1969 did not know the historical significance of the subject matter. World War II had been over for almost a quarter of a century and the typical person under 25 knew little if anything about specific battles within the war.

However, military historians and veterans all know the significance of the capture of the Ludendorff Bridge. In 1945, the Allied Powers in Europe were on the offensive but the Germans were not giving up easily. The Allies knew that it was vital to launch a major assault into the heart of Germany to win the war. But the German Wehrmacht had destroyed all of the bridges leading into the homeland, except for the Ludendorff Bridge at Remagen. When the 27th Armored Infantry Battalion secured this bridge, it was a stunning and unexpected victory for the Allies. The definitive account of the battle can be found in Ken Hechler's book, *The Bridge at Remagen* (Balantine;1957, Presidio Press; 2005). During the war, Hechler was a military historian assigned to the 9th Armored Division of which the 27th Armored Infantry was a unit.

The movie of the same title begins with the destruction of the Obercassel Bridge over the Rhine by the Wehrmacht to prevent its capture by American troops. The Nazis realize the imperative of also blowing up the last remaining bridge at Remagen to prevent Allied forces from entering the homeland. German commanders order General Von Brock to destroy the bridge, despite his pleas to leave it standing to enable 75,000 German soldiers to return home. Von Brock then conspires with Major Kreuger to delay blowing up the bridge for as long as possible. However, U.S. General Shinner wants to trap the retreating Germans before they can return to the safety of their country and orders a company of men to contain them. At this stage, Shinner doesn't consider the bridge important because he assumes that either the Germans or the U.S. Air Force will blow it up.

The 27th Armored Infantry Battalion, commanded by Captain Colt, is caught in the middle of these strategic decisions. Though numerous battles have already exhausted the 27th, Shinner's subordinate, Major Barnes, volunteers the unit to spearhead the assault at the town of Mechenheim. After Captain Colt is killed, Lieutenant Hartman reluctantly accepts command of the unit. When the men of the 27th find that German troops have left the town, General Shinner orders the unit to Remagen. After a fierce battle, they are surprised to see the bridge still standing. Shinner decides to secure the bridge before it is blown up and Barnes again volunteers the 27th for the hazardous task. As Hartman's missions become increasingly dangerous as well as increasingly futile, he becomes torn between following orders or keeping his men alive. Simultaneously, as the pressure on Kreuger intensifies, he is equally torn between obeying the command to blow up the bridge or saving the lives of thousands of civilians and soldiers. These opposing forces will meet in increasingly bloody skirmishes and culminate in an explosion of twisted metal and shattered bodies.

A summary of the film cannot convey the complexities of the intricate script. Besides being an action-filled war film, it is a story about people and how war affects their interactions. Two relationships are the primary focus of the story. The first is that of Lieutenant Hartman and Sergeant Angelo of the U.S. Army. The tension between Hartman and Angelo becomes quite clear as the story shifts to the men of the 27th. Lieutenant Hartman is shaving, trying to retain some degree of civilization in the aftermath of a battle. But he can't avoid the sight of Angelo who is looting valuables off the dead bodies of German soldiers. He tersely expresses his contempt for Angelo who responds with equal scorn. They obviously detest one another and hatred is a dangerous emotion in combat when each man may have to depend upon the other for his life.

The boy is scared. He fires out of the hotel window at the enemy, hitting American soldiers. He trembles with fear as return fire shatters the glass that cuts into his face. But he holds onto the rifle and prepares to fire again. Then Angelo kicks the door open and fires upon the sniper. He walks to the body and turns it over, seeing the youthful face of a boy. He kneels down beside the boy, agony on his face. Hartman reaches the door, surveys the scene and tells Angelo that he can rob the body later. Angelo slowly stands and turns furiously to Hartman, raising his rifle and pointing it at the officer. Then he walks out of the room. Hartman walks to the body and looks down at it.

Lieutenant Hartman and Major Kreuger form the second relationship. Although a patriot, Kreuger is becoming increasingly disenchanted with the Nazi regime, particularly after seeing fellow officers executed. Since he realizes that his superiors, excluding Von Brock, have no concern for the lives of the thousands of troops and civilians, he confronts an agonizing dilemma. The memory of his father, whose gold cigarette case he cherishes, has always inspired him to do his duty but now he is gambling with his life so that he can satisfy both his superiors and his conscience. Kreuger is on a collision course with Hartman. Their fates are intertwined. They will never meet and neither will ever know the other's name. They will sight each other once through binoculars but neither man will realize who is in his sights. They will exchange brief words over a telephone in the midst of battle but neither will know to whom he is talking.

The hatred that Hartman and Angelo share is only the first indication that the unit is not the standard Hollywood military group composed of stereotypical soldiers. Hartman deliberately doesn't get close to any of his men, because he knows they could die at any moment. Angelo admits that he wants to make a profit out of the war. And the rest of the soldiers are just hoping the war will end so they can go home. They hope to survive the war but they also know that their chances of dying increase with each battle. Each of these individual soldiers will have at least one scene which will allow his character to evolve into a genuine human being. Captain Colt's life ends suddenly but his expression of total fatigue is difficult to forget. Private Glover has a moment when fear catches up with him. Private Slavek makes a thoughtless remark about Hartman and regrets it. Private Bissell looks directly into the face of a captured soldier and sees only the bloodied countenance of an old man.

German lobby card for *The Bridge at Remagen*

The military commanders who can see the overall picture have the lives of these men in their hands. General Shinner has the responsibility of winning battles. When he changes strategy, he realizes that more American soldiers will die but, from his perspective, that is a price they will have to pay. He is so far removed from the actual fighting that he considers the men to be only expendable means to an end. Major Barnes sees each battle as a closer step to a promotion and glory. He volunteers Hartman and his men for any mission, no matter how dangerous, so he will reap the rewards of victory. His pretense of concern for the soldiers doesn't fool Hartman or anyone else.

Eager to please General Shinner, Barnes hurries to the 27th and orders Hartman to blow up the bridge. Exasperated, Hartman tells him that such an act would unnecessarily risk the lives of his men and would be pointless since the Germans are going to blow it up. When Barnes persists, Hartman replies angrily and sarcastically, mimicking the major's acquiescence to his general, risking reprimand and possible court-martial. Angelo stares at Hartman, as if seeing him for the first time.

This movie is not only about soldiers but civilians and the effect war has upon them. An innkeeper keeps a picture of Hitler prominently displayed when Kreuger visits him but quickly removes the picture upon arrival of the Americans. His wife barely speaks to him but merely looks at him with contempt. A French girl lives on scraps in the jail when Americans arrive and her young face conveys total despair. A German child stands helplessly in the middle of the street just before the building next to her

Sgt. Angelo (Ben Gazzara) and Lt. Hartman (George Segal) battle enemy forces.

explodes. The wounded and the displaced clutch their meager belongings while trying to cross the bridge. The faces of the children and the elderly evoke terror as they try to escape the bombs dropping upon them from the American planes above. Though some U.S. veterans' groups objected to this scene, it is historically truthful. In his book, *Among the Dead Cities: The History and Moral Legacy of the WWII Bombing of Civilians in Germany and Japan* (Walker & Company; 2006), A.C. Grayling documents the extensive strategic bombing campaigns which killed approximately 800,000 civilians.

This movie is also about bravery and how ordinary men become heroes when placed in situations that can draw out the best or the worst in them. As Hartman and his men are pushed into one dangerous mission after another, the reward for those who survive is to be forced into even more perilous situations. But yet they keep following orders, keep risking their lives, keep dying. When they reach the bridge after a bloody battle, they are in desperate need of a rest and time to regain their strength but they are given neither.

Hartman and his surviving men are huddled in a shell crater, exhausted and depleted. But General Shinner won't let them rest and tells Barnes to order the 27th to defuse the explosives, though they could explode at any moment. Even Barnes is taken aback by the command. But Shinner knows Barnes' weakness and plays into it. Barnes races to the crater and gives Hartman a direct order. Hartman is incredulous and refuses to obey, knowing that he will be leading his men into a death trap. Incensed, Barnes raises his rifle toward Hartman. Then

Angelo kicks the rifle out of Barnes' hands and slams his fist into the major's face, knocking him to the ground.

The scene that perhaps most illustrates the senselessness of war as well as the heroism of the men occurs when Shinner's latest change in strategy reaches Hartman and his men, many of whom will probably die because of the general's decision. After initially resisting, Hartman realizes that it is useless to disobey the order. They have to run into the face of enemy fire like cattle to a slaughter, hoping that luck will be on their side. But the men are systematically cut down as they desperately try to cross the bridge. As each of his men falls, Hartman can feel a piece of himself die but he keeps on fighting, trying to gain some kind of advantage before they all are killed.

Some German soldiers also display heroism. General Von Brock risks his career to save the German troops. A young German soldier makes a perilous run across the bridge to light the emergency fuse that will blow it up. When Major Kreuger realizes that he cannot delay blowing up the bridge any longer, he becomes determined to stop the Americans from capturing it. In the face of enemy fire, he races across the bridge and is wounded but quickly picks himself up, not realizing that his father's cigarette case has dropped out of his pocket. He becomes increasingly unable to withstand the pressure which becomes agonizing when two soldiers

German lobby card for *The Bridge at Remagen*

run away and he fires upon them. He knows that his last hope is with Von Brock and rushes back to headquarters to plead for re-enforcements. He finds only that he and Von Brock are doomed. And he realizes that his patriotism is misplaced. The Third Reich has corrupted the Germany that he loved and would willingly die for. He finally understands who the real enemy is but it is too late. One of his last acts as he faces his executioners is to reach for his cigarette case.

The film illustrates the horror of war in a hauntingly brutal manner. The battle scenes are viciously realistic on both a grand and intimate scale. The spectacle of the military firepower and the destruction is colossal but never eclipses the human drama of the individuals caught in the midst of the devastation. Private Glover huddles for safety in the middle of the bridge and notices the gold cigarette case lying in the rubble. He reaches out to grab it as bullets slam into his body. Other soldiers die just as quickly and brutally. In the heat of battle on a barge below the bridge, Hartman hears his name cried out and turns to see Angelo clutching his chest and falling backward into the river. Hartman runs to the rail and can see only darkness below. The immediacy of death repeatedly explodes upon the screen, thanks to highly talented filmmakers.

David Wolper, the recipient of many awards for his television documentaries and miniseries, is the producer. In 1959, he produced his first television special and, in 1964, produced his first theatrical movie, *Four Days in November*, a documentary about the assassination of President Kennedy. His second motion picture was *The Devil's Brigade*. In his memoir, *Producer* (Scribners; 2003), he relates the extraordinary circumstances under which he produced his third feature, *The Bridge at Remagen*. This was the first American movie to be filmed in Czechoslovakia, which the Soviet Union had ruled since the end of World War II. When the U.S. film crew arrived, the country was in flux because the Czechs were demanding freedom from Soviet oppression. Filming was proceeding smoothly in Prague until the crew awakened one morning to find themselves encircled by tanks and in the midst of the Russian invasion to suppress the uprising.

Leaving the country proved to be difficult because the Russians suspected that the film company was a camouflage for an American intelligence operation. This was ironic because the Pentagon had denied assistance to Wolper; U.S. Army officials objected to the unfavorable depiction of military commanders. Under threat of arrest by the Russians for espionage, the film crew was finally able to escape to Austria in a taxicab caravan arranged by the U.S. Embassy. The following autobiographies contain additional accounts of these perilous events: *A Fortunate Life* by Robert Vaughn (Thomas Dunne; 2008), *In the Moment: My Life as an Actor* by Ben Gazzara (Carroll & Graf; 2004) and *Are You Anybody: An Actor's Life* by Bradford Dillman (Fithian Press; 1997).

Once safely out of harm's way, Wolper had to frantically search for other locations and eventually settled on Italy and Germany. The scenes of the crossing of the bridge by American forces actually were filmed in three different countries but it is impossible to detect this in the movie. This is a tribute to all of the filmmakers, including the Czech film crew which was not as fortunate as their American counterparts; although they had worked extremely hard to display their aptitude in hope of developing their country as a popular film location, many of them were unable to leave the country due to the Russian occupation or unwilling to leave due to the emerging Czech resistance.

John Guillermin, a veteran of the Royal Air Force, is the director. Ten years earlier, he had directed *Tarzan's Greatest Adventure* (1959), the best Tarzan film of all time. In the intervening years, his reputation steadily grew with such British films as *The Day They Robbed the Bank of England* (1960) and *Guns at Batasi* (1964). Critical praise for these relatively small films led to his first big-budget Hollywood movie, *The Blue Max* (1966). The spectacle of this World War I aerial adventure and

John Guillermin prepares for a scene.

the intimacy of his low-budget movies merge seamlessly in *The Bridge at Remagen*. Although the battle scenes are horrifying as well as spectacular, Guillermin never loses sight of the fact that human beings are the main focus of the story. (Incidentally, at one point, Wolper reports that he fired Guillermin but the two men resolved their differences and he rescinded the firing.) Aiding the director immensely is the cinematography of Stanley Cortez whose panoramic vistas convey the magnitude of the conflict while his camera's immersion in the center of the battle scenes creates a feeling of unmitigated chaos and desolation.

George Segal graduated from Columbia University with a degree in drama and served in the U.S. Army during the peacetime late 1950s. After some New York theater work, he made his first film appearance with a small role in *The Young Doctors* (1961), which starred Ben Gazzara. This led

George Segal as Lt. Hartman

to a contract with Columbia Pictures and his first starring role in *King Rat* (1965). Following his memorable performance as the cynical agent in *The Quiller Memorandum* (1966), he demonstrated his versatility by portraying diverse characters, including a ruthless gangster in *The St. Valentine's Day Massacre* (1967). It was also in 1967 that he appeared on television on *The Smothers Brothers Comedy Hour* singing Phil Ochs' anti-war protest song,

"The Draft Dodger Rag." In 1968, critics praised his portrayal of George Milton in a television production of John Steinbeck's *Of Mice and Men*. As Lieutenant Hartman, he perfectly conveys his character's increasing anguish as his pretense of not caring slowly crumbles. After the climactic devastation and slaughter, the actor's expression clearly suggests that Hartman doesn't care about anything anymore, not even his life, which is why the reunion that follows is so gratifying. This is another of Segal's many unappreciated and superb performances. Two years later, he would electrify the screen with his portrayal of a hairdresser turned drug addict in *Born to Win* (1971) but, due in part to poor distribution, the movie and his brilliant performance were unrewarded.

Ben Gazzara was a struggling actor in 1952 when he received his draft notice in the midst of the Korean War. But the draft board classified him as 4-F (not acceptable for military service) because he was seeing a psychiatrist. He subsequently achieved fame for his portrayal on Broadway as the sadistic military school cadet in *End as a Man*, for which he won the 1954 Theater World Award. The film version, entitled *The Strange One* (1957), was his first film role and brought him equal acclaim. He subsequently divided his career between the stage, film and television. After starring on television from 1965 to 1968 in the series, *Run for Your Life*, he returned to films with his portrayal of Angeol. Initially, Angelo appears to be a hu-

Ben Gazzara as Sgt. Angelo

Robert Vaughn as Lt. Krueger

man vulture but it gradually becomes evident that he has created another personality to obscure his pain. As the horrors of the war steadily erode his facade, he becomes increasingly unable to conceal his agony and his inherent warmth fully emerges in the finale. Gazzara perfectly conveys Angelo's outwardly differing emotions which seem to be waging a battle within him. For example, in the sequence with the French girl, Angelo displays lustful delight upon first seeing her, paternal tenderness when he is alone with her and then contempt when he finds her half-naked with Hartman. This is a virtuoso performance that is typical of Gazzara.

Robert Vaughn received rave reviews that equaled Ben Gazzara's for his portrayal of the same brutal cadet in the Los Angeles stage production of *End as a Man* in 1956. As a result, he won a significant role in Alexander Mackendrick's *Sweet Smell of Success*, but lost the role when the Army drafted him; Martin Milner, who had been drafted in 1952, replaced him. Upon his return to civilian life, he acted steadily, mostly on television, though he did star in *Teenage Caveman* (1958); he was 26 years old but must have had bills to pay. In 1963, he won the starring role in the television series, *The Man from U.N.C.L.E.* From 1964 to 1968, his portrayal of super-spy Napoleon Solo brought him — and co-star David McCallum — tremendous popularity. While the series was still on the air, he starred in *The Venetian*

Affair (1967), but it was a box-office failure. He then had a supporting role in his first post-series movie, *Bullitt* (1968). The increasingly frantic Major Kreuger was a challenging role because the character was the opposite of the unruffled and charming Solo with whom he was still identified. In addition, he was playing a character who has to suppress his emotional turmoil beneath a rigid exterior as his composure gradually erodes. Vaughn does a commendable job of making his character sympathetic and, ultimately, tragic. Six years later, Vaughn would guest star in an episode of *Columbo* directed by Ben Gazzara.

In a supporting role, Bradford Dillman as Lieutenant Barnes is the epitome of mock sincerity with his expressions and tone perfectly projecting his character's inner ambition and outer hypocrisy. While a student at Yale, Dillman had joined the U.S. Naval Reserve and was subsequently commissioned as a 2nd Lieutenant in the Marine Corps. He first attracted acclaim on Broadway when he won the Theater World Award in 1957 for his performance in *Long Day's Journey into Night*. He subsequently starred in several films, most notably *Compulsion* (1959), but Hollywood rarely utilized his admirable skill to full capacity. In the 1960s, he acted mostly on television while occasionally appearing in movies, such as *A Rage to Live* (1965) with Ben Gazzara. In 1967, he played a villain in a two-part episode of *The Man from U.N.C.L.E.* entitled "The Prince of Darkness Affair;" which played in some countries as a theatrical feature called *The Helicopter Spies*.

Also providing effective support are E.G. Marshall (who was the prosecuting attorney to Dillman's psychopathic killer in *Compulsion*) and Peter van Eyck as opposing generals while Hans Christian Blech stands out as Captain Schmidt. And it is difficult to forget the expression of absolute desolation on the faces of Anna Gael and Sonja Ziemann representing civilians caught in the crossfire. All of the performers in the film, whether playing soldiers or civilians, look believably weary and hardened beyond the point of caring, as though they are actually living in the hell known as war.

Elmer Bernstein's score is noteworthy. Bernstein was drafted during World War II, during which he arranged and composed scores for U.S. Army Air Force propaganda radio shows. After the war, he struggled to earn a living until Columbia Pictures hired him in 1950, thus beginning a distinguished career (which was interrupted when the House of Un-American Activities Committee, a prominent member of which was Congressman Richard Nixon, blacklisted—actually "greylisted"—him for his alleged leftist sympathies). In addition to scores for such films as *The Man with the Golden Arm* (1955), *The Ten Commandments* (1956) and *The Magnificent Seven* (1960), he also scored the war films *Men in War* (1957), *Kings Go Forth* (1958) and *The Great Escape* (1963).

The main title theme for *The Bridge at Remagen* is martial and energetic, conveying the heroism of the soldiers as well as the relentless power of the armed forces. In contrast, subdued themes accompany intimate scenes which suggest the fragility of the civilians, as well as the vulnerability of soldiers, whose lives are inconsequential to the military command. In these interludes, the human cost of the war that is represented by scenes of human carnage and societal devastation is meaningfully enhanced by the music. United Artists Records did not issue an LP soundtrack album upon the film's release. Leroy Holmes and His Orchestra recorded the title theme but this version was not available in the United States; ironically, UA released the 45 rpm single record in Germany and Japan. In 1975, UA Records in Britain released an LP album entitled *Great War Film Themes* which included the Holmes version. In 1997, the City of Prague Philharmonic Orchestra recorded the theme for a Silva Screen CD entitled *Great Movie Themes: War*. In 2007, almost four decades after the film's release, Film Score Monthly released the complete soundtrack on CD.

At the center of the film is the literate and perceptive script. This is the only screen credit of critically acclaimed author Richard Yates. Just as his most celebrated novel, *Revolutionary Road*, is an indictment of the American dream of 1950s suburban life, the script for *The Bridge at Remagen* is an indictment of the sanitization of WWII as "the good war." Since Yates had served in the Army in Germany during World War II, he had some direct experiences with the topics of the film. However, according to Blake Bailey's biography of Yates, *A Tragic Honesty* (Picador; 2003), the author disowned the movie and claimed that the final screenplay was almost a total alteration of his initial script, though he did take credit for the humanizing of the Germans as well as the symbolism of the ending (with the cigarette case). Problems with producer Wolper may have affected his opinion of the film. During pre-production, Wolper fired Yates and, on this occasion, did not rescind the firing. As a result of his dismissal, Yates was quite angry and may have been too biased to recognize the virtues of the film. Furthermore, as a highly praised author, his ego must have suffered to know that a Hollywood screenwriter would re-write his script.

William Roberts receives credit as co-writer of the final screenplay and probably deserves praise for many of its qualities. Since the previous credits of Roberts included the famed Western, *The Magnificent Seven*, as well as the mediocre *The Devil's Brigade*, his scripts ranged from high to middling quality. (According to some sources, Roberts only revised Walter Newman's screenplay for *The Magnificent Seven* but, as Newman felt that he shouldn't have to share authorship, he removed his name from the credits.) Since Yates made no secret of his disapproval of the final script for *The Bridge at Remagen*, the contributions of Roberts must have been considerable. In addition, Roger Hirson is credited with the story

The Obercassell Bridge is about to be destroyed.

basis. To further complicate the subject, Steven Jay Rubin's article on the making of the movie in *Cinema Retro* #33 reveals that, through the lengthy development of the screenplay, Ted Strauss, Sam Thomas, Ray Rigby and even Rod Serling made uncredited contributions to the script. Regardless of precise authorship, the end result of the involvements of the all of the writers produced a splendid screenplay.

There are many unforgettable scenes in the film that stand out but one at the end is indicative of the script's resonance. As Hartman and Angelo watch the stream of evacuees cross over the war-torn bridge into the custody of the American forces, he takes out the gold cigarette case he retrieved from Glover's dead hand and offers a cigarette to Angelo. At that moment, Captain Schmidt walks by and sees the case which he recognizes as Kreuger's. He asks Hartman where he got the case and Hartman replies, "From a friend." Hartman, who had tried to deny all friendships, now realized how many friends he had, though he would never know that the owner of the cigarette case had also been his friend.

Many soldiers lost friends at Remagen. However, from a larger perspective, military commanders considered the price to be relatively low and historians tend to concur. The capture of the Ludendorff Bridge altered the course of history. Besides the military significance, the psychological impact upon the morale of the German army was disastrous. The capture led to the surrender of over 50,000 German troops. Furthermore, establishing a bridgehead at Remagen was essential in developing the

Angelo and Hartman lead the charge across the Ludendorf bridge.

southern and eastern pincers for the Allied Powers that trapped 300,000 German soldiers within the heart of the country. In effect, seizure of the bridge saved thousands of Allied lives and ended the war sooner than it would have otherwise. General Eisenhower, Supreme Commander of the Allied Forces, called the capture of the bridge "completely unforeseen;" he added that, as a consequence, "the final defeat of the enemy was now just around the corner." (Ten years later, President Eisenhower created "The Society of the Remagen Bridge" to honor the men who fought and died at the battle.)

Compared to other battles, the number of lives lost at Remagen was not enormous. But history's tendency to measure the significance of losses by numbers loses sight of the fact that each of those soldiers was a human being with his entire life ahead of him and their loss also affected the families at home who loved them. The movie justly confirms their sacrifices but it also shows that many of them died needlessly. Multitudes of soldiers might well have come home from Remagen and from other battles if not for the capriciousness, the stupidity and the egotistical ambition of some of their commanders.

Some historians quibble with the film's fictional characterizations but the movie doesn't pretend to be a documentary. The script changes the names of the main characters, composites of actual soldiers, to permit dramatic license. In reality, Lieutenant Karl Timmermann led the charge across the bridge in the face of enemy fire and was the first officer to set foot on the east side of the Rhine. Sergeant Alexander Drabik is credited as the first enlisted man to cross the bridge, though some military historians believe that either Sergeant Michael Chinchar or Sergeant Joseph De Lisio deserve the title. It's a technicality since all of them along with Timmermann and many other soldiers of the 27th received the Distinguished Service Cross (the second highest award after the Medal of Honor) for "extraordinary heroism." In addition, several other soldiers received the Silver Star (the third highest decoration). The movie may change their names as well as their characterizations but their bravery remains intact, as does the valor of all of all of the soldiers depicted. Timmermann, incidentally, was born about 100 miles from Remagen and moved to the U.S. with his parents when he was an infant. Ken Hechler wrote a biography of Timmermann entitled *Hero of the Rhine* (Pictorial Histories; 2004), a fitting companion to his book on the historic battle.

Ken Hechler also served as special technical advisor for the movie. He was one of the historians who didn't approve of the fictionalization of the main characters. In the book, *Guts and Glory* by Lawrence H. Suid

Some of the men of the battle-hardened 27th Infantry.

One of the many battle scenes in *The Bridge at Remagen*.

(University Press of Kentucky; 2002), Hechler is quoted as saying that the movie transformed the characters into Hollywood stereotypes. But he also admits that "the filmmakers had patterned most of the characters on real people and those who had fought for the bridge or who had read his book could readily identify perhaps 75% of the characters." Hechler also objected to some of the scenes with excessive military action that he believed were exaggerated, including the firefight at the end of the movie. However, the film's other technical advisor, retired Colonel Cecil Roberts, also disagreed with some of the script's details but thought that "the major events were there."

Colonel Roberts is correct. The movie depicts numerous historical events reported in Hechler's book. These include the initial expectation of U.S. military commanders that the Germans would destroy the bridge before the Americans reached it, the surprise of American troops who found it still standing, the failed attempts by the Germans to blow it up, the explosion which failed due to cheap explosives and the last-minute decision by American commanders to save the bridge. A major did indeed order Timmermann and his men to cross the explosive-laden bridge in what was virtually a suicide mission and some troops did resist. The attempt by the soldiers to cut wires connected to demolition charges while expecting the bridge to be blown up at any moment happened as depicted. And, following the capture of the bridge by American forces, the Nazis executed five German officers with most of them, like Kreuger, falsely labeled cowards and used as scapegoats.

Hartman feels tired and depressed. The dead bodies are everywhere. He feels guilty to be alive. As the tanks roll victoriously across the bridge, he walks

The men of the 27th try to enjoy a fresh meal.

recklessly alongside, almost hoping that a bullet will crash into him. And then he hears his name called out in the darkness. The voice sounds familiar. But the man that voice belonged to is dead. He looks toward the sound of the voice and can't believe his eyes. It is Angelo, his friend; his closest friend. And he is alive. Hartman runs to him as Angelo smiles warmly at him. They are so happy to see one another that tears well up in their eyes. Out of the horror of war has been born a friendship that is as deep and true as either of them had ever known.

And in the midst of the tumultuous years of the late 1960s, a powerful movie about the Second World War educated an angry generation about a piece of history that made it possible for them to demonstrate their anger against another war.

The Bridge at Remagen belongs on the list of great World War II movies.

CREDITS: Producer: David L. Wolper; Director: John Guillermin; Screenplay: Richard Yates, William Roberts, Based on a Story by Roger Hirson; Cinematographer: Stanley Cortez; Editors: William Cartwright, Harry Knapp, Marshall Neilan; Music: Elmer Bernstein

CAST: George Segal (Lt. Phil Hartman); Ben Gazzara (Sgt. Angelo); Robert Vaughn (Major Paul Keruger); Bradford Dillman (Maj. Barnes); E.G. Marshall (Gen. Shinner); Peter van Eyck (Gen. von Brock); Hans Christian Blech (Capt. Schmidt); Heinz Reincke (Holzgang); Anna Gael (French Girl); Sonja Ziemann (Greta Holzgang); Joachim Hansen (Capt. Beaumann); Vit Olmer (Lt. Zimring); Bo Hopkins (Cpl. Grebs); Robert Logan (Pvt. Bissell); Matt Clark (Cpl. Jellicoe); Steve Sandor (Pvt. Slavek); Frank Webb (Pvt. Glover); Tom Heaton (Lt. Pattison); Paul Prokop (Capt. Colt); Richard Munch (Gen. von Sturmer); Gunter Meisner (Gen. Gerlach)

LAWMAN

By the 1970s, the end of the Western as a popular film genre was in sight as the number of Westerns steadily declined with each year. Furthermore, many Westerns of the decade criticized the values traditionally associated with the genre while others emulated the Italian Westerns of the 1960s by featuring immoral anti-heroes and graphic bloodshed. Anti-Westerns debunking popular heroes were also fashionable. And some Westerns were political allegories for the tumultuous years in which they were released.

In 1971, United Artists released a Western that appeared to be both traditional and modernist. On the surface, it pits an austere frontier lawman against a land baron, a theme used in numerous oaters. The complaisant town marshal who has seemingly lost his nerve was also a familiar ingredient of many Westerns. However, the film develops these characters with psychological depth and infuses them with contemporary shadings. The graphic violence and shocking climax also place the film within a modernist category. Moreover, the story is a reflection of the Vietnam era and the government response to the dissension on the home front. The movie is entitled *Lawman*.

There is one falsehood about the creation of this movie that deserves an official burial. In his book, *Western Films*, (Rawson Associates; 1982), Brian Garfield reviews *Lawman* and writes: "Ostensibly an original, the story is an unacknowledged remake of the 1955 Robert Mitchum movie *Man With the Gun* with only a few changes." Phil Hardy repeats this in his book, *The Western* (William Morrow; 1983), calling it "an unofficial remake of *Man With the Gun*." In the annual *Time Out Film Guide* (Penguin), Nigel Floyd also writes that it is "a remake of *Man With the Gun*." They are all mistaken.

Richard Wilson, who co-wrote (with N.B. Stone) the script for *Man With the Gun*, was born in McKeesport, Pennsylvania in 1915. He began his Hollywood career in the late 1930s and was a production associate of Orson Welles. He acted occasionally (for Welles) but was primarily a producer and director as well as writer. *Man With the Gun* was the first movie that he directed. He co-wrote and directed one other Western, *Invitation to a Gunfighter* (1964), which was based upon a story that Arthur Penn had directed for television in 1957.

The protagonist of *Man With the Gun* is Clint Tollinger who has become a town tamer to avenge the murder of his pacifist father that he witnessed as a boy. He journeys to Sheridan City to find his estranged wife, Nelly, and their daughter. Rancher Dade Holman controls the town and the surrounding valley. Nelly, who left Clint because of his violent profession, manages a saloon owned by one of Holman's underlings. The town's weak-willed sheriff hires Clint to be his deputy, despite warnings about his extreme methods. To establish his authority, Tollinger bans guns and institutes a curfew. Meanwhile, Jeff Castle is building a farm in the valley against Holman's wishes. Jeff refuses Tollinger's offer of protection because he wants to prove to his fiancée, Stella, that he is his own man. When Nelly tells Tollinger that their daughter died, he angrily burns down the saloon. Holman uses the resentment of the townspeople to set a trap for Clint who is wounded before Jeff kills Holman. Tollinger then reunites with Nelly.

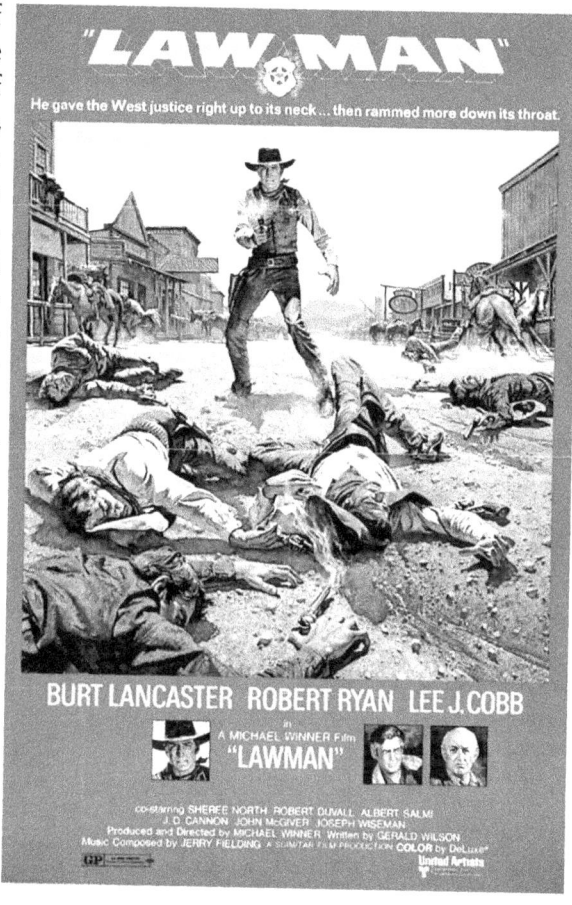

Gerald Wilson, who wrote the script for *Lawman*, was born in Pittsburgh, Pennsylvania in 1930. Gerald Wilson and Richard Wilson are not related. In *Cinema Retro #14*, John Exshaw provides biographical information on Gerald Wilson. His parents were Canadian and were traveling from Mexico to Canada at the time of his birth. He grew up in Ontario. At various times in his life, he worked as a miner, a seaman and a geologist. While working as an exploration geologist, Wilson "lived for seven years among various Indian tribes and the Eskimo in the Arctic Circle, the Northwest Territories and the Yukon." He moved to London in 1955. He began his writing career with a play and then wrote episodes for British television series in the 1960s. His first theatrical screen credit is the story basis for *Robbery* (1967). *Lawman* is his first credited screenplay. The very few common elements that *Lawman* shares with *Man With the Gun* are those shared with innumerable Westerns, just as other genres share basic elements. The characterizations and relationships as well as the plot development and resolution are totally dissimilar. It is an original script. It is not a remake, unofficial or otherwise.

Marshal Jared Maddox (Burt Lancaster) with his prisoner Vern Adams (Robert Duvall).

Lawman begins with a group of rowdy cowboys celebrating the end of a cattle drive by shooting up the town of Bannock, accidentally leaving one man dead. The protagonist then appears as he rides across the barren terrain. He is Bannock Marshal Jared Maddox and he has warrants for the men responsible for the killing. The men, who live near the town of Sabbath, include cattle baron Vincent Bronson and his closest friend, Harvey Stenbaugh, along with two of his ranch hands, Choctaw Lee and Jack Decker. The other men are smaller ranchers Vern Adams and Hurd Price. A seventh name is on the list, that of Mark Korman, whose lifeless body lies across the saddle on the horse behind Maddox.

Upon arriving in Sabbath, Maddox presents his warrants to town marshal Cotton Ryan who informs him that he will not serve them. Cotton is a formerly honorable lawman who, like everyone else in town, owes his livelihood to Bronson. As word spreads through the town, some of the townspeople want to confront Maddox but saloon-owner Lukas, who knows Maddox, warns them to avoid him. Cotton visits Bronson who offers to make amends for the killing. Stenbaugh's anger increases but Bronson cautions him against violence. He only wants to live in peace on his ranch with his son, Jason. But Jason agrees with Stenbaugh and doesn't think that his father should surrender to a lawman from another town. Meanwhile, Laura Shelby visits Maddox in his hotel room. In the past, they had been very close. However, she is now living with Hurd Price and has come to ask Maddox to spare him. Maddox refuses to bend the law for her but he assures her that Hurd will not be harmed if he turns himself in. "No one has to die," he tells her, making it clear that what happens to the men will depend upon them.

That evening, Bronson meets with all of the wanted men. Stenbaugh remains defiant while Decker and Choctaw also vote to resist the warrants. Adams cannot afford to leave his ranch while Price is too frightened to make his own decision and agrees with the others. Bronson, who has painful memories due to the violence of the past, still hopes that he can avoid bloodshed and that Maddox will accept his financial offer. But Maddox refuses, which infuriates Stenbaugh who comes into town with young cowhand Crowe Wheelwright. Stenbaugh provokes Maddox into a gunfight and is killed. Since Maddox knows that Crowe is not on his list, he persuades the younger man to back down. Upon learning of Stenbaugh's death, Bronson is grief-stricken and enraged. For Bronson, his friend's death ends any chance of a peaceable solution. Now all he wants is vengeance.

Back in town, storekeeper Luther Harris has instigated a group of townspeople who attempt to force Maddox to leave town but the lawman humiliates them into withdrawing. Harris, shamed in front of his friends, seethes with hatred. That night, Decker tries to kill Maddox who believes that Crowe set him up for the ambush. Cotton, who despises back shooters,

Crowe Wheelwright (Richard Jordan) and Cotton Ryan (Robert Ryan) stand over the body of Harvey Stenbaugh (Albert Salmi).

finds Decker and angrily drags him to jail. The incident earns the respect of Maddox who remembers Cotton as a fearless lawman. After Cotton tells Maddox how he fell from grace, his current status doesn't seem as simple as it previously did to Maddox. It is also revealing that, when Cotton initially visited Bronson, he gave him advice which, if followed, would have prevented the resulting tragedy. Now he also tries to reason with Maddox but is equally unsuccessful. Maddox sums up his life by explaining: "You play it by the rules; without rules, you're nothing."

The next day, as Maddox leaves town to serve his first warrant, he exchanges brief words with Lukas. The conversation indicates that Maddox's inflexible adherence to the law ended their friendship, just as it ended his relationship with Laura. But Maddox assumes no responsibility for the breach and seems indifferent to the anguish that Lukas displays. He has his duty to perform and rides away from Lukas toward the Adams ranch. Crowe, who feels obliged to convince Maddox that he didn't know of Decker's ambush, follows and confronts him. The young man's sincerity impresses the lawman. Later, after Adams and Price try to bushwhack him, Maddox captures Adams and takes the wounded man to the Price ranch where he finds Laura alone. That evening, Maddox realizes that he and Laura still love one another. He asks Laura to return to Bannock with him but she explains that she cannot live with a killer. Her words have a distinct effect upon him.

But it appears to be too late. Bronson now is determined to kill Maddox and he rides toward Sabbath, accompanied by Jason, Choctaw, Crowe and a reluctant Hurd Price. In town, Maddox tells Cotton that he is leaving without serving his warrants. However, Lukas arrives to tell them that Bronson and his men have just arrived in town. Maddox remains determined to leave without causing any more bloodshed. He starts to ride out of town, pausing only upon seeing Laura who represents a new beginning. But Luther Harris raises his rifle and starts the bloodshed that leaves virtually everyone dead or dying—except for Maddox and Hurd Price. And Price will soon die, but not facing Maddox like the others and not from his own hand like Bronson. He will die unarmed and running in terror as a bullet smashes into his back ands hurls him to the ground at Laura's feet. As Maddox rides away, he leaves in his wake misery and death.

The climactic sequence of *Lawman* is powerful, not only because of the bloodshed but, more significantly, because the changes within Maddox could have prevented it. Due to two recent events in his life, he has concluded that his obstinate devotion to justice has cost him what he values the most. His fishing interlude with Crowe makes him aware of the kind of peaceful life that he might have had with a son of his own. His meal with Laura makes him equally aware of the fulfilling life he could have

Maddox returns fire after trying to leave the town peacefully.

had with her. These two incidents shatter his rigidity and provide him with a new perspective of the law as well as of himself. Because he now sees the barrenness of his life, he decides for the first time to bend the law and let the remaining men on his list go free. This will prove to Laura that he can be a different man. But the blind pride that Maddox formerly felt about his profession is the same kind of pride that brings Bronson and his men into town just as Maddox is about to leave. Bronson now feels that he must resort to violence as a solution while Maddox is now determined to reject that very same violence.

Upon seeing Maddox start to leave town, Bronson realizes that he has made the wrong decision and starts to back away. For a brief moment, it appears that there will be no bloodshed. And there would not have been any if not for one man's hatred. Just as Maddox is about to approach Laura with proof that he is capable of changing, Luther Harris tries to kill him. The tragedy is that it is Harris and neither Maddox nor Bronson who precipitates the slaughter. Once the violence explodes, Bronson's only hope is to save his son from joining his comrades in death. Sadly, Jason does not have the maturity and wisdom of his father to understand that he also is wrong. He will not back down and seals his own fate as well as his father's. Maddox is not responsible for the bloodbath but, once it starts, he is a victim of his own past.

Japanese poster for *Lawman*

This applies to the original perpetrators as well. While the cowboys are innocent of deliberate murder in Bannock, they are not free of guilt. Vern Adams invites sympathy when he explains why he cannot afford to leave his small ranch. However, in the opening sequence, Adams gleefully terrorizes the citizens of Bannock. And it is this same Vern Adams who has no hesitation about trying to kill Maddox from ambush. Hurd Price was also willing to assist Adams and then panicked and ran away, leaving Adams to be caught by Maddox. Similarly, Harvey Stenbaugh was all too willing to shoot down Maddox in the street just as Choctaw would later try to do. Stenbaugh was filled with self-righteous arrogance and Choctaw fancied himself better with a gun than Maddox. Both men gave Maddox no choice at all. Jack Decker lost all sense of honor by trying to murder Maddox while hiding in a dark room.

Of all of the men on the list, only Bronson emerges with honor and he is the one who will suffer the most. And, as it is made clear in the prologue, he was not doing any shooting at Bannock. In view of this, he is the most innocent as well as the most honorable man of the group. In the climactic sequence, when he loses everything dear to him, he does not raise his gun against Maddox. He doesn't want to live in a world that has caused him so much pain and will not inflict similar pain upon anyone else, not even the man who kills his son. And so he elects to leave the world to Maddox and others like him.

But this does not mean that Maddox is a villain, despite his final controversial act. In Bill Harding's book, *The Films of Michael Winner* (Frederick Muller Limited; 1978), screenwriter Wilson states that he wanted to write an "almost archetypal Western, except pushing it to a sense of extreme (and) moving it off center slightly." Maddox's inflexibility may border on extremism but, prior to this act, he goes out of his way to avoid killing anyone. He has lived by rules all of his life because he believes that he would be no better than the men he hunts without such rules. The law and his sense of morality support those rules. Maddox executes Hurd Price because the men who have tried to kill him have destroyed his dream for a new life, because of what he has just experienced with Laura and because of his own past.

In all of the killings leading up to and including the climactic gunfight, Maddox reacts in self-defense and there is always an expression of regret on his face. But when he shoots down Hurd Price, it is not self-defense and his expression is one of rage and contempt. Why does he raise his gun and fire at Price? Why does he violate his most sacred rule and shoot the unarmed man in the back, thus becoming contemptible even to Cotton Ryan? There are two possible reasons, one professional and one personal. Professionally, after killing brave men in a fair fight, perhaps he believes that the spineless Price doesn't deserve to live. Personally, perhaps he feels that Laura deserves a better man than a sniveling coward. Either way, he is breaking the rules but not to save lives as his earlier decision would have done but to take a life.

However, there is one other reason for the killing and that lies within Maddox. At this point, he has lost his belief in the infallibility of the law. He is now willing to replace the law with his love for Laura. He has to start clean to prove to her that he can change. However, after the bloodshed, with so many dead bodies in the street, he knows that he has lost her forever. Now he has nothing and no one to replace the law that he had served so faithfully. When he saw Bronson take his own life, he completely understood that act. Bronson had lost everything in his life that was meaningful and now Maddox similarly has nothing in his life that is meaningful. Maddox murders Price because he has no more rules to live by, no one to live for and, therefore, no reason to live. As he rides out of Sabbath, Jared Maddox is already dead inside.

Gerald Wilson's screenplay is notably incisive, due in no small part to his own experiences. "My years in the wilderness increased both my interest and knowledge of certain things," he told John Exshaw, "which indirectly leaks into my films." The dialogue has an authentic ring to it while the characters appear to inhabit the real West. Many scenes that could have been formulaic seem fresh and genuine. For instance, the sequence that follows Vern's ambush of Maddox is particularly interesting.

Cotton tries to convince Vincent Bronson (Lee J. Cobb) to cooperate with Maddox.

After his horse is shot, Maddox in an almost casual manner proceeds to catch his quarry. He is in no hurry, secure in the knowledge that he will succeed. His manner conveys so much morality that, when he takes two horses from an Indian rancher without asking, there is no doubt that he will have them returned. And when he stops to have a meal and patiently waits for Adams, it is obvious that the ambusher does not have a chance. It is a beautifully written, deceptively simple sequence that expands upon the characterization of Maddox. Similarly, each scene within the film has meaning within the fuller context and leads inexorably to the conclusion. And the shock of the protagonist's final act is not superfluous or exploitative since it thematically follows everything that has preceded it.

Director Michael Winner was also a producer, writer and editor. After working as a film critic in the 1950s, he entered the film industry as an assistant director and writer for BBC television. During the latter half of the decade, he directed several shorts and wrote the screenplay for *Man With a Gun*, not the similarly titled 1955 Hollywood Western but a 1958 British crime thriller. He directed his first feature film, *Shoot to Kill*, in 1960 and then received acclaim for several films (*The System* in 1964, *The Jokers* in 1967, *I'll Never Forget What's 'Isname* in 1968) that scorned established social conventions in Britain. The critical success of these movies brought offers from Hollywood.

After reading Gerald Wilson's script for *Lawman*, Winner proposed it as his first Hollywood film, surprising studio moguls who believed that a Western would be an unlikely project for an Englishman noted for biting social dramas. But the director was determined to prove that he could direct a variety of genres, including one as intrinsically American as the Western. Executives at United Artists told him that if he could get Burt Lancaster to star, he could make his Western. He then arranged for a meeting with Lancaster who accepted and the director's Hollywood career officially began.

Winner's substantial skill is definitely in evidence in *Lawman*. The director, who had a reputation for not shooting in studios, captures the look and feel of the Old West, from the arid plains to the ramshackle dwellings, from the frontier town to the lavish estate inhabited by the town patriarch. His frequent use of zoom shots, which was often the subject of criticism, actually is of great assistance in conveying the relationship of the specific characters, either to one another or to their environment. His trademark intense pacing also moves the story along at a rapid tempo with all of the scenes serving the purpose of furthering the storyline and characterizations without unnecessary exposition.

Winner's insistence on accuracy created this authenticity. In his autobiography, *Winner Takes All* (Robson Books; 2004), the director relates how he visited several sets from Spain to Arizona and finally settled on Durango, Mexico and the surrounding area which included the village of Chupaderos. After consulting American historians, he recreated virtually everything that would be used in the film, even if seen only fleetingly, from costumes to flowers, from furniture to oil lamps, from newspapers to antique glass bottles. He even had the existing adobe Western town revamped to suit his vision of what Sabbath should look like. Robert Paynter's cinematography complements this vision and is invaluable in making the landscape surrounding Sabbath look so inhospitable.

Some critics censured Winner for the film's violence and accused him of imitating the Italian Westerns as well as the recent controversial film, *The Wild Bunch* (1969). But the violence is tame by comparison with not only Sam Peckinpah's classic but with other Westerns of the era, such as Ralph Nelson's gory *Soldier Blue* (1970). Furthermore, Winner depicts the violence swiftly and doesn't linger upon it. More significantly, the scenes of bloodshed are an essential part of the story and of the characterizations. Because of such scenes, Maddox's decision to abandon his violent past is clearly understandable. And Bronson's loathing of the same violence is equally explicable.

The relationship of the film's violence to the social environment in which it was made—specifically regarding the Vietnam War and an emerging police state—was deliberate. Bill Harding quotes screenwriter

Maddox casually awaits his quarry.

Wilson as saying that the law and order policy of the United States during this tumultuous period was not the best way to impose justice and that he conceived *Lawman* to reflect this viewpoint. Protests against the draft and the war were increasing across the nation. Terrorist groups and anarchists took advantage of the protests to instigate violence and destruction. Police officers often responded with extreme brutality against not only the minority radicals but against the majority peaceful protestors. In May, 1970 following the expansion of the war into Cambodia, the Kent State University campus in Ohio was the site of three days of anti-war protests and vandalism, during which arsonists destroyed the campus ROTC building. On the fourth day, over 2,000 students demonstrated on campus. National Guardsmen fired at the protesters, killing four students—two of whom were not involved in the protest—and wounding nine others. Eleven days later, at Jackson State College in Mississippi, protesters rioted and started fires. Police shot at the students, injuring 12 and killing two, one of which was a 17-year-old high school student who was walking home. The police state was not just emerging; it was in full force.

Lawman attempts to display the futility of violence on both sides. However, this viewpoint develops logically from the characterizations and their relationships within the storyline. Though many films during that era hammered home their political messages, *Lawman*'s message is subliminal. This is why the movie succeeds as stimulating entertainment while so many other message-driven films of the era emerged as preachy and patronizing.

The three major actors of *Lawman* bring dynamic screen presence to their roles. Burt Lancaster joined the U.S. Army after Pearl Harbor and was assigned to Special Services, the branch of the military that provided entertainment for the troops. Following the war, he began his acting career on Broadway and became a star with his first film, *The Killers* (1946). Throughout his career, he starred in 12 Westerns, including *Vera Cruz* (1954), *Gunfight at the O.K. Corral* (1957) and *The Professionals* (1966). Lancaster's forceful portrayal of Jared Maddox is at the center of *Lawman*. Since Maddox is ostensibly so inflexible, Lancaster could have played the entire film in the same range, with unmoving features and brusque delivery of his lines. Instead, he imparts the character with a wide range of emotions through subtle gestures and expressions. Many scenes effectively convey the complexity beneath the rigidity. The scene in which he plays his flute suggests veiled sensitivity. When he sits alone in the crowded saloon, his expression of resignation implies that he doesn't want or need companionship. But yet he conveys suppressed emotion by a slight shift in his tone when he asks Crowe to join him for a meal or when he develops respect for Cotton Ryan. Similarly, his eyes moisten almost imperceptibly when Laura leaves his side. Lancaster expertly brings a complex character fully to life.

Robert Ryan was a former U.S. Marine drill instructor. He started his film career in 1940 but it was after the war that he attracted acclaim, particularly as a film noir protagonist. When he saddled up, he was equally fine, most memorably in *The Naked Spur* (1953), *The Professionals* and *The Wild Bunch* (1969). Ryan has never given a less than stellar performance and his portrayal of the pragmatic Cotton Ryan in *Lawman* is impeccable. This is due in part to the depth he brings to the role of a formerly noble man, a depth that is notably poignant when he describes his gradual humiliation. In other Westerns, similar characterizations of peace officers who have sold out have been depicted as pitiable or contemptible but Ryan invests his character with some degree of dignity in part because his low opinion of himself is soon revealed to be too harsh and actually inaccurate. His expression of righteous anger when persuading Bronson to listen to his opinion and his expression of pleasure after re-discovering his courage are just two examples of the intensity and shading he brings to his character.

Lee J. Cobb appeared in a couple of B Westerns in the 1930s. After serving in the Army Air Force during the war, he had some supporting roles in films but achieved his greatest fame on Broadway in 1949 in

Lee J. Cobb as Vincent Bronson.

Death of a Salesman. His subsequent film career included occasional Westerns, including *Man of the West* (1958). Cobb brings his customary authority to his role of Vince Bronson in *Lawman* but yet there is a trace of vulnerability lurking beneath his hardened surface. He makes Bronson an essentially good man who is increasingly powerless to stop events over which he has no control. He is particularly effective in the scenes in which he quietly tries to persuade his men to refrain from violence, his tone and expression making it clear that he senses the folly of such action. And later, when his best friend is killed, the fury he displays is complex since his manner still suggests that he knows his action will unleash more deaths but is unable to resist his own urges. The last scene in which he kneels beside his son's body is heartbreaking because of his expression of total loss. It is a very poignant performance and Cobb makes Bronson the most sympathetic character in the film.

All of the supporting players bring gravity to their roles. Sheree North as Laura divests herself of glamour and looks as worn out as her faded attire. Robert Duvall brings credibility to Vern Adams, a man whose pride will not let him accept charity but will allow him to ambush Maddox. J.D. Cannon is particularly fine as Hurd Price, making him uncomfortably pathetic. Joseph Wiseman projects all facets of Lukas' repressed emotions. Even minor players invest their role with conviction despite the brevity of their scenes. John McGiver, who stood out in every movie in which he appeared, is particularly effective as the Mayor and a symbol of the spineless townspeople.

Sheree North as Laura Shelby.

Jerry Fielding's score adds to the film's impact. The harshness of the main title theme reflects Maddox's personality as well as the desolate landscape that seems to suit him. The score is frequently grating and out of kilter; just when it seems to be entering familiar Western motifs, it shifts to a bizarre tone which is jarring. In the climactic showdown, the brutality of the images is perfectly matched by the barbarous tone of the music. Ironically, as Maddox rides out of town, there is a brief note of tenderness suggesting what might have been, but then it is quickly followed by the ferocious title theme which defined Maddox at the beginning and now sums up his entire life. (There was no soundtrack album for the movie in the year of its release. However, in 1978, Citadel Records issued a double-LP set entitled *Four Film Suites by Jerry Fielding*, one of which was *Lawman*. In 2004, Intrada released the complete soundtrack on CD.)

Reviews for *Lawman* varied. "Rich" in *Variety* called it "a quite entertaining film [and] a commendable Western that should do reasonably good business." In London, where it premiered in March 1971, it received excellent reviews. Alexander Walker in *The Evening Standard* wrote: "*Lawman* is outstanding; it is a Western in the classic tradition that manages to give its theme a serious and unexpected twist to put it, like a noose, round some contemporary dilemma." Robin Bean in *Films and Filming* called it "an extraordinarily perceptive Western," adding that, "there is little conso-

lation in this deadly intrusion into the land of myth; everything is dirt, dust and death." But when it opened in the U.S. in August, reviews were negative. Howard Thompson in *The New York Times* wrote that the film has "some cutting dialogue and boiling psychological tension" but concluded that it is "a potent but exasperating Western [that] doesn't hold water or convincing fire." Archer Winsten in *The New York Post* wrote that it was "a Western of simple confrontations [and] is basically a compendium of previous Westerns rolled up into one violent homage." And Roger Ebert in *The Chicago Sun-Times* wrote that it was "a movie with a lot of sides but no center," whatever that means.

On *Variety*'s list of Top-Grossing Films for 1971, *Lawman* is 45th with $2.7 million in domestic theatrical rentals, which placed it in the category of box-office disappointments. The list reveals the decreasing interest among moviegoers for Westerns, especially traditional ones. Since *Lawman*'s modernist elements and allegorical message were not apparent in the film's publicity, it appeared to be quite conventional and, consequently, did not appeal to the counter-cultural moviegoer. And the bad reviews certainly didn't help.

In contrast, the most successful Western on the list is Arthur Penn's *Little Big Man*. Boasting anti-Western and anti-establishment credentials in vogue with the turbulent era, it appealed to revisionist audiences and earned $15 million. But it is dreadful not only because the filmmakers approach the Western genre with condescension but because they assume a superior tone while perverting history. The sardonic jabs at Western legends are especially banal, including the politically correct but unjustly erroneous portrayal of George Armstrong Custer. The attempt to correlate the Cheyenne and the Battle at the Washita River with the Vietnamese and the My Lai massacre is particularly distasteful. At the actual Washita battle, many warriors were armed and Custer's soldiers refrained from firing at non-combatants; it was the Osage scouts who killed women and children in retaliation for past killings by the Cheyenne. But the film distorts this fight as well as the battle of the Little Big Horn. Definitive books on these controversial subjects are *Washita: The U.S. Army and the Southern Cheyennes, 1867-1869* by Jerome A. Greene (University of Oklahoma Press; 2008) and *A Terrible Glory: Custer and the Little Big Horn* by James Donovan (Little, Brown; 2008).

Little Big Man was not the first Western to distort history to make a My Lai analogy. The previous year, Ralph Nelson's *Soldier Blue* earned $2.8 million. This film dramatizes the Sand Creek Massacre that, unlike the Washita battle, was a deliberate act of genocidal butchery; more than 700 volunteer soldiers from the Colorado Territory Militia under the command of Colonel John Chivington murdered and mutilated scores of helpless Cheyenne and Arapaho women and children. A U.S. Congressional investigation concluded that the massacre was "cowardly slaughter sufficient to cover its perpetrators with indelible infamy." The film trivializes this atrocity with its sanctimonious tone, gruesome violence and clichéd characters, including a pseudo-hippie flower child who seems to have wandered onto the prairie from Woodstock. The movie doesn't even include Black Kettle, the noble and pacifist Cheyenne chief who escaped this slaughter only to die tragically at Washita. (Five years earlier, Nelson's *Duel at Diablo* was far more effective because the story about racism and miscegenation between the Apaches and Americans took precedence over the implicit message.)

Additional Westerns on the 1971 list met with varying degrees of success. Two John Wayne films scored: veteran director George Sherman's last movie, *Big Jake*, was Number 10 with $7.5 million and the renowned Howard Hawks' last movie, *Rio Lobo*, was Number 22 with $4.5 million. Without the Duke, traditional westerns on the list were scarce. Robert Altman's self-indulgent anti-Western, *McCabe and Mrs. Miller*, with Warren Beatty was Number 25 with $4.1 million. Broadway director Edwin Sherin's first movie, *Valdez is Coming*, with Burt Lancaster was Number 39 with $3 million, though Lancaster's portrayal of an elderly Mexican constable is not quite convincing. William Fraker's melancholic *Monte Walsh* with Lee Marvin was Number 50 with $2.3 million. Frank Perry's fatuous *Doc* with Stacy Keach was Number 52 with $2.2 million; it equates Wyatt Earp with Richard Nixon, Tombstone with Vietnam and the outlaws at the O.K. Corral gunfight with Vietnamese villagers, thus reaching a

Cotton won't help Maddox but he won't hinder him either.

new level of cinematic stupidity. Burt Kennedy's humorous *Support Your Local Gunfighter* with James Garner was Number 54 with $2.1 million and Blake Edwards' studio-butchered *Wild Rovers* with William Holden was number 57 with $1.8 million. Westerns that didn't earn a position on the list include *Shoot Out* with Gregory Peck, *Something Big* with Dean Martin, *The Beguiled* with Clint Eastwood and *A Gunfight* with Kirk Douglas.

Burt Lancaster's subsequent career included many other fine films. The following year, he starred in another outstanding Western, Robert Aldrich's *Ulzana's Raid*, a brutal Cavalry vs. Apaches story which contains distinct parallels to the Vietnam War. In 1973, he and Robert Ryan appeared together again in *Executive Action*, portraying conspirators involved in the assassination of President Kennedy. In 1977, Lancaster and Aldrich collaborated on the superb *Twilight's Last Gleaming*, in which he plays a dishonored Air Force general who is determined to expose the truth about the government's ruthlessness regarding the Vietnam War. And in 1978, he portrayed a heroic Army major in *Go Tell the Spartans*, which illustrates the futility of the American military's intrusion into Vietnam. Lancaster took numerous chances in his career and left a legacy of many exceptional performances.

Director Michael Winner with Burt Lancaster and Robert Ryan on the set of *Lawman*

Lawman was the beginning of a fruitful collaboration for Michael Winner and Gerald Wilson. Wilson wrote another original script for the second and last of Winner's Westerns, *Chato's Land* (1972), about a half-breed Apache who defeats a posse that pursues him on his home turf. This film, the first of six that Winner would direct with Charles Bronson, succeeds primarily as an exciting Western but, secondarily, as an effective Vietnam allegory. Wilson revised David W. Rintels' original screenplay for *Scorpio* (1973), an excellent Cold War thriller that re-united Winner with Burt Lancaster; this film demonstrates the ease with which the CIA conducts its illegal activities, including murder. Wilson also wrote the screenplays for two other Winner films, though neither was an original. *The Stone Killer* (1973), based upon a John Gardner novel, is a gripping crime story about a Mafia don who hires Vietnam veterans to commit mass murder. *Firepower* (1979) is based upon a story by Winner and Bill Kerby and is an action movie about an assassin called out of retirement. This was their last collaboration. Wilson subsequently taught screenwriting at the London Film School.

It was without Wilson that Winner made his most commercially successful and most controversial movie, *Death Wish* (1974). Though the film's screenplay alters Brian Garfield's novel and regretfully reverses

Maddox realizes how much he needs Laura.

its message, Winner's direction is effectively manipulative, even though Charles Bronson is miscast. He directed two sequels with diminishing returns. *The Nightcomers* (1971) and *The Sentinel* (1977) are uneven but deliberately disturbing horror films. *The Mechanic* (1972) is a clever thriller about a contract killer and seems particularly good today compared to its 2011 remake. His remake of Raymond Chandler's *The Big Sleep* (1978) unwisely transports private eye Philip Marlowe from pre-war 1939 Los Angeles to swinging London of the 1970s. Winner's later films indicate that he may have sacrificed his creativity for a paycheck and include such dreadful movies as *Bullseye* (1990), *Dirty Weekend* (1993) and his last film, *Parting Shots* (1999). In 1994, he began an alternate career as a restaurant critic for *The Sunday Times*, for which he wrote a weekly column until 2012.

Despite Winner's prior inexperience with Westerns, *Lawman* displays his total command of the genre. His career included 36 movies over four decades. Some of his early British films received more critical acclaim and some of his Hollywood films did bigger box office but *Lawman* stands out among them all. The movie's reputation today is undeservedly poor. In most reference books, it is castigated. Brian Garfield writes that "the film is terrible; the characterizations are cardboard, the script turgid and the film is neither plausible nor palpable." (Garfield was perhaps biased against Winner since he understandably did not approve of the director's film version of his novel, *Death Wish*.) Nigel Floyd calls it a "would-be thoughtful Western which ultimately resorts to killing and ketchup to make up for its lack of style and originality." Phil Hardy calls it "a traditional Western deformed by Winner's excessive reliance on blood and gore in imitation of the Italian Western."

Nevertheless, *Lawman* is memorable not only because of its overall quality but because of the questions it raises about the relation of law and order to justice. The movie would perhaps be more comforting if the characterizations were less complex or if Jared Maddox was not so flawed and, ultimately, so human. And, of course, it would be so much less troubling if Hurd Price had drawn his gun at the climax and had not been racing away in terror as a bullet slammed into his back and extinguished his life. However, Winner and Wilson declined to patronize audiences and refused to dispel the troubling questions raised by the movie.

Lawman is a superb Western.

The lawman and the lawbreaker.

CREDITS: Producer/Director: Michael Winner; Screenplay: Gerald Wilson; Cinematography: Robert Paynter; Editor: Freddie Wilson; Music: Jerry Fielding

CAST: Burt Lancaster (Jared Maddox); Robert Ryan (Cotton Ryan); Lee J. Cobb (Vincent Bronson); Sheree North (Laura Shelby); Joseph Wiseman (Lucas); J.D. Cannon (Hurd Price); Robert Duvall (Vern Adams); Richard Jordan (Crowe Wheelwright); John Beck (Jason Bronson); Albert Salmi (Harvey Stenbaugh); William Watson (Choctaw Lee); Ralph Waite (Jack Dekker); Walter Brooke (Luther Harris); John McGiver (Mayor Bolden); Charles Tyner (Minister); Robert Emhardt (Hersham); Lou Frizell (Cobden); John Hillerman (Totts); Richard Bull (Dusaine); Hugh McDermott (Moss)

AFTERWORD

I

I was drafted into the Army during the Vietnam War and was stationed at Fort Devens, Massachusetts. One evening in 1967, *The Dirty Dozen* was playing at a base theater. During the climactic scene in which American soldiers incinerate German soldiers and civilians, a loud scream erupted from the audience. The film stopped and lights filled the theater. Two soldiers helped a third soldier, who had a very youthful face, walk up the aisle. The young soldier was barely able to stay on his feet and was sobbing uncontrollably. The sound of his crying gradually got lower and then disappeared.

In that theater, the cinematic world of war collided with the real world of war. But World War II, which the movie depicted, was different than the Vietnam War, which every person in the audience was experiencing in one way or another. For instance, in WWII, draft-dodging was unforgivable; in the Vietnam War, it was understandable. In WWII, it was shameful for servicemen to deviously avoid combat; in Vietnam, it was justifiable.

The four presidents who were engaged in various stages of the nation's involvement in Vietnam had all served in WWII, but in vastly different capacities. Dwight D. Eisenhower was the Supreme Commander of the Allied Forces and was in charge of Operation Overlord, known as D-Day, which signified a turning point in the war in Europe; the 1962 film, *The Longest Day*, depicts his leadership in this historic invasion. As president, he was susceptible to manipulation by the CIA due to his abhorrence of communism. Taking advantage of this, the Agency created conditions in Vietnam that were designed to lead inevitably to American participation in a war. Toward the end of his administration, Eisenhower became increasingly suspicious of the CIA and of his vice-president, Richard Nixon.

John F. Kennedy was awarded the Navy and Marine Corps Medal during WWII; the 1963 film, *PT 109*, depicts his heroism. As president, he fired the CIA's director, Allen Dulles, and defied the Agency's plans for war in Vietnam. He was also determined to end the Cold War and signed the Nuclear Test Ban Treaty with Russia. His policies curtailed profits from the Cold War and threatened the enormous profits that the military-industrial complex was anticipating from a war in Vietnam. The Warren Commission Report on JFK's assassination blamed "a lone nut" but knowledgeable people knew that the Report was fraudulent. *Breach of Trust: How the Warren Commission Failed the Nation and Why* by Gerald D. McKnight (University Press of Kansas; 2005) verifies that the Commission was created to conceal the truth from the American people and was simply a public relations hoax designed to validate a predetermined deception.

David Miller's impressive 1973 film, *Executive Action*, with a screenplay by Dalton Trumbo, reveals some of the facts suppressed by the Warren Report. Quite courageous since it was made only 10 years after the actual event and hampered by the limited research available at the time, the movie still exposes the dishonesty of the government account of the assassination. It also naturally aroused the fury of the establishment. Consequently, many media outlets refused to advertise it and many theaters cancelled its showings. Also hurting the movie's commercial prospects was the fact that the subject was still too painful for a large segment of the population and its implications too distressing to confront.

Almost two decades later, the public had become conditioned to the perfidy of the government and flocked to Oliver Stone's 1991 film, *JFK*. Artistically innovative and scrupulously researched, the movie brilliantly exposes the treason of the military industrial complex and shoves the burning iron of truth right up the well-oiled rumps of the national mass media puppets. Expectedly, the movie incensed the CIA and its media sycophants who viciously attacked the film even while it was in production, though this was merely a prelude to the vitriolic condemnation that greeted it upon its release. *JFK: The Book of the Film* (Applause Books; 1992) presents the meticulously annotated screenplay by Stone and Zachary Sklar accompanied by articles illustrating the controversy the film engen-

dered. Since then, persistent investigative research has vindicated Stone and irrefutably established the certainty of a conspiracy.

Nevertheless, the cover-up of the assassination of President Kennedy continues with the aid of government flunkies such as Stephen King and Bill O'Reilly whose fictional books, respectively in 2011 and 2012, endorse the fallacious Warren Report. And then there is actor and self-styled historian Tom Hanks who in 2010 announced plans to produce a miniseries based upon a pro-Warren Report book by Vincent Bugliosi. "We're going to do the American public a service," Hanks pompously declared, displaying both ignorance and arrogance. Hanks eventually abandoned this project, perhaps due to the rapidity with which researchers exposed the book's incalculable deceptions, and produced the worthless 2013 movie, *Parkland*.

(In 2010, Hanks stated that World War II was a racist war in which the United States "wanted to annihilate the Japanese because they were different." Hanks apparently didn't know that China was an American ally; the Rape of Nanking may have claimed more civilian casualties than the atomic bombings of Japan. And the Filipinos, among other "different" people, fought and died with American forces. In a similar vein, Clint Eastwood in his 2006 movie *Letters from Iwo Jima* depicts American marines killing unarmed Japanese soldiers. Will Eastwood make a movie about the Bataan Death March, the Sook Ching Massacre, the Bangka Island Massacre, the Alexandra Hospital Massacre or the Manila Massacre?)

Following the huge commercial success of *JFK* all over the world, the CIA was determined to ensure that Hollywood would never again produce such a movie. In his book, *Reclaiming Parkland: Tom Hanks, Vincent Bugliosi and the JFK Assassination in the New Hollywood* (Skyhorse Publishing; 2013), Jim DiEugenio not only thoroughly demolishes Bugliosi's book but also chronicles how the CIA subsequently influenced the film colony and pressured studios and filmmakers to portray the Agency and the military-industrial complex in a favorable light. The author reports the extent to which Hollywood surrendered its independence and why so many Hollywood personalities rolled over like little puppies and became government lapdogs.

Lyndon B. Johnson's only WWII "combat" experience was 15 minutes as an observer over New Guinea in a bomber that never came within sight of enemy forces; his Silver Star for that uneventful plane ride was an insult to all worthy recipients of the medal. After JFK's murder, Johnson appointed Allen Dulles to the Warren Commission, thus indicating its intrinsic corruption. As president, he fabricated the Gulf of Tonkin incident as a pretext to begin a full-scale war.

Richard M. Nixon also never came close to seeing combat. But, like Johnson, he acceded to the CIA's mandates and was more than willing to shed the blood of young Americans to satisfy the inexhaustible greed of the profiteers. When Nixon resigned in disgrace in 1974, Gerald Ford succeeded him. Ford was the member of the Warren Commission who concealed a crucial element pertaining to JFK's autopsy in order to prop up the Report's mendacity.

During the Johnson and Nixon administrations, the United States dropped 7.5 million tons of bombs on Southeast Asia. The U.S. military sprayed the area with 20 million gallons of Agent Orange, a poisonous herbicide that killed and maimed hundreds of thousands of civilians and caused untold numbers of birth defects. Estimates of Southeast Asian civilian deaths during the Vietnam War range from 800,000 to 3 million.

During the Johnson and Nixon administrations, the U.S. government drafted more than 1.7 million men into the military. Over 100,000 men evaded the draft by leaving the country. Over 3 million Americans served in Southeast Asia; almost 40 percent were draftees. More than 58,000 Americans, average age 23, were killed; almost 30 percent were draftees. Over 350,000 were wounded and more than 75,000 were disabled. The number of psychiatric casualties, like the young Fort Devens soldier, is unknown.

After the Vietnam War ended, the military-industrial complex proceeded with business as usual. After a suitable period of time, industrialists began to lobby the U.S. government to normalize relations with Vietnam, notwithstanding its poverty, slave labor, religious suppression and prison camps. Both Republicans and Democrats were receptive to their associates in the industrial world.

Currently, trade between the United States and Vietnam generates billions of dollars annually into the coffers of the military-industrial complex.

Thus, it is understandable that many movies from the Vietnam era reflected cynicism about the United States government. During the 1960s and 1970s, millions of Americans perceived the insidious corruption within the soul of the nation's government and lost their faith in the United States of America. This disillusionment had an enormous influence upon Hollywood and its films.

II

Once again, in this third volume of *Celluloid Adventures*, I have attempted to address egregious omissions in Hollywood's past by shining a spotlight on films and artists that have been neglected or even disparaged with the passage of time.

Glenn Ford never received an Academy Award nomination, despite numerous outstanding performances. Ford's son and innumerable fans lobbied for years to get an Honorary Academy Award for him but

Glenn Ford

the Academy members refused. For his military service (he was promoted to Commander in 1963), he received the Navy Commendation Medal, the Marine Corps Reserve Ribbon and the Vietnam Service Medal for a month's tour of duty in 1967 to scout locations for a documentary.

Victor Mature was considered a movie star as opposed to an actor. Mature often belittled his talents with self-effacing modesty. When applying for entry to a country club and being told that actors were not allowed, he stated, "I am not an actor and I have 64 films to prove it." It is an amusing statement and typical of his humility but the evidence proves otherwise. Nevertheless, he was never nominated for an Academy Award and was often denigrated.

Compare Sabu's portrayal of Mowgli to 17-year-old Mickey Rooney's performance in *Babes in Arms* (1939), for which he received a Best Actor nomination—or to 14-year-old Peggy Ann Garner's performance in *A Tree Grows in Brooklyn* (1945), for which she received an Outstanding Child Actress award—or to 12-year-old Bobby Driscoll's performance in *The Window* (1949), for which he received an Outstanding Juvenile Actor award. Yet the film capital never bestowed upon Sabu similar acknowledgement of his talents. At least he received several medals, including a Distinguished Flying Cross, for his service in the Army Air Force during WWII.

Despite the neglected performances cited in this book, stars such as Gregory Peck, Burt Lancaster and Anthony Quinn received praise and Academy Awards for other film roles. However, many other artists that I have paid tribute to in this volume deserved but never received even a nomination for an Oscar. Robert Ryan, Lee J. Cobb and Dana Andrews consistently gave exceptional performances but were repeatedly overlooked. Ben Gazzara and Richard Basehart always excelled but were consistently ignored at Oscar time.

Although he received a Best Supporting Actor Academy Award nomination for *Who's Afraid of Virginia Woolf* (1966), George Segal never received a Best Actor nomination despite many memorable starring roles. However, he has continued to display his commendable talents on the small screen, his likeable screen presence and flair for comedy making him an asset to the many series in which he has appeared. He is currently enjoying the sixth decade of his career.

Television also allowed supporting actors in films, such as Peter Falk and Telly Savalas, to achieve the stardom that eluded them in the cinema. Ricardo Montalban and E.G. Marshall along with Richard Basehart, Hugh O'Brian and Lloyd Bridges also became the stars of successful series, which allowed these actors to become household names. But too many talented actors like Richard Egan, Stephen McNally and Arthur O'Connell, who starred in series that failed, have unjustly been forgotten in the sands of time.

George Segal

And then there is that great gallery of character actors who always went that extra mile. Undeservedly unknown actors — except to film buffs — like Joseph Calleia, J. Carrol Naish, Morris Ankrum and Frank Silvera always stood out, regardless of how small their roles. Reliable performers like Simon Oakland, John McGiver and John Anderson consistently added immeasurably to their roles with their outstanding talents. Anderson, incidentally, memorably guest-starred in a 1971 episode of the television series *Hawaii Five-0* entitled "To Kill or Be Killed," which is one of the most poignant and haunting anti-Vietnam War dramas ever filmed — on either the small or big screen.

Many actors discussed in the text may not have become major movie stars but successfully pursued other interests. Robert Vaughn earned a

PhD in communications in 1970 and published his thesis on the Hollywood blacklist entitled *Only Victims*; he also achieved some renown for being the first Hollywood actor to publicly protest the Vietnam War. Bradford Dillman retired from acting in 1995 and became a successful author of both fiction and non-fiction. Hugh O'Brian, who was the youngest Drill Instructor in the history of the Marine Corps, founded HOBY in 1958 and devoted his life to this organization dedicated to developing leadership in youth.

Directors Frank Capra, Alexander Mackendrick, Zoltan Korda, John Sturges and Robert Mulligan have received praise for films other than the ones discussed herein. And Richard Fleischer is finally receiving overdue acclaim. But John Guillerman, Michael Winner and Brian Hutton should enjoy better reputations than they have. Irving Pichel and Kurt Neumann may have made too many forgettable movies but, when provided with quality material, they rose to the occasion. And it isn't easy to make a good movie in 10 days.

III

When viewing these movies today, it may be surprising to learn about some of the problems that plagued their production. Quite often, when any motion picture is being made, events occur which can be interesting, dramatic or even alarming. The films highlighted in this volume are no exception.

Some of the incidents are amusing.

While filming *They Won't Believe Me*, Robert Young was in a restaurant with his wife when a woman asked for his autograph and told him that she loved him in the two *Claudia* movies. After she left, Young said to his wife, "If she sees what I'm making now, she'll probably throw my autograph away."

While rehearsing for *Violent Saturday*, J. Carrol Naish who had recently portrayed Sitting Bull said to Victor Mature who had recently played Crazy Horse, "My Sioux chief is more historically accurate than your Sioux chief." Mature replied, "So sue me."

Other incidents are typical of Hollywood productions.

Character actor Joseph Calleia memorably portrayed the villain in *Jungle Book* because Jerome Cowan, who was originally cast in the role, was fired after disappearing for three days with the film company's hairdresser.

Bette Davis was infuriated with Glenn Ford throughout the production of *Pocketful of Miracles* because he reportedly said in an interview that he had arranged for her to be in the film to repay her for the favor she had given him 15 years earlier.

Jane Greer and Robert Young

After two weeks of clashes with actress Joan Hackett while filming *The Satan Bug*, John Sturges told producer Walter Mirisch that he couldn't work with her. Anne Francis, with just one day's notice, replaced Hackett.

Brian Hutton had had only four more scheduled days of filming *Sol Madrid* when John Cassavetes became ill and was unable to complete his role. Rip Torn replaced him and Hutton had to re-film all of the scenes in which Cassavetes had appeared.

Other incidents are alarming.

In the midst of filming *The Bridge at Remagen* in Czechoslovakia, Bradford Dillman rushed into Robert Vaughn's hotel room to tell him about the Russian invasion. Vaughn looked out his window and, upon seeing tanks and armored cars, said quite calmly, "I would say that your appraisal is accurate."

During the filming of a scene in *Lawman*, when Michael Winner told Burt Lancaster that he had the wrong gun, the actor furiously grabbed him by the lapels and dragged him to the edge of a cliff. Winner relented, explaining later that he didn't want to die on a mountain in Mexico.

But after all the humor, after all the conflicts, after all the problems and strife, the films emerged as terrific motion pictures. Though the primary purpose of these movies is to entertain, they may also be disturbing and provocative. They may even have a moral.

Jungle Book depicts man's destruction of nature and of the animals with which it shares the Earth.

They Won't Believe Me suggests that immorality has a price, however unfashionable that may be today.

The blind Martian woman and her barbaric tribesmen in *Rocketship X-M* foretell the possible future of humanity.

Violent Saturday proposes that it may be necessary to resort to violence to destroy violence.

Pocketful of Miracles shows that the spirit of self-sacrifice exists within the most destitute members of human society.

The Satan Bug asserts that biological weapons can be more dangerous than nuclear weapons.

A High Wind in Jamaica suggests that children should be loved, protected, cherished — and feared.

The tactics of the agent in *Sol Madrid* may be merciless and brutal but are still necessary.

The Stalking Moon illustrates that the United States was founded upon bloodshed and heartache.

The Bridge at Remagen shows how the inhumanity of war is the result of the nature of humanity.

Lawman proposes that violence is self-perpetuating, like a force of nature that cannot be controlled once it is unleashed.

These messages are effective because they are implied and because talented artists were primarily intent on making enjoyable and compelling movies. They succeeded admirably.

It is my hope that this book will bring belated appreciation and praise for the artists responsible for these movies and perhaps atone for their perceived failure.

"Perceived" is the key word, because, in the final analysis, the movies didn't fail. Decades later, they still entertain and excite and thrill and amuse and sadden.

That is proof of their success.

INDEX

Absent-Minded Professor, The 114
Adler, Buddy 88
Adler, Larry 157
Adler, Renata 162
Aero Theater 101
AFI Silver Theater 61
Agent Orange 253
Air America 164, 168
Alan J. Pakula: His Films and Life (book) 187
Aldrich, Robert 246
Alexander Korda (book) 31
Alexander Korda Award 37
Alexander Korda's The Thief of Bagdad: An Arabian Fantasy (book) 19
Alexandra Hospital Massacre 252
Alfred Hitchcock Hour, The (television series) 57
Alfred Hitchcock Presents (television series) 57, 58, 172
All the Young Men 162
Allied Artists 65
Allied Powers 9, 39, 84, 39, 213, 226
Almeida, Laurindo 176
Altman, Robert 245
American Cinematheque 60, 101
American Indian Wars 11, 180
American Madness 106
American Tragedy: Kennedy, Johnson and the Origins of the Vietnam War (book) 208
Amis, Martin 158
Among the Dead Cities: The History and Moral Legacy of WWII Bombings of Germany and Japan (book) 216
Among the Living 53
Anderson, John 136, 255
Anderson, Maxwell 25
Anderson, Warner 70
Andersonville Trial, The (television movie) 135

Andrews, Dana 135, 254
Anglo-Japanese Alliance 8
Anhalt, Edna 128
Anhalt, Edward 128, 129
Ankrum, Morris 77, 80, 81, 225
Annie Get Your Gun 79
Ann-Margaret 120
Ansara, Michael 176, 179
Anzio 211
Apache Wars 180, 182
Apache-Mexico War 181-182
Apaches (history) 180-182
Arabian Nights 38
Archer (television series) 177
Archer, John 70, 81
Are You Anybody: An Actor's Life (book) 218
Arrow in the Sun (novel) 183
Arsenic and Old Lace 108
Arthur Lyons Film Noir Festival 61
Ashanti Sanket 39
Asner, Ed 136
Asphalt Jungle, The 84
Atomic City, The 92
Attack of the Monster Movie Makers (book) 81
Attack On the Iron Coast 211
Axis Powers 9, 39

Babes in Arms 254
Baby the Rain Must Fall 185
Bachelor and the Bobby-Soxer, The 57
Bad Day at Black Rock 92, 127, 135
Bailey, Blake 224
Balcon, Michael 147, 148
Bangka Island Massacre 252
Barabbas 93, 96
Barack-Room Ballads (poems) 19
Barker, Lex 74
Baron of Arizona, The 65
Barter Theater 96, 186
Bartlett, Hall 166
Baseheart, Richard 134, 135, 254, 255
Bass, Gary J. 41

Bataan Death March 252
Battle Cry 99
Battle of Britain 212
Battle of Britain 8
Battle of Okinawa 42
Battle of Saipan 96
Battle of the Atlantic 39
Battle of the Bulge 42
Battle of Washita River 245
Battleground 79
Baxter, Deborah 145, 157
Bay of Pigs 207
Bean, Robin 242
Beatty, Warren 245
Becket 128
Beery, Noah Jr. 77, 78, 80
Beguiled, The 246
Behlmer, Rudy 41
Benjamin, Robert 64, 79
Berger, Ludwig 17
Bernstein, Elmer 223-224
Best Years of Our Lives, The 57
Betting On the Africans: John F. Kennedy's Courting of the African Nationalist Leaders (book) 212
Bhaumik, Kaushik 197
Biesen, Sheri Chinen 42
Big Clock, The 48, 58
Big Combo, The 100
Big Country, The 186
Big Heat, The 92, 97
Big Jake 245
"Big Kick, The" (television episode) 172
Big Parade, The 25
Big Sleep, The (1978) 248
Billboard (magazine) 146
Billy Budd 148
Billy Two Hats 202
Biological Weapons Laboratory 125
Black Hawk War 180
Black Kettle 245
Black Narcissus 39
Black Swan, The 34
Black Tuesday 104
Blackboard Jungle 99, 111
Blackout: World War II and

Good Movies...Evil Wars   259

the Origins of Film Noir (book) 42
Blech, Hans Christian 223
Block, Irving 71
Blood Rage (novel) 182
Blood Telegram: Nixon, Kissinger and the Forgotten Genocide, The (book) 41
Blue Dahlia, The 54
Blue Max, The 219
Body and Soul 57
Boehm, Sidney 88, 92
Bon Voyage 114
Bonestell, Chesley 67
Bonine, Abby 146
Booth, Shirley 111
Borgnine, Ernest 90, 96, 97, 124
Born to Kill 55
Born to Win 221
Boston Strangler, The 95
Bouchey, Willis 119
Boys' Night Out 134
Bravados, The 186
Breach of Trust: How the Warren Commission Failed the Nation and Why (book) 250
Breakheart Pass 124
Brian, David 119
Bridge at Remagen, The (book) 212
Bridge at Remagen, The 204-229, 257, 258
Bridges, Lloyd 76, 77, 78, 80, 255
Briskin, Samuel 108, 112
Broadway Bill 107, 108
Brode, Douglas 100
Brog 78
Broken Arrow 79
Bronson, Charles 140, 247, 248
Brown University 93
Brown, Jared 187
Brown, Jim 124, 197
Brute Force 57
Buchanan, Patrick J. 105
Bugliosi, Vincent 252
Bull, Richard 188
Bullitt 162, 178, 223
Bullseye 249

Burr, William 209
Burton, Richard 177, 212
Bush, George H. W. 164
Butch Cassidy and the Sundance Kid 197
Butcher of Budapest 206
Butler, Lawrence 34
By Love Possessed 128
Byrd, Ralph 32

Cagney, James 107
California Institute of the Arts 159
Call Northside 777 58
Calleia, Joseph 31-32, 255, 256
Calling, The 157
Camelot Theater 60
Canby, Vincent 197
Cannan, Dennis 149
Cannon, J.D. 242
Cannon, Jimmy 110, 118
Cape Fear 186
Capra, Frank 105, 106, 107, 109, 110, 111, 112, 113, 114, 115, 118, 120, 121, 122, 139, 256
Caretakers, The 157
Carnival Story 72
Cash McCall 134
Cassavetes, John 257
Castle Keep 212
Castro Theater 60
Castro, Fidel 207
Cat Ballou 98
Cat Women of the Moon 65
Central Intelligence Agency (CIA) 40, 62, 126, 163, 164, 165, 205, 206, 207, 208, 209, 250, 251, 252
Ceplar, Larry 73
Chan, Jackie 121
Chandler, Raymond 248
Changes 157
Changi Prison 123, 128
Charro 198
Chato's Land 135, 247
Che 177
Cheaper by the Dozen 79
Chicago Deadline 58
Chicago Sun-Times (newspaper) 244
Chief Crazy Horse 95

Children's Hour, The 112, 115, 134
Chinchar, Michael 227
Chino 140
Chivington, John 243
Churchill, Hitler and the Unnecessary War (book) 105
Churchill, Winston 8, 39, 105
Churchill's Secret War: The British Empire and the Ravaging of India During World War II (book) 39
Cinema Retro (magazine) 173, 225, 230
Circle of Danger 57
Circle Theater 185
Circus World 116
Citadel Records 242
City of Prague Philharmonic Orchestra 224
Civil War (American) 82, 187
Classic Movie Guide (book) 58
Claudia 52, 256
Clavell, James 128, 129
Clay, Noland 192, 195
Cobb, Lee J. 238, 241-242, 254
Coburn, James 156-157
Cocaine Politics: Drug Armies of the CIA in Central America (book) 164
Cochise 182
Cohn, Harry 105, 107, 109
Cold War 9-10, 40, 41, 62, 64, 69, 71, 84, 87, 92, 100, 124, 126, 139, 163, 247, 250
Collier, John 16
Colorado Territory Militia 245
Columbia Pictures 195, 105, 106, 107, 109, 110, 111, 127, 223
Columbia University 219
Columbo (television series) 223
Columbus, Christopher 143
Comanche-Mexico War 181
Communist Party USA 72

Connolly, Walter 120
Conquest of Space 70
Conspirator, The 64
Cook, Bruce 73
Cooper, Gary 108
Cooper, Merian C. 45
Cornered 45, 55
Cosmopolitan (magazine) 88, 102, 104
Coursodon, Jean-Pierre 203
Cowan, Jerome 119, 256
Creeping Unknown, The 65
Crist, Judith 138, 212
Criterion (DVD label) 41
Criterion Theater 69
Crossfire 57, 58
Crowther, Bosley 34, 99, 138
Cuban Missile Crisis 40, 207
Cummings, Bruce 85
Curtis, Tony 147
Custer, George Armstrong 245

Dakota Wars, The 180
Dalton Trumbo (book) 73
Dalton Trumbo: Blacklisted Hollywood Radical (book) 73
Dalton Trumbo: Hollywood Rebel (book) 73
"Dark Alliance" (article) 164
Dark Alliance: The CIA, the Contras and the Crack Cocaine Explosion (book) 184
Dark City: The Film Noir (book) 58
Dark Passage 57
Davenport, Nigel 142
Davis, Bette 111, 113, 119, 120, 121, 256
Day the Earth Stood Still, The 65
Day They Robbed the Bank of England, The 219
Day, Doris 115
Days of Glory 186
De Lisio, Joseph 227
Dead Reckoning 55
Deadline at Dawn 53
Dean, Isabel 142
Death of a Gunfighter 199
Death of a Salesman (play) 241-242
Death of Billy the Kid, The (teleplay) 185
Death Wish (novel) 248
Death Wish 247, 249
DeCamp, Rosemary 31, 32, 33
Decision Before Dawn 134
Defenders, The (television series) 167
Demetrius and the Gladiators 96
Democratic National Convention (1968) 209
Denham Studios 17
Dennis, Sandy 186
Desperate Hours, The 100
Destination Moon 57, 62, 65, 66, 657, 68, 69-70, 73, 77, 79, 81
Detective, The 162
Devil Girl from Mars 65
Devil's Brigade, The 218, 224
Devil's Chessboard: Allen Dulles, the CIA and the Rise of America's Secret Government, The (book) 126
Devil's Disciple, The 148
Dexter, Brad 99
Diem, Ngo Dinh 205, 206
Dien Bien Phu 205
DiEugenio, James 252
Dilllman, Bradford 218, 223, 256, 257
Dirty Dozen, The 98, 211, 250
Dirty Dozen: The Next Mission, The (television movie) 98
Dirty Harry 170
Dirty Weekend 248
Discovery Doctrine 182
Disney, Walt 14, 36, 37, 93, 94 114, 115, 148
Distant Thunder 39
Distinguished Flying Cross 254
Distinguished Service Cross 227
Distinguished Service Medal 108
Doc 245
Dogs 178
Don is Dead, The 95
Don't Go Near the Water 111
Don't Make Waves 159
Donovan, James 245
Double Indemnity 43, 54
Douglas, Kirk 246
Drabik, Alexander 227
"Draft Dodger Rag" (song) 221
Dressler, Marie 1107
Driscoll, Bobby 25
Drum, The 16, 41
Duel at Diablo 245
Dulles, Allen 125, 126, 205, 206, 208, 252
Dulles, John Foster 204, 205, 206, 208
Duvall, Robert 232, 242

Eagle Has Landed, The 140
Eagle-Lion Films 64, 65, 68, 69, 79
Ealing Studios 146, 147, 148, 159
Earp, Wyatt 80, 139, 245
Eastwood, Clint 140, 177, 212, 246, 252
Easy Rider 212
Ebert, Roger 244
Eclipse (DVD label) 41
Egan, Richard 95, 255
Egg and I, The 57
Egyptian Theater 60, 101
Egyptian, The 95
Eisenhower, Dwight D. 126, 204, 205, 206, 208, 226, 250
Elam, Jack 120
Elephant Boy 16, 19, 30, 41
Emery, John 77, 78, 81
Emperor of the North 98
Enchanted Cottage, The 41
End As a Man (play) 221, 222
End of the River, The 39
Enemies List 202
Enemy from Space 65
Entr'acte Records 36
Escape Artist (book) 132
Escape from Fort Bravo 127
Evans, M. Stanton 62
Evening Standard (newspaper) 243

Executive Action 246, 251
Exshaw, John 231, 237
Eye Witness 57

50 Years of American Cinema 202-203
Factories of Death: Japan's Biological Warfare 1932-1945 and the American Cover-Up (book) 125
Fairbanks, Douglas 16
Falk, Peter 120, 121, 255
Fall, Bernard 205
Fallen Angel 55
Fantastic Voyage 93
Farrell, Glenda 120
Fatal Politics: The Nixon Tapes, the Vietnam War and the Casualties of Reelection (book) 210
Father Knows Best (radio series) 51
Father Knows Best (television series) 51, 52
Fear Is the Key 124
Fear Strikes Out 185
Federal Bureau of Investigation (FBI) 62
Feld, Fritz 119
Ferdinand, Franz 146
Ferguson, Frank 53
Fielding, Jerry 242
Film Daily (trade paper) 78, 197
Film Forum Theater 101
Film Music Society 35
Film Noir Foundation 54
Film Noir: An Encyclopedia (book) 59, 60
Film Noir: An Encyclopedic Reference to the American Style (book) 58
Film Score Monthly (CD label) 137, 176, 224
Film Society of Lincoln Center 203
Filming of the West, The (book) 139
Films and Filming (magazine) 243
Films of Michael Winner, The (book) 237

Films of the Fifties, The (book) 100
Fire Maidens from Outer Space 65
Firepower 247
First Deadly Sin, The 177
First Indo-China War 204
First Men in the Moon 66
Five Million Years to Earth 66
Flaherty, Robert 16
Flamingo Road 162
Fleischer, Richard 88, 93, 94, 96, 97, 99, 101, 256
Flight to Mars 65
Flin 34
Floyd, Nigel 230, 249
Fly, The 81, 82
Flying Saucer, The 64
Flying Saucers Are Real, The (book) 63
Fonda, Henry 162, 198
Foote, Horton 185, 187
Forbidden Planet 65
Ford, Glenn 110-111, 118, 120, 198, 199, 253, 256
Ford, Peter 111, 253
Fordham Law School 96
Foreign Correspondent 44
Foreman, Carl 148
Forster, Robert 192, 195
Fortunate Life, A (book) 218
Four Days in November 218
Four Film Suites (LP) 243
Fraker, William 245
Francis, Anne 130, 133, 135-136, 257
Franco-Prussian War 145
Frank Capra: The Catastrophe of Success (book) 116
Frank, Nino 42
Frankenland State Symphony Orchestra 36
Freedom Betrayed: Herbert Hoover's History of the Second World War and Its Aftermath (book) 105
From Hell to Texas 187
From Here to Eternity 96
Fruit of the Poppy (novel) 162, 165-166, 167, 178
Fuller, Samuel 65

Gael, Anna 223
Gambit 187
Gangster Film: The Overlook Film Encyclopedia, The (book) 116
Gardner, John 247
Garfield, Brian 230, 247, 248
Garmes, Lee 33
Garner, James 134, 197, 246
Garner, Peggy Ann 254
Gay, John 136
Gazzara, Ben 212, 216, 219, 221-222, 253, 254
General Service Studios 32-33
Genn, Leo 36
Geronimo 182
Gershwin, Jerry 166, 167, 176
Get Yourself a College Girl 159
Gigot 119
Gilda 111
Girl Named Tamiko, A 128
Glass Key, The 45
Glasser, Albert 77
Glenn Ford: A Life (book) 111
Glory Brigade, The 95, 96
Go Tell the Spartans 203, 246
Golden Age of Piracy 145
Golden Triangle 163
Golden Turkey Awards, The (book) 95
Golding, William 142
Goldsmith, Jerry 137
Gomer Pyle U.S.M.C. (television series) 126
Grand Canyon Suite 77
Graves, Richard Percival 14-143, 154
Grayling, A.C. 216
Great Adventure Films, The (book) 31
Great Depression 104, 105, 106, 107, 114, 115, 116, 121
Great Escape, The 128, 133, 134, 136, 157, 174, 223
Great Movie Themes: War (LP) 224
Great Sioux War 180

Great War Film Themes (LP) 224
Green Berets, The 211
Greene, Jerome A. 245
Greene, W. Howard 33
Greer, Jane 53, 55, 58, 257
Grofe, Ferde 77-78
Guillermin, John 210, 256
Gulf of Tonkin 252
Gulf of Tonkin Resolution 208
Gunfight at the O.K. Corral 128, 139, 172, 241
Gunfight, A 246
Gunfighter, The 186
Gunga Din (poem) 19
Gunga Din 128
Guns at Batasi 219
Guns of Navarone, The 123, 124, 148
Guts and Glory: The Making of the Military Image in Film (book) 227-228
Guy Named Joe, A 72

H.M. Pulham, Esq. 52
Hackett, Joan 257
Hallelujah Trail, The 132, 136, 138, 139
Halliwell, Leslie 116
Hammer Films 79
Hampton, Orville 72
Hanging Tree, The 187
Hanks, Tom 252
Hanson, Peter 73
Harding, Bill 237, 239
Hardy, Phil 66, 116, 230, 249
Harris, Robert 125
Harris, Sheldon 125
Harrison, Joan 44, 55, 57, 58
Harvard University 45
Harwood, Ronald 149
Have Gun Will Travel (television series) 172
Hawaii Five 0 (television series) 255
Hayes, Helen 111
Hayes, Margaret 99
Hayward, Susan 47, 53, 58
Hayworth, Rita 111
He Walked by Night 65, 134
Heath, W. L. 86, 87
Heaven with a Gun 199

Hechler, Ken 212, 227, 228
Heinlein, Robert 67
Helicopter Spies, The 222
Hell in a Very Small Place: The Siege of Dien Bien Phu (book) 205
Hell Is for Heroes 134
Hell On Frisco Bay 100
Helms, Richard 126
Hendrickson, Al 196
Here Comes the Groom 108
Hero of the Rhine: The Karl Timmerman Story (book) 227
Heroin Gang, The 168, 178
Herring Farm, The 147
Herron, Julia 33
Heston, Charlton 133
Higgins, Jack 140
High and the Mighty, The 100
High Road to China 177
High Wall, The 55
High Wind in Jamaica, A (novel) 142-145, 146, 151, 154
High Wind in Jamaica, A 142-160, 258
Higher Form of Killing: The Secret History of Chemical and Biological Warfare, A (book) 125
Hingle, Pat 176, 178
Hirson, Roger 224
Hitchcock, Alfred 44, 52, 57, 58, 172
Hitler, Adolph 105
Ho Chi Minh 204, 205, 206
Hobbs, Halliwell 120
HOBY (Hugh O'Brian Youth Leadership) 256
Holden, William 197, 246
Hole in the Head, A 109, 110
Holliday, Doc 139
Hollywood Nineteen 57
Hollywood Reporter (trade paper) 113
Hollywood Ten 72
Hollywood's Frontier Captives: Cultural Anxiety and the Captivity Plot in American Film (book) 202
Holmes, Leroy 224

Homolka, Oscar 146
Honeymoon Machine, The 134
Hoover, Herbert 104, 105
Horton, Edward Everett 119
Hour of the Gun 139
House of Bamboo 100
House of Strangers 58
House Un-American Activities Committee (HUAC) 58, 62, 72
How the West Was Won 186
Hudson Bay 45
Hudson, Rock 134
Hughes, Ken 210
Hughes, Richard 142, 146, 147, 148, 154, 158, 159
Hunt, Linda 125
Hutton, Brian G. 167, 172, 173, 174, 175, 176, 177, 256, 257

I Died a Thousand Times 100
I Shot Jesse James 65
I Thought We Were Making Movies, Not History (book) 133
I'll Never Forget What's 'Isname 238
I'll Take Sweden 159
Ice Station Zebra 124, 139
Il Bidone 135
In the Moment: My Life as An Actor (book) 218
Incubus of Intervention: Conflicting Indonesia Strategies of John F. Kennedy and Allen Dulles, The (book) 207-208
India's First War of Independence 145
Indian Quarterly (magazine) 197
Indian Rebellion of 1857 145
Indio-China War 40
Indio-Soviet Treaty of Peace, Friendship and Cooperation 41
Innocent Voyage, The - see *A High Wind in Jamaica* (novel)
Innocent Voyage, The (play) 146

Inside Daisy Clover 185
Interns, The 175
Intrada (CD label) 243
Invaders from Mars 65
Invasion of the Body Snatchers 65
Invasion of the Saucer Men 65
Invitation to a Gunfighter 230
It Came from Outer Space 65
It Happened One Night 107, 121
It's a Wonderful Life 108, 116

Jackson State College 240
Jaffe, Sam 16
Jamaica (history) 143
Jeopardy 127
Jewell, Richard 59
JFK 251-252
JFK and Vietnam: Deception, Intrigue and the Struggle for Power (book) 208
JFK: Ordeal in Africa (book) 207
JFK: The Book of the Film (book) 251
JFK: Vietnam and the Plot to Assassinate John F. Kennedy (book) 208
JFK's Forgotten Crisis: Tibet, the CIA and the Sino-Indian War (book) 40
Ji Ji 121
Joe Kidd 140
Joe Smith, American 52
Johnny Belinda 96
Johnny Get Your Gun (novel) 72
Johnson, Lyndon 163, 164, 200, 208, 209, 210, 252, 253
Johnson, Nunnally 148
Johnson, Rita 53, 55, 58, 59
Jonathan Livingston Seagull 167
Jones, Kent 203
Jones, Shirley 111
Jordan, Richard 233
Journey for Margaret 52
Judgment at Nuremburg 112, 114

Jungle Book (1942) 14-41, 256, 258
Jungle Book, The (1967) 14, 36
Jungle Book, The (1994) 36-37
Jungle Book, The (2016) 37
Jungle Book, The (stories) 19, 20, 26, 28, 29

Kael, Pauline 201, 203
Kaiser, David 208
Kanter, Hal 110, 117
Karate Killers, The 179
Karlin, Fred 196
Karp, David 167, 177
Kastner, Elliott 166, 167, 176, 177
Kauffman, R. J. 88
Keach, Stacy 245
Keen, Leslie 63
Keep Watching the Skies (book) 69
Kelly's Heroes 177
Kemp, Philip 148, 149
Kennedy, Burt 246
Kennedy, John F. 40, 41, 200, 206, 207, 208, 218, 246, 250, 251, 252, 253
Kennedy, Johnson and the Nonaligned World (book) 207
Kennedy, Robert 200, 209
Kent State University 240
Kerby, Bill 247
Keyhoe, Donald E. 63
KGB 206
Khrushchev, Nikita 40, 206
Kibbee, Guy 120
"Kill or Be Killed" (television episode) 255
Kill the Messenger 164
Kill the Messenger: How the CIA's Crack Cocaine Controversy Destroyed Journalist Gary Webb (book) 164
Killers from Space 65
Killers, The 241
Killing, The 84
Kim (novel) 19
Kim Il-sung 85
Kimball, Jeffrey 209

King Rat (novel) 128
King Rat 220
King Solomon's Mines 79
King, Martin Luther 209
"King's Ankus, The" (story) 28
Kingfisher Caper, The 178
Kings Go Forth 223
Kings Row 100
Kipling, Jack 20
Kipling, Rudyard 14, 16, 19, 20, 21, 26, 28, 29, 30, 31, 34, 35, 36, 37, 83, 102
Kipling's Jungle Book Suite (78 rpm) 35
Kipling's Jungle Book Suite (LP) 36
Kiss Me Deadly 100
Kiss of Death 55, 95
Kissinger, Henry 41, 209
Klaw, Barbara 88
Knight, Arthur 113, 197
Korda, Alexander 15, 16, 17, 18, 20, 37, 146
Korda, Vincent 15, 17, 32, 33, 37
Korda, Zoltan 15, 16, 18, 20, 30, 37, 256
Korean War 10, 69, 84-86, 126, 221
Korean War: A History, The (book) 85
Kramer, Stanley 112
Krim, Arthur 64, 79
Kulik, Karol 31

La Cattura 178
La Strada 135
Lady for a Day 107, 109, 110, 116, 121
Lady in the Lake 55
Ladykillers, The 147
Lalo Schifrin Film Scores (CD) 176
Lancaster, Burt 138, 147, 148, 232, 241, 245, 246, 247, 254, 257
Lane, Mark 209
Lang, Charles 193
Lange, Hope 119, 120
Langelaan, George 81
Last Frontier, The 95

Last Run, The 95
Last Train from Gun Hill 172
Lastfogel, Abe 111
Latimer, Jonathan 45, 58
Laughton, Charles 146
Law of the Plainsman (television series) 176
Lawman 230-249, 257, 258
Lawrence, T. E. 20
Leibfried, Philip 16, 19
Leith, Virginia 99
Lend-Lease Act 8
Leonard, Sheldon 119
Leroy, Mike 157
Lethal Innocence: The Cinema of Alexander Mackendrick (book) 148-149
Letters from Iwo Jima 252
"Letting in the Jungle" (story) 27
Liberty Films 108
Life (magazine) 197
Life and Legend of Wyatt Earp, The (television series) 80
Life with Father 57
Lippert Pictures 64, 65, 68, 69, 79, 82
Lippert, Robert 65, 68, 77, 78, 79, 81
Lister, Richard 88
Little Big Horn 245
Little Big Man 244-245
London Film School 247
London Films 16, 19
Long Day's Journey into Night (play) 223
Longest Day, The 250
Lord of the Flies (novel) 142
Los Angeles Times (newspaper) 164
Lost Horizon 107, 116
Love Bug, The 212
Love with the Proper Stranger 185
Lovell, Glenn 132, 133, 136, 140
Lover Come Back 114
Ludendorf Bridge 212, 225
Lukas, Paul 176, 179

Mackendrick, Alexander 146,
147, 148, 149, 151, 152, 153, 155, 156, 157, 158, 159, 160, 222, 256
Mackenna's Gold 186, 197
MacLane, Barton 119
Maclean, Alistair 123, 124, 125, 127, 140, 141, 177
"Madame La Gimp" (story) 102, 105, 106
Madigan 162
Mafia 163, 165
Magnificent Seven, The 99, 128, 136, 157, 223, 224
Maharis, George 130, 132, 133, 134, 135, 136, 138, 139
Mahoney, Richard D. 207
Mahoney, Richard D. 207
Maltin, Leonard 57, 58
Man from Bitter Ridge, The 96
Man from Planet X, The 70
Man from U.N.C.L.E., The (television series) 162, 179, 222, 223
Man in the White Suit, The 147
Man of the West 242
Man Who Would be King, The (novella) 19
Man with a Gun 238
Man with the Golden Arm, The 223
Man with the Gun 230, 231
Manifest Destiny 182
Manila Massacre 252
Mann, Anthony 65
Mann, Delbert 96
Mao Zedong 85
Marcelino, Muzzy 196
Marcus Welby, M.D. (television series) 52
Marin, Edward L. 44
Marine Corps Reserve Ribbon 254
Marks, John 126
Marooned 116, 139
Marshall, E. G. 223, 255
Marshall, Jonathan 164
Martin, Dean 110, 128, 246
Marty (teleplay) 96
Marty 96, 97
Marvin, Lee 93, 96, 97, 100,
162, 245
Mason, James 147
Massen, Osa 77, 78, 80
Master List of Political Opponents 202
Mature, Victor 90, 95, 96, 101, 254, 256
Mayes, Wendell 187, 203
Mayfair Theater 69
Mazurki, Mike 119
McBride, Joseph 111, 116
McCabe and Mrs. Miller 243
McCallum, David 162, 165, 173, 174, 175, 177, 178, 179, 222
McCoy, Alfred 163
McDonell, Gordon 44
McGiver, John 242, 255
McGoohan, Patrick 124
McKnight, Gerald D. 250
McNally, Stephen 93, 96, 255
McQ 140
McQueen, Steve 134, 162, 185
Mechanic, The 248
Medal of Honor 227
Medved, Harry 95
Medved, Michael 95
Meet John Doe 108, 116
Menzies, William Cameron 18
Metropolis 62
Mexican War of Independence 181
Mexican-American War 182
MGM 52, 65, 66, 108, 124, 127, 139, 146, 161, 162, 166, 173, 174, 177, 179, 185
MGM Records 176
Mid-Century Films 70
Midnight Cowboy 212
Military-industrial complex 20
Miller, David 251
Mills, Hayley 148
Milner, Martin 132, 222
Miracle On 34th Street 115
Miracles 121
Mirisch Corporation 128
Mirisch, Walter 133, 257
Mister Roberts 99
Mitchell, Thomas 119

Mitchum, Robert 199, 230
MKULTRA 126
Mojave War 180
Montalban, Ricardo 162, 176, 179, 255
Monte Walsh 245
Montgomery, Robert 57
Moon and Sixpence, The (television movie) 185, 186
Moon is Down, The 45
Morgenstern, Joseph 197
Morrison, Ann 90
Mortimer, Barbara 202
Mosquito Squadron, The 178
Most Dangerous Game, The 45
Mother Wore Tights 57
Motion Picture Guide, The (book) 59
Motion Picture Herald (trade paper) 55
Mowgli 35
"Mowgli's Brothers" (story) 26
Mr. Canton and Lady Rose 121
Mr. Deeds Goes to Town 107
Mr. Smith Goes to Washington 107, 108
Mrs. Miniver 35
Muehlenbeck, Philip E. 207
Mukerjee, Madhusree 39
Muller, Eddie 60, 61
Mulligan, Robert 185, 186, 187, 193, 197, 199, 201, 203, 256
Murder My Sweet 45, 55
Murph 196
My Gal Sal 33
My Lai Massacre 209, 245
Mystery Street 127
Mystery Writers of America 92

Naish, J. Carroll 93, 98, 255, 256
Naked Spur, The 241
Name Above the Title, The (book) 110
Narcisco, Nathaniel 193, 195
Narrow Margin, The 93
Nash, Alfred 105
Nash, Jay Robert 59
Nation (magazine) 88
National Film and Television Archives 41
National General Pictures 180, 185
National Liberation Front 206
National Mobilization Committee To End the War 209
National Security Action Memorandum (NSAM) 263 208
National Security Action Memorandum (NSAM) 273 208
National Security Action Memorandum (NSAM) 288 208
Navaho War 180
Navy Commendation Medal 254
NBC Symphony Orchestra 35
NCIS (television series) 178
Neumann, Kurt 64, 68, 72, 74, 78, 81, 82, 256
Never So Few 128
New Centurions, The 95
New Statesman (magazine) 88
New York Confidential 100
New York Herald Tribune (newspaper) 88
New York Post (newspaper) 244
New York Times (newspaper) 34, 55, 78, 99, 113, 138, 162, 164, 197, 212, 244
New Yorker (magazine) 201, 212
Newman, John 208
Newman, Paul 197
Newman, Walter 224
Newsweek (magazine) 34, 99, 113, 138, 197
Nez Perce War 180
Night Has a Thousand Eyes 58
Night Watch 177
Nightcomers, The 248
Nightmare Alley 55
Nixon, Richard 41, 200, 202, 206, 207, 208, 209, 210, 223, 245, 250, 252, 253
Nixon's Nuclear Specter: The Secret Alert of 1969, Madman Diplomacy and the Vietnam War (book) 209
Nocturne 45
Noir City Festival 60, 61
Noonan, Tommy 91, 99
Nora Prentiss 57
North, Sheree 242, 243
Northwest Passage 52
Northwestern University 95
Now, Voyager 34
Nuclear Test Ban Treaty 25

100 Rifles 197

Oakland, Simon 136, 255
Obercassel Bridge 213, 225
O'Brian, Hugh 77, 78, 80, 255, 256
Ochs, Phil 220
O'Connell, Arthur 119, 120, 255
Odds Against Tomorrow 84
Of Mice and Men (television movie) 221
Office of Strategic Services (OSS) 125, 126, 163
Office of War Information 108
O. K. Corral gunfight 245
Old Gringo 203
"Old Is Not Gold, It's Mackenna's Gold" (article) 197
Old Man and the Sea, The 128
Olsen, Theodore V. 182
On the Waterfront 186
Once a Crooked Man (novel) 178
Once More My Darling 57
Once Upon a Time in the West 198
One (novel) 167
One Million B.C. 95
One, Two, Three 112, 114
Only Victims (book) 255
Operation Crossbow 139
Operation Overlord 250
Operation Paperclip 125

O'Quinn, Kerry 77
O'Reilly, Bill 252
O'Rourke, Patricia 21, 32
Origins of the Second World War, The (book) 105
Osborn, Paul 146
O.S.S. 45
Out of the Past 55, 57, 58

Pad and How to Use It, The 173
Paiute War 180
Pakula, Alan J. 185, 186, 187, 197, 199, 201, 203
Pal, George 64, 67, 68, 69, 70, 79
Panic in the Streets 128
Parallax View, The 203
Paramount Pictures 65, 108
Parent Trap, The 114
Parker, Jean 120
Parkland 252
Parsons, Milton 54
Parting Shots 248
Pasadena Playhouse 52, 54, 95
Paxman, Jeremy 125
Paynter, Robert 239
Pearl Harbor 9, 35, 93, 96, 108, 127, 241
Peck, Gregory 185, 186, 187, 193, 197, 198, 202, 203, 246, 254
Peckinpah, Sam 239
Penn, Arthur 230, 244
Perry Mason (television series) 80
Perry, Frank 245
Pete Kelly's Blues 100
Petit, Chris 139, 140
Peyton Place 100
Pfeiffer, Lee 173, 177
Phenix City Story, The 100
Philantropist, The (play) 178
Philco Television Playhouse (television series) 96, 185
Philippine War of Independence 102
Philippine-American War 102
Phoenix Program 209
Pichel, Irving 45, 57, 58, 67, 69, 256

Pigeon That Took Rome, The 114
Pirie, David 140
Planet of the Apes 66
Plumes (novel) 25
Pocketful of Miracles 102-122, 256, 258
Point Blank 162
Politics of Heroin in Southeast Asia, The (book) 163
Politics of Heroin: CIA Complicity in the Global Drug Trade, The (book) 163
Porfirio, Robert 58
Post Traumatic Stress Disorder 97
Pouligrain, Greg 207-208
Powell, Michel 17, 39
Powell, William 107
Power, The 70
Powers, Tom 54, 58, 70
Prelude to War 108
Presley, Elvis 162, 198
Pressburger, Emeric 39
Price, Dennis 145
"Prince of Darkness Affair, The" (television episode) 223
Private Life of Henry VIII, The 16
Producer: A Memoir (book) 218
Producers Releasing Corporation 64, 65
Professionals, The 241
Project Artichoke 126
Project Bluebird 126
Prouty, Fletcher 208
PT 109 250
Puglia, Frank 31, 32

Qualen, John 31, 32
Quatermass and the Pit 66
Queen of Outer Space 65
Quick Before It Melts 133
Quicksand 57
Quiller Memorandum, The 220
Quinn, Anthony 149, 155, 156, 254

Rabin, Jack 68, 71
Radio City Music Hall 107, 139
Rage to Live, A 223
Raintree County 187
Rakove, Robert B. 207
Rampage 40
Rank, J. Arthur 64, 146
Ransom 111
Rape of Nanking 252
Rattlesnake (novel) 183
Raw Deal 65
Rawhide (television) 177
Ray, Satyajit 39
RCA Victor (record label) 36
Reagan, Ronald 164
Reap the Wild Wind 34, 35
Rebecca 44
Recessional (poem) 19
Reclaiming Parkland: Tom Hanks, Vincent Bugliosi and the JFK Assassination in the New Hollywood (book) 252
Red Danube, The 64
"Red Dog" (story) 28
Red Menace, The 64
Redford, Robert 197
Reel Music Down Under (CD label) 196
Regal Films 81
Rembrandt 16
Remick, Lee 138
Return of the Man from U.N.C.L.E., The (television movie) 178
Revengers, The 203
Revolutionary Road (novel) 224
Reynolds, Burt 199
Rhee, Syngman 85
Rich 243
Richard Hughes (book) 142
Ride the Pink Horse 57
Riding High 108
Riedel, Bruce 40
Rigby, Ray 225
Rintels, David W. 247
Rio Lobo 245
Riskin, Robert 106, 107, 108, 109, 121, 122
RKO Radio Pictures 42, 44, 45, 64, 55, 57, 59, 65,

70, 74, 93, 108
RKO Story, The (book) 59
Robbery 231
Robbins, Jerome 112
Roberts, Cecil 228
Roberts, William 224
Robson, May 107, 120
Rocketship X-M 62-83, 258
Rockford Files, The (television series) 81
Rogow, Lee 99
Romenstein, Herbert 52
Rooney, Mickey 254
Roosevelt, Franklin D. 8, 62, 104-105, 125, 204, 208
Ross, Stanley Ralph 59
Route 66 (television series) 132, 135, 136
Royal Academy of Dramatic Art 174
Royal College of Physicians 126
Rozsa, Miklos 21, 34, 35, 36
Rubin, Benny 119
Rubin, Steven Jay 225
Rudyard Kipling's Jungle Book - see *Jungle Book* (1942)
Run for Your Life (television series) 221
Runyon, Damon 102, 104, 107, 110, 113, 121
Russian Revolution 9
Ryan, Robert 233, 241, 246, 247, 254

Saboteur 44
Sabu 16, 17, 19, 20, 21, 22, 26, 30, 31, 33, 35, 37, 38, 40, 254
Saint, Eva Marie 186, 187, 193, 198
Salmi, Albert 233
Sam Whiskey 199
Sammy Going South 148, 149
Samson and Delilah 79, 95
Sand Creek Massacre 245
Sanders of The River 16
Sands of Iwo Jima 79
Sargent, Alvin 185, 187
Satan Bug, The 123-141, 257, 258
Saturday Review (magazine)

99, 197
Savalas, Telly 165, 175, 176, 178, 179, 255
Scarlet Coat, The 135
Scarlet Pimpernel, The 16
Scene of the Crime 43
Schickel, Richard 107
Schifrin, Lalo 176
Schou, Nick 164
Science Fiction: The Film Encyclopedia, Volume Two (book) 66
Scorpio 247
Scott, Peter Dale 164
Screen Guild Productions 65
Sea Chase, The 99
Sea Hunt (television series) 80
Search for the Manchurian Candidate: The CIA and Mind Control, The (book) 126
Second Anglo-China War 145
Second Indio-China War 209
Second Jungle Book, The (stories) 19, 20, 27, 28
Second Opium War 145
Second Woman, The 58
Secret Agenda: The United States Government, Nazi Scientists and Project Paperclip (book) 125
Secret Agent 45
Segal, George 212, 216, 219, 220-221, 255
Selby, Spencer 58
Selective Service Act of 1948 10
Selleck, Tom 177
Selznick, David O. 44
Sergeants 3 128
Serkis, Andy 37
Serling, Rod 225
Seven Cities of Gold 96
Shack-Out on 101 100
Shadow of a Doubt 44
Shaik, Selar - see Sabu
Shauburg Cinerama Theater 197
Shaughnessy, Mickey 120
She 45
She-Devil 80
Sherin, Edward 245

Sherwood Forest 32
Shoot to Kill 238
Shoot-Out 203, 246
Sidney, Sylvia 91, 98-99,
SIFF Cinema 58
Silva Screen (CD label) 224
Silver Star 227
Silver, Alain 58
Silvera, Frank 188, 195, 255
Sinatra, Frank 109, 110, 128, 162
Sino-Indian War 40
Siodmak, Robert 44
Sklar, Zachary 251
Sleep My Love 48
Smith! 198
Smothers Brothers Comedy Hour, The (television series) 220
So Ends Our Night 110
Social Security Act 104
Society for Preservation of Film Music 35
Society of the Remagen Bridge 226
Sol Madrid 161-179, 257, 258
Soldier Blue 183, 239, 245
Solomon's Vineyards (novel) 45
Something Big 246
Sook Ching Massacre 252
Spanish Flu 105
Spanish-American War 102
Speedway 162
Spikes Gang, The 97
Split Second 96
"Spring Running" (story) 28
Spy With My Face, The 179
St. Valentine's Day Massacre, The 220
Stalin, Joseph 8, 10, 85, 204, 205
Stalin's Secret Agents: The Subversion of Roosevelt's Government (book) 62
Stalking Moon, The (novel) 182, 183-185
Stalking Moon, The 180-203, 258
Stallings, Lawrence 25, 26, 27, 28, 29, 30, 34

Stanford University 95
Star of India: The Life and Films of Sabu (book) 16
Star Wars 66
Stark, Richard 162
Starlog Records 77
State of the Union 108
Steiger, Rod 96
Steiner, Max 34
Stevens, George 108
Stevens, Leith 70
Stevens, Stella 162, 172, 175, 178
Stolen Life, A 111
Stone Killer, The 251
Strange Affair of Uncle Harry, The 44
Strange One, The 221
Stranger Wore a Gun, The 97
Strauss, Ted 225
Struss, Karl 74
Stuart, Ian 124
Sturges, John 123, 124, 127, 128, 131, 132, 133, 136, 137, 138, 139, 140, 141, 157, 172, 256, 257
Submarine X-1 211
Suid, Laurence H. 227
Sunrise 74
Support Your Local Gunfighter 247
Support Your Local Sheriff 197
Surtees, Robert 131
Suspicion 44
Sutton, Frank 136
Sweet Rosie O'Grady 52
Sweet Smell of Success 147, 222
Swiss Family Robinson 148
Sykes-Picot Treaty 20
Sylvia 133, 138
System, The 238

20,000 Leagues Under the Sea 93
2001: A Space Odyssey 66
20th Century Fox 65, 66, 81, 84, 87, 88, 95, 147, 159
3:10 to Yuma 111
Talbot, David 126
Tangier 38
Tarzan and the Amazons 74

Tarzan and the Leopard Woman 74
Tarzan and the She-Devil 74
Tarzan's Greatest Adventure 219
Tavernier, Bernard 203
Taylor, A. J. P. 105
Taylor, Elizabeth 177
Teenage Caveman 222
Teenagers from Outer Space 65
Ten Commandments, The 223
Terrible Glory: Custer and the Little Big Horn, A (book) 246
That Touch of Mink 114
Theater World Award 221, 223
These Thousand Hills 96
They Fought in the Creature Features (book) 76
They Were So Young 72-73
They Won't Believe Me 42-61, 67, 256, 258
Thief of Bagdad Suite, The (LP) 35
Thief of Bagdad, The (1924) 17
Thief of Bagdad, The (1940) 17, 19, 30, 34, 41
Thieves Highway 58
Thing from Another World, The 65, 70
Things to Come 16, 62
Thirty Seconds Over Tokyo 72
This Gun for Hire 43
This Island Earth 65
Thomas Crown Affair, The 162
Thomas, Sam 225
Thomas, Tony 31
Thompson, Howard 78, 212, 244
Three Bites of the Apple 174
Thunderbolt 127
Tiger Walks, A 40
"Tiger, Tiger" (story) 27
Tight Little Island 147
Time (magazine) 34, 55, 99, 146, 197
Time Limit 134
Time Machine, The 70

Time Out Film Guide (book) 139, 140, 230
Times (newspaper) 141
Timmerman, Karl 204, 227
To Hell and Back 99
To Kill a Mockingbird 185
Todd-AO 70mm Festival 197
Tomlinson (poem) 83
"Toomai of the Elephants" (story) 16
Tora! Tora! Tora! 93
Torn, Rip 172, 178, 257
Toscanini, Arturo 36
Tourneur, Jacques 57
Tragic Honesty: The Life and Work of Richard Yates, A (book) 224
Treasure Island 159
Treaty of Versailles 8, 105
Tree Grows in Brooklyn, A 254
Trial 100
Trial of the Catonsville Nine, The 202
Triple Alliance 146
Triple Entente 20, 146
True Grit 197
Truman, Harry 85, 125, 126, 204
Trumbo, Christopher 73
Trumbo, Dalton 72, 73, 74, 251
Try and Get Me! 80
Tube 112
Tugend, Harry 110, 117
Tusca, John 139
Twilight Time (DVD label) 101
Twilight's Last Gleaming 246
Tyne, George 53, 56

UCLA Film and Television Archives 41
UFOs: Generals, Pilots and Government Officials Go On the Record (book) 63
Ulzana's Raid 246
Unchained 167
Unconquered 57
Undefeated, The 197
Underwater 96
Unfriendly Nineteen 57
Unit 731 125

United Artists 14, 15, 21, 35, 70, 79, 110, 111, 112, 114, 115, 124, 128, 137, 139, 211, 212, 230, 239
United Artists Records 36, 137, 224
United States in the Philippine Islands, The (poem) 102
Universal-International 38, 40, 65
University of California at Berkeley 186
Unsuspected, The 55
Untamed 96
Up the Down Staircase 186
USC School of Law 81
Ustinov, Peter 148

Valdez is Coming 245
Van Eyck, Peter 223
Variety (trade paper) 34, 35, 55, 78, 79, 95, 99, 114, 137, 138, 159, 161, 162, 196, 197, 212, 243, 244
Vaughn, Robert 162, 178, 212, 218, 222-223, 255-256, 257
Venetian Affair, The 222-223
Vera Cruz 241
Victor Symphony Orchestra 36
Vidor, King 52
Vietnam Service Medal 254
Vietnam War 10, 11, 163, 177, 180, 200, 202, 204-210, 211, 239, 246, 247, 250, 253, 255, 256
View from Pompey's Head, The 96
Vikings, The 93, 96
Village of the Damned 66
Violent Saturday (novel) 86-87
Violent Saturday 84-101, 256, 258
Voyage to the Bottom of the Sea (television series) 135

Wake Island 35
Wald, Jerry 148
Walk a Crooked Mile 64

Walker, Alexander 243
Walking Hills, The 127
War Lover, The 134
War of the Worlds, The 65, 70
War on Drugs 164, 165
Ward, Elizabeth 58
Warner Bros. 37, 108, 111, 146
Warren Commission Report 250, 251, 252
Warren, Bill 68
Warren, Earl 200
Washington Post (newspaper) 164
Washita: The U.S. Army and the Southern Cheyennes 1867-1869 (book) 245
Watergate 140
Wayne, John 140, 197, 211, 245
Weaver, Tom 76, 81, 135
Webb, Gary 164
Webb, Roy 46, 54-55
Webster, Ferris 135, 136, 140
Weiler, A. H. 55, 113, 158
Weissmuller, Johnny 74
Werker, Alfred 65
Wesson, Dick 70, 77
West Side Story 112, 114
Western Films (book) 230
Western, The: The Film Encyclopedia (book) 230
What Price Glory (play) 25
Whelan, Tim 17
When Eight Bells Toll 124
Where Eagles Dare 124, 177, 212
Whiskey Galore 147
Whit 55, 137, 161, 212
White Man's Burden (poem) 19, 102
White Savage 35
Who's Afraid of Virginia Woolf? 255
Why We Fight 108
Widmark, Richard 162, 199
Wild Bunch, The 197, 239, 241
Wild One, The 97
Wild Rovers 246
Wild Seed 173
Wild, Harry 45
Wilder, Billy 112

Wilder, Robert 16, 163, 166, 167
William, Warren 107, 120
Williams, Elmo 157
Willis, Malcom 19
Wilmarth, William 34
Wilson, Gerald 230, 231, 237, 239, 240, 245, 247
Wilson, Richard 230, 231
Wilson, Woodrow 20, 105
Winchell, Walter 147
Wind and the Lion, The 157
Window On Main Street (television series) 52
Window, The 254
Winner Takes All (book) 239
Winner, Michael 135, 238, 239, 247, 248, 256, 257
Winsten, Archer 274
Wise, Robert 112
Wiseman, Joseph 242
Wolper, David 218, 219, 224
Woman on Pier 13, The 64
Wood, Natalie 186
Work Progress Administration 104
World War I 8, 19-20, 25, 104, 105, 146
World War II 7-9, 10, 11, 17-18, 35, 38, 39, 42, 43, 45, 52, 62, 71, 72, 84, 85, 87, 89, 95, 96, 99, 104, 105, 108, 110, 121, 123, 125, 127, 128, 155, 163, 167, 177, 180, 186, 204, 211, 212-213, 225-229, 241, 250, 252
Writers Guild of America 73
Written On the Wind 162
Wyler, William 108, 112, 127
Wyoming Mail 96

X,Y and Zee 177

Yale School of Drama 93
Yankee Doodle Dandy 35
Yates, Richard 224
You Can't Take It with You 107
Young Billy Young 199
Young Doctors, The 219
Young Rebel 167
Young, Betty 57, 256

Young, Robert 47, 51, 52, 53, 55, 57, 58, 59, 256, 257
Yuma War 180

Zanuck, Darryl F. 88, 89, 147, 148, 149
Ziemann, Sonja 273
Zorba the Greek 155

If you enjoyed this book,
write for a free catalog of
Midnight Marquee Press titles
or visit our website at
http://www.midmar.com

Midnight Marquee Press, Inc.
9721 Britinay Lane
Baltimore, MD 21234
410-665-1198
mmarquee@aol.com

www.ingramcontent.com/pod-product-compliance
Lightning Source LLC
Chambersburg PA
CBHW071305110526
44591CB00010B/780